Baseball in
Beertown
AMERICA'S PASTIME IN MILWAUKEE

TODD MISHLER

PRAIRIE OAK PRESS

BLACK EARTH, WISCONSIN

Library of Congress Control Number: 2004115841
ISBN: 1-879483-94-7

Photos: courtesy of the Milwaukee Brewers Baseball Club unless otherwise noted
Editor: Stan Stoga
Design: Colin Harrington

Printed in the United States of America by Sheridan Books, Inc.

10 09 08 07 06 05   6 5 4 3 2 1

Prairie Oak Press, a division of Trails Media Group, Inc.
P.O. Box 317 • Black Earth, WI 53515
(800) 236-8088 • e-mail: books@wistrails.com
www.trailsbooks.com

Dedication

To those who've ever picked up a bat, ball, or glove, and those loved ones who've cheered them on.

Contents

Introduction

The fans of Milwaukee couldn't believe how lucky they were, and, as players, we felt even luckier. We thought we were playing in the best town in the world. Then, 13 years after John Quinn passed out those caps with M's on them, we became the first team ever to leave a city without baseball. It seemed unthinkable that it could happen to Milwaukee. Not with those fans. Not with our team.

To this day, whenever I'm in Milwaukee, which is often, I'm reminded that the people there still haven't gotten over the Braves leaving. If it helps, they should know that the players haven't either.

Hank Aaron wrote those painful words in his 1991 book *I Had a Hammer: The Hank Aaron Story.*

Amazing that it happened, but still true nonetheless. Those who don't still hate the organization for packing its bags and scurrying off to Atlanta after the 1965 season absolutely adore the old Milwaukee Braves and what they represented. They miss the times in which they played. It's a heartfelt yearning for an era, the 1950s and early '60s, when all seemed right with the world, and more times than not those fans shared their lives at County Stadium to watch their heroes or gathered nearby to listen to the ball games on the radio.

It was baseball's version of Green Bay. Old-timers won't—and can't—let younger generations forget about Vince Lombardi's Packers and their five championships in seven years, a legacy that probably never will be matched in the National Football League.

Such has been the unenviable position that Bud Selig's Brewers found themselves in, especially during the past 20-plus years. All everyone remembers and longs for is a return to the days of "Stormin'" Gorman, Rockin' Robin, calls for "Cooooop," and the fun-loving playoff teams of 1981–82.

Milwaukee's teams won pennants and were the darlings of Major League

Baseball in Beertown

Baseball during both periods, and those players captured the imaginations of thousands of fans across the region. Still, the rest of the country showed little respect. However, folks in these parts didn't, and don't, really care, as Frank Clines pointed out in his *Milwaukee Journal Sentinel* column in September 2000 while the Brewers prepared to leave County Stadium for good and move into their new palace called Miller Park: "Face it. The self-important big shots on both coasts still think of us as, well, bumpkins. When the super-cool "Sports Center" crowd shows Bernie Brewer's chalet or the Sausage Race, more often than not the real message is: 'Aren't they amusing, those quaint, out-of-touch Midwesterners?' That isn't going to change, no matter what kind of stadium Milwaukee has. But so what? This is a nice place to live, in part because we have big-league baseball."

That we do, but it wasn't always that way. The American Association's Milwaukee Brewers provided the city's only professional baseball entertainment, albeit a pretty good franchise, from 1902 to 1952. However, it wasn't the same thing as being in places such as Saint Louis, Chicago, New York, Pittsburgh, and Boston—cities that could boast, regardless of how horrible their teams were, that they belonged in the big time.

Speaking of Boston, the National League organization from that Massachusetts city had been a losing proposition for many of those same 50 years and, since its inception in the 1870s, had gone under such names as the Red Stockings, Beaneaters, Doves, Rustlers, and Bees.

But when news spread that the owner of this sad-sack squad had picked Milwaukee as his team's new home, it was as if the city had been reborn. Mayor Frank Zeidler announced a week's worth of celebrations. The city was finally major league, and to everyone's surprise, even the organization's, the Braves performed that way from the beginning, finishing second in their first season on Lake Michigan and accumulating winning records all 13 years they played in Milwaukee.

Attendance averaged almost 20,000 fans per game for more than 1,000 contests at County Stadium, including 22,700 or better during the team's first seven seasons, setting league marks in the process. The high-water standard was 28,403 in the Braves' World Series championship season of 1957.

The Braves rewarded their supporters on the diamond, posting winning home records against eight of the nine franchises they played against. The only exception was the Brooklyn/Los Angeles Dodgers, against whom Milwaukee finished 62–74 for a .456 percentage.

Baseball historian and writer Curt Smith once said, "The time was without peer in baseball history and really without peer in Wisconsin history. The smallest city in baseball led baseball in attendance through just about the entire 1950s. Milwaukee was baseball's capital."

Longtime and current Brewers announcer Bob Uecker, who suited up for the Braves in 1962–63, recalled during an interview with the *Journal Sentinel* in 2002 what it was like growing up in his hometown back then: "It was every kid's dream to go to a major league game," Uecker told the newspaper.

For me it was down in Chicago at Wrigley Field or the White Sox. But when the Braves came, it was an immediate identity. And, of course, some of the guys who came here to play for the Braves, I had already seen in Milwaukee with the Brewers at that time. I used to hang around at Borchert Field. But to come down here each and every day to see County Stadium being built. I used to live around 47th and Galena. It was a major happening. To see what they did and to remember Charlie Grimm and all of those players who came here through all those years, that's been a big part of my life. And it always will be. The Braves were here first.

That they were, and Mike Fuss, 57, attended his first big-league game in 1955 and fondly recalled those seven or eight annual trips to County Stadium with his father, his grandfather, and sometimes his uncle.

"I can remember the Braves losing that first game I went to, 5–4, to the Cubs," Fuss said via phone from his Madison home. "Del Rice was catching for the Braves, and there was a close play at home plate. The ump called the runner safe, and Rice slammed the ball down on the plate and it bounced 15 to 20 feet in the air. Those images are so vivid in my mind."

So much so that Fuss, who retired in 2000 after 31 years with the Madison Fire Department, purchased old Fire Station Number 8 on North Street in 1990. He has turned it into his personal museum, transforming it into a shrine to the Milwaukee Braves in general and to third baseman Eddie Mathews in particular. Mathews was his boyhood idol and later became a good friend after the two met in 1984.

"I know lots of kids who wanted to be like Hank Aaron and Warren Spahn, but I've talked to tons of people around Wisconsin, and Eddie Mathews was the most loved," Fuss said. "Those players were so down-to-earth, and people around here worshipped them."

So, why the huge drop in attendance despite pennants and world titles?

"The biggest reason was because they changed owners, and for their last three years in Milwaukee those guys denied they wanted to move the team when they knew damn well they were going to," Fuss said about a team that ended up winning almost 59 percent of its games and coming within a whisker of claiming four or five consecutive NL crowns. "They dumped the tomahawk [emblem] and changed the uniforms. When it became official, fans dropped them. I know for a fact that some people still hate them for leaving."

Fuss said it still pains him to talk about the Braves' controversial departure. "I was sick when it happened, and it still eats me up inside," Fuss said. "It was a thrill for me to go to County Stadium, which I thought was a grand old park. I was so mad when they tore it down. I hate Miller Park. I'm from the old school in that I think baseball, like football, should be played outdoors like it was meant to be. That's why I try to keep those Braves memories alive."

He tries to accomplish that as a board member of the Milwaukee Braves Historical Association. The group is responsible for three monuments near Helfaer Field, a Little League diamond outside Miller Park, that commemorate the Braves' stay. One represents the team's first game in Milwaukee, a second honors the 1957 champions, and the third is for September 22, 1965, the team's last appearance in County Stadium. The monuments were unveiled April 14, 2003. Ironically, the smallest crowd in Miller Park history attended the Brewers' game against the Cardinals a few hours later, after then-team president Ulice Payne had talked about reestablishing a Braves-like connection with fans.

The group's president is none other than former Braves shortstop Johnny Logan, who along with ex-teammates Andy Pafko and Jack Dittmer attended the ceremony. "I got my biggest break in baseball when I got traded to Milwaukee," said Pafko, a Boyceville, Wisconsin, native who lives in the Chicago area. "It was a baseball city when I played. The support we got was almost indescribable. I played for Cub fans, and I played in Brooklyn. They were all excitable years, but when I went back to Milwaukee, I never saw anything like that."

One person who vowed to see that kind of joy return to the old ballpark was Allan H. "Bud" Selig, who was among the 12,577 fans who watched the Braves take the field for a final time. "It was heartbreak," Selig said in a phone interview. "It was such a poignant reminder of what baseball had meant. People didn't know me as well back then, but a woman came up to me after the game and asked if I was Bud Selig, and I'm thinking, 'Uh-oh.' I'll never forget her words. She said, 'Don't you fail us.' She was so brokenhearted that she wept."

Well, it may have taken a while, but Selig didn't fail. And some of that nostalgia and magic reoccurred when George Bamberger and Harvey Kuenn unleashed "Bambi's Bombers" and "Harvey's Wallbangers," respectively, on American League pitching staffs in the late 1970s and early '80s, and Fuss said it was similar to what he had witnessed while growing up.

"That's the one thing about the Brewers, back in the late '70s, it was just like when the Braves were here," Fuss said. "They were loved. You knew all of the players and had your heroes. It was a good time, and they had so many characters on those teams."

One of the biggest characters was Gorman Thomas, who is still a folk hero. "I swear to God, you'll never hear about, or ever see, a cast of characters like we had," Thomas said in 2002 as he gathered with several former teammates for a reunion of the '82 squad. "We did so many crazy things. Oh, man, we had so much fun."

"Our fans were some of the most loyal, blue-collar, good-hearted, down-to-earth people I ever met," relief pitcher Bob McClure said.

Milwaukee's faithful, minus that pennant fever for 25 years, rejoiced in the Brewers' success and created bonds with the players, guys they could share brats and beverages with and who made them forget about their troubles.

"Today's player has so much money that he doesn't really think he has to blend in or have any kind of affiliation with the fan," Thomas said. "Back when I played, we really didn't look at it that way. We established a lot of friendships, a lot of different people and families. It's actually harder and takes more effort to be rude than it does to be nice."

One of the unsung heroes on those teams, catcher and outfielder Charlie Moore, said that group deserved to be remembered. "Hopefully, someday another group will come in here and do the same thing because there's nothing like it," Moore said. "You wish everybody could have the memories that we had, playoffs, World Series. It's just a shame we didn't win it."

Long-suffering Milwaukee fans are still waiting. They haven't even been able to enjoy a winning season since 1992. But what about fans' part in this whole equation? Attendance has eclipsed the two million mark only twice since 1983, the first time occurring when droves came to take in the spectacle of Miller Park's first season in 2001 and again, surprisingly, in 2004.

Maybe Michael Ellis, a Republican from Neenah who still serves in the state Senate, was correct when he had this to say during the stadium debate in 1996: "They could line up orange crates and people would get slivers in their butts to watch Michael Jordan, but you could put recliners in and they wouldn't watch the Brewers." He's got a point, although one can't blame even the staunchest Brewers supporters for not paying good money to see millionaires play terrible baseball, which has happened quite often in Milwaukee the past 12 seasons.

In the meantime, the situation came full circle on November 6, 1997, when the Brewers officially became the first team in modern history to switch leagues, moving from the American League to the National League. Fittingly, they opened the 1998 season against the Atlanta Braves and dropped a 2–1 decision at Turner Field.

Despite the team's obvious shortcomings and disastrous second half, fans showed their appreciation for the effort the young club showed during 2004. A prime example of that enthusiasm was the continued and growing presence of those lovable, colorfully attired faithful known as the "Buckethead Brigade," who have been made famous on Tuesday nights by TV announcers Daron Sutton and Bill Schroeder and usually are among the first fans shown during broadcasts.

New manager Ned Yost, like Schroeder a former backup catcher for the Brewers, said that's why he accepted the job and challenge of resurrecting the moribund franchise. "We were all stunned by the success of the section as it sold out every single Tuesday home game," Yost said. "You can already feel the excitement welling up in our fans. Those are special fans and that doesn't happen everywhere. There are only a few places in baseball that they have fans like that. That's why I'm here to bring that excitement back. Everything that I do is with the fans in the back of my mind. If a player doesn't hustle, do you think I'm screaming at him for me? Half of it is 'yes,' but the other half is that they let the fans down, too. They are there with us all the time."

People in that section should be commended, but unfortunately many fans are waiting, some impatiently, for another winner. They reacted angrily in late 2003 and early 2004 amid the backlash of Payne's abrupt and troubling departure.

Uecker sincerely didn't understand such harsh attacks against the Seligs and the team. "That's not what Milwaukee's all about," he said in a *Journal Sentinel* interview. "I was born and raised here, and I hate to see this. I don't understand why people have gone after the Seligs."

More of this saga will be addressed later in the book, but suffice it to say that it shouldn't be surprising because discord has been part of the sport's history in Milwaukee too. It took decades of arguing and negotiating to finally decide where, when, and how to build County Stadium. Then came the ugly final years before the Braves left and the four-year void until the Brewers came along.

New Yorkers referred to Milwaukee as "Bushville" during the '57 Series, and in some ways, deserved or not, that moniker has stuck. So the question remains: Are the city of Milwaukee and the state of Wisconsin big-league?

Bob Buege, author of the 1988 book *The Milwaukee Braves: A Baseball Eulogy*, said in a phone conversation that the question is up for debate. "Milwaukee always has been a baseball city, but it's not as good as some," Buege said. "Saint Louis doesn't have a much larger population, but that is a terrific baseball town. They support their team no matter what, but Milwaukee prefers a winner. They're more fair-weather."

The numbers back up Buege's assessment, but that's not to say that Major League Baseball doesn't belong here. Fans can only hope for another return to the glory days, when Hall of Famers such as Hank Aaron, Warren Spahn, Eddie Mathews, Red Schoendienst, and Phil Niekro played for the Braves and Robin Yount, Paul Molitor, Don Sutton, and Rollie Fingers led the Brewers.

Baseball in Beertown tries to weave those two wonderful periods together while capturing as many great moments and not-so-great moments as possible—from before, in-between, and ever since.

Acknowledgments

To the players, coaches, team officials, and fans who made this project possible, especially those who agreed to be interviewed. To the staff members of the Wisconsin State Historical Society and Janesville Public Library. A big thanks to the Milwaukee Brewers and their media relations staff, especially Robbin Barnes for her diligence and patience in providing photographs. And kudos to Stan Stoga, Erika Reise, Candy Parrell, and others at Trails Media.

Chapter One

The Minor League Brewers and the Boston Braves (1902–52)

Depending on how old they are, people may think that baseball didn't start in Milwaukee until the Seattle Pilots became the Brewers in 1970, or maybe when Boston's Braves moved to the western shore of Lake Michigan in 1953. However, to experience Milwaukee's introduction to baseball, you'd have to take a time machine back to November 30, 1859, when the first organized game was played at what was then the State Fairgrounds on Spring Street on a site that today is part of Marquette University's campus. The three-inning contest ended with a score of 40–35.

Rufus King, editor of the *Milwaukee Sentinel* who later became a Union general in the Civil War, helped organize the city's initial professional club April 5, 1860. But Milwaukee didn't join the major-league ranks until 1877 (December 5), when the National League awarded the city a franchise. It didn't officially enjoy its first taste of the big-league experience until the next year.

Primarily known as the Cream Citys, the visiting Milwaukee club downed Indianapolis, 2–1, in the season opener on May 9, 1878, with Sam Weaver pitching a no-hitter. On May 14, the Creams downed the Cincinnati Reds, 8–5, in the first major league outing in Milwaukee as 1,500 fans showed up at the field at North Tenth Street and West Clybourn. Unfortunately, the team went into bankruptcy and folded after only one year in business.

The locals fielded a squad in the Union League five years later, and then a team joined the Western League for 11 seasons starting in 1888. Cornelius McGillicuddy managed the latter squad, and later earned fame as one of the sport's all-time greats with the Philadelphia Athletics under his better known name of Connie Mack.

Milwaukee jumped into the spotlight again as one of eight teams in the fledgling American League, which was founded January 28, 1901. Three of the entries (Chicago, Philadelphia, and Boston) were located on prime National League turf, thus setting off a two-year battle for territory, fans, and players as stars such as Cy Young, John McGraw, and Jimmy Collins jumped ship to what became called the Junior Circuit.

The Milwaukee Brewers opened their American League schedule April 25, 1901, losing 14–13 at Detroit after the Tigers rallied for 10 runs in the ninth inning. It was an omen of things to come as Milwaukee finished in the cellar.

History again wasn't kind to Milwaukee. A few months later, league president Ban Johnson announced that the franchise would move to Saint Louis to become the Browns. And there they remained until Bill Veeck tried to bring them back to Milwaukee more than 50 years later. But that's getting a little too far ahead of the story.

MILWAUKEE IN THE MINOR LEAGUES

The city was forced to settle for the minor-league Brewers, struggling with that image as a minor-league burg for the next half-century. At least crowds were treated to pretty decent baseball. The Brewers claimed eight American Association championships. They earned crowns in 1913 and 1914, winning a combined 198 contests, but didn't reach first place again until '36, when the Shaughnessy playoff system was instituted and included the top four teams in the standings. Milwaukee won postseason titles that first season and again in 1951, while the franchise finished with three Junior World Series championships in which the AA's top team squared off against the International League's finalist. The Brewers reached or surpassed the 100-victory plateau three times, including a record 102 triumphs in 1944.

These teams played at Athletic Park, which had been built for $40,000 in 1888 and occupied a city block in a residential area between West Chambers and Burleigh streets on a spot that became a playground when County Stadium came along and was eliminated in the early 1960s with the construction of Interstate 43.

The park's most distinctive feature was its rectangular shape—one in which the right- and left-field fences stood only 266 feet from home plate. The configuration meant that the so-called power alleys were farther away from home plate than in straightaway center field, which measured 395 feet.

Milwaukee native Otto Borchert purchased the franchise in 1919 and owned it until his death in 1927. The stadium was renamed in his honor and kept that name until the autumn of 1952, when it and the land were sold to the city for $123,000. Pieces of Borchert Field can still be found at the Milwaukee Public Museum and the county's historical society. The ballpark was home to some of baseball's pioneer executives, managers, and players.

Borchert didn't win a pennant as Milwaukee's owner, but his relationship with Mack helped two of the state's greatest early stars get their opportunity to play in the majors. Their names were Joe "Unser Choe" Hauser and Al Simmons (born Aloysius Semanski), both Milwaukee natives.

Hauser, whose nickname means "Our Joe" in German, joined the Brewers in 1920 and quickly became a fan favorite. In 1924, Hauser established a then-AL mark with 14 total bases August 2 and finished with 27 home runs that summer, second only to Babe Ruth. Hauser's big-league career was cut short because of a knee injury, but he ripped minor league pitchers for thunderous home runs for years afterward. He became the first pro performer to belt 60 or more round-trippers twice, accomplishing the feat with 63 for Baltimore in 1930 and 69 for Minneapolis in 1933.

Simmons was tabbed the "Duke of Mitchell Street" by those on the city's south side. He went on to lift the A's to consecutive World Series titles in 1929 and '30. It was easy to see why he was considered one of the game's best players. He batted higher than .380 four times and was inducted into the Hall of Fame in 1953.

Brewers players also turned in some of the league's best individual performances, including batting champions George Stone (.405 in 1904), Alex Chappelle (.349 in '13), Wheeler "Doc" Johnston (.374 in only 31 games in '18), Glenn Myatt (.370 in '22), Lester Bell (.365 in '24), Art Shires (.385 in '31), Earl Webb (.368 in '34), Lou Novikoff (.370 in '41), Eddie Stanky (.342 in his Most Valuable Player season of '42), Lewis Flick (.374 in '45), Heinz "Dutch" Becker (.363 in '47), and Bob Addis (.323 in '50).

Other sterling numbers included Lancelot Richbourg's 28 triples in 1928; U.S. "Stony" McGlynn's 446 innings pitched, 27 wins, and 14 shutouts in 1909; and Frank Schneiberg's dubious honor of hitting 34 batters during the 1907 campaign.

Anthony "Bunny" Brief was one of the game's top sluggers, leading the American Association in homers five times with Milwaukee and Kansas City. He had played for the Browns, the Chicago White Sox, and the Pittsburgh Pirates from 1912 to 1917.

And people probably don't know that the man many recognized as the world's greatest all-around athlete, Jim Thorpe, suited up for the Brewers, who purchased him from the New York Giants on April 1, 1916. He spent the entire season in Milwaukee and led the league with 48 stolen bases. Unfortunately, the Brewers finished in last place with a 54–110 mark.

Crowds also had the privilege of seeing some of the biggest names in the managerial ranks ply their trade from the Milwaukee dugout, including Charlie Grimm and Casey Stengel. Grimm led the Chicago Cubs to three World Series appearances, although he lost all three. He directed the second-place 1942 Brewers squad that then won the league crown the next season, and was replaced by Stengel during the '44 season. Grimm also helped write another chapter in Milwaukee baseball history 10 years later.

Borchert Field, on Milwaukee's near north side, was home to the minor league Brewers from 1902 to 1952.

Grimm and Stengel both served under perhaps the biggest showman in major league history. Bill Veeck, the son of an ex-Cubs owner, bought the rights to the Milwaukee franchise for $25,000 during 1941—and sold them for $250,000 four years later. The city and Borchert Field hadn't seen many characters like the guy nicknamed "the P. T. Barnum of Baseball."

Veeck improved the stadium and increased attendance while being named minor league baseball's executive of the year in 1942, at age 28. His innovative promotional tactics included such stunts as conducting morning games so third-shift defense workers could attend, having ushers wear nightgowns and pass out cereal and doughnuts to the crowds, and dressing band members in pajamas to play between innings. He conducted wacky giveaways of items such as ladders, butter, vegetables, and livestock.

The Brewers played about 4,000 games between 1902 and their final contest in Milwaukee in 1952. The franchise drew an estimated 8.3 million fans before being banished to Toledo, Ohio, when it was announced in March 1953 that the Braves were coming to town. The largest crowd at Borchert was 18,000, and more than 365,000 attended games in the high-water season of 1927, one of four years in which the franchise reached the 300,000 mark. One of the team's fans in the 1940s and early '50s was none other than Bud Selig, who did a lot of traveling and attended major league games at Yankee Stadium, Ebbets Field, and the Polo Grounds in New York and Wrigley Field and Comiskey Park in Chicago. "I went to a lot of games at Borchert Field, attending my first game there in 1941 or '42," baseball's commissioner said in a phone interview from his Milwaukee office in September 2004. "They had a lot of terrific players and teams. I had a number of favorites with those old Brewers, especially Herschel Martin. He got sold to New York and that's why I became a Yankee fan at the time."

THE BOSTON BRAVES

Meanwhile, halfway across the country, nobody was laughing it up in certain parts of Boston, where the NL representative Braves had suffered more defeats than any team except for the Philadelphia Athletics, finishing no higher than fourth place between 1917 and 1946. The team's only pennants since the turn of the century had come in 1914 and 1948 as the organization compiled 11 winning seasons in 52 years, while it finished last or second to last 24 times.

From 1903 to 1912, the misfits known as the Beaneaters languished through 10 straight finishes of sixth place or lower. The '06 team suffered the indignity of a franchise-record 19-game losing skid. The next season they became the Doves, named after their new owners, and made the final change to Braves in 1912, but mostly they were called losers.

The 1928 squad included future Hall of Famers Rogers Hornsby (.387) and George Sisler (.340), but it finished in seventh place at 50–103.

One particularly pitiful group was the 1935 gang, which turned in a franchise-worst 38–115 record for its 11th and final 100-loss season since 1905. That occurred despite the presence of the great Babe Ruth. It was the Bambino's final hurrah, as he hit only .181 with 13 hits in 72 plate appearances, although he crunched the last six of his 714 homers.

The truly miraculous 1914 champions and the '48 team, whose magnificent pitching duo coined the phrase "Spahn and Sain and pray for rain," were the only seasons to remember. The Braves of 1914 lost 18 of their first 22 contests and still sat in the basement as late as July 18, but they couldn't be stopped after that, posting an incredible 51–16 mark the rest of the way. The underdogs then whipped heavily favored Philadelphia in four straight games in the World Series. Former Cubs great Johnny Evers and Walter "Rabbit" Maranville, both future Hall of Famers, and Bill James were the stars of the otherwise unheralded bunch.

The 1948 season saw five players hit above .300 and the return of Warren Spahn and Johnny Sain from duty in World War II. Spahn won 15 games, while Sain was outstanding with a 24–15 record and nifty 2.60 earned run average. However, Cleveland turned the tide, winning the World Series in seven games.

The organization's hapless performances weren't helped any by the fact that the crosstown Red Sox were a much bigger draw, despite their not winning a championship since the 1918 squad gave the team its third trophy in seven seasons. The Braves' attendance was a stupefying 281,000 in their final

A worker positions the first message on the scoreboard at County Stadium in the spring of 1953.

season in Boston, and something had to give, or go. And it was the Braves, who finished in seventh place, a whopping 32 games behind the pennant-winning Dodgers, who in 1952 would lose the first of two consecutive World Series matchups with the New York Yankees. However, as bad as things appeared—and actually were—in Boston, the foundation for a strong rebound had been laid.

Eddie Mathews had hit only .242 but showed his awesome potential with 25 homers, while Sid Gordon and Johnny Logan were mainstays. On the mound, Spahn, Lew Burdette, and Max Surkont had fashioned losing records despite respectable ERAs. The Braves, through several key acquisitions and promotions from the Brewers farm club, were poised to make a run at respectability.

The Braves left after calling Boston home for 77 years, assuming Pittsburgh's place in the Western Division. But nobody was prepared for the welcome the boys from Beantown received in Milwaukee, and their quick rise in the standings took a city and the league by storm.

LEAGUES OF THEIR OWN

The city also fielded a representative, the Milwaukee Bears, in the National Negro League in 1923, and 21 years later the Milwaukee Chicks spent one season in Beertown as part of the All-American Girls Professional Baseball League.

The Bears participated in the Negro League's fourth season, but they played their final series in July of that year before folding. Competing at Borchert Field, the Bears were led by player-manager Preston "Pete" Hill, who had been a standout outfielder with the Philadelphia Giants and the Chicago American Giants early in the twentieth century. Other top performers included first baseman Percy Wilson, second sacker Anderson Pryor, shortstop Leroy Stratton, and pitcher Fulton Strong.

In 1944, the Chicks joined the AAGPB, which existed from 1943–54 and fielded teams in Racine and Kenosha. The Chicks made the most of their one year in Milwaukee, compiling a 70–45 record and winning the league championship as they downed Kenosha for the title.

During the season, Thelma "Tiby" Eisen, a California native, stole 91 bases. Right-hander Connie Wisniewski, also an outfielder, was Milwaukee's best pitcher. She finished 23–10 for the league's top winning percentage (.697) despite wearing a brace because of a knee injury after starting 5–0; she also won four games in the league championship.

Future Major League Hall of Famer Max Carey managed the team before it moved to Grand Rapids, Michigan, where it won two more titles.

Chapter Two

A Love Affair with the Braves (1953–65)

"It was as if a girl who'd sat alone night after night at George Devine's Million Dollar Ballroom—everybody saying she was a good sport, but nobody wanting to dance with her—it was as if such a girl suddenly found herself elected Miss Sex Symbol of 1953." That's how Robert W. Wells, in his 1970 book *This Is Milwaukee: A Colorful Portrait of the City that Made Beer Famous*, described the euphoria surrounding the news that Milwaukee had finally, after 52 years, become a major league city again.

Owner Lou Perini's Boston Braves club had suffered a horrendous 80 percent decline in attendance from the pennant-boosted totals of '48. Only 3,700 fans per game walked through the Gaffney Street turnstiles during 1952, proving that the Braves were falling way behind the Red Sox in fan loyalty and the almighty dollar in Boston.

While Perini later admitted that Toronto had been his first preference to set up shop, he grabbed his luggage and announced on March 13, 1953, that he wanted to head for the Midwest because he feared losing his territorial rights to the Milwaukee Brewers minor league franchise and there was talk about the possible relocation of the Saint Louis Browns. Five days later, his National League counterparts unanimously (8–0) approved the decision. Meanwhile, Browns' owner Bill Veeck, the Brewers' former president, was forced to take his beleaguered bunch to the East Coast, where they enjoyed much more success as the Baltimore Orioles.

Perini couldn't have made a wiser choice, but even he and the team's brass couldn't have prepared themselves for such a transformation in scenery and the outpouring of support they received upon arriving in their new home. An estimated 12,000 people greeted the players at the train depot in Milwaukee, and another throng of 60,000 well-wishers packed the parade route along Wisconsin Avenue.

Besides filling County Stadium regularly and conducting numerous spontaneous celebrations in the city's streets, faithful followers showered their new heroes with gifts. A Lutheran group gave outfielder and Wisconsin native Andy Pafko two cars and $6,000 worth of other merchandise. Warren Spahn received a $5,000 tractor and a 500-acre farm in Oklahoma, which he owned until his death in 2003, from the Federation of German-American Societies. More fans raised $5,500 for rookie outfielder Billy Bruton as a down payment on a house.

Newspapers around Wisconsin hailed the team's arrival, including this commentary in the *Manitowoc Herald-Times*: "It is safe to assume that the Braves, like the Green Bay Packers, will become a team claimed by the entire state as its own." The *La Crosse Tribune* said, "The new Braves indeed must have statewide support if they are to succeed box office-wise, and especially if the club's fortunes in the percentage column of wins and losses ever become grievously disappointing." That never came close to happening. The love affair had officially started, and it lasted for the remainder of the decade.

Jack Dittmer can attest to that. The left-handed-hitting second baseman played with the Milwaukee Brewers in 1952 before Boston called him up. Dittmer played 93 games, and although he hit just .193, he belted seven homers and knocked in 41 runs in 1952.

"Boston was a Red Sox town," Dittmer said via telephone from his office in Elkader, the small town in northeastern Iowa where he still works for the auto dealership that his father used to own. "Going from Boston to Milwaukee was like night and day. We went from drawing a couple thousand to having County Stadium full almost every game."

Dittmer played with the Braves through the 1956 season, finishing his Boston-Milwaukee career with a .232 average and 24 homers. However, he was the team's regular second sacker and enjoyed his best campaign in '53, batting .266 with nine round-trippers and 63 RBIs in 138 games. He said players felt like royalty during those years.

"The people adored us, and we couldn't do anything wrong," Dittmer said. "Businesses gave us cases of Miller, bought us gas, and did our dry cleaning. They treated us like kings. We had plenty of characters on those teams and did some things that maybe we don't want to remember. I can still recall a lot of stuff from those days, but I can't remember what my wife told me today."

Right-handed relief pitcher Dave Cole was another role player who witnessed the transition and move from a losing team on the East Coast to one of baseball's best organizations in the Midwest, but he also labored with the American Association's Brewers. "I played at Borchert Field, and it was the worst place to play," Cole said via phone from his native Maryland. "Depending on which dugout you were sitting in, you couldn't see the left-field or right-field corners. It was unbelievable. County Stadium was beautiful."

Cole compiled a 3–7 mark in 59 appearances with the Braves before being traded to the Cubs in March 1954 and then bouncing around the majors and minors for several years. Even though he didn't get many opportunities to shine, Cole remembers one special moment in 1953.

"I only pitched about 15 innings that year, and the funny thing was I had four of them in this one game," Cole said. "It was against the Giants and Sal Maglie. They jumped ahead 15–0 after four innings, and [manager Charlie] Grimm looks down the bench at me and says, 'Cole, you're pitching if it takes us all night to get outta here.' Well, my first time up to bat I hit a home run and the second time I hit a fly ball to the wall, so I hit .500 and had a slugging percentage of 2,000."

Unlike Cole, Lew Burdette was one of the stars on the Braves' outstanding pitching staff during their glory days, ones the Louisiana native recalled fondly via phone from his home in Florida. "I loved playing there and had a wonderful time," Burdette said. "We couldn't draw any fans in Boston, which was an American League city. But in Milwaukee it seemed like everybody jumped on the bandwagon. It was great winning a championship there."

Burdette said it was unfortunate that Milwaukee didn't bring home more World Series titles. "We had some pretty good ball clubs," he said. "We had [Warren] Spahn, [Bob] Buhl, and myself, and Don McMahon was in the bullpen. But we could never find that fourth starter. We had a bunch of super guys. We had different personalities, but we hardly ever had any arguments or fights."

They saved those for their National League opponents. The Braves' average finishing position in 1953–59 was 1.7 as they never fell below third place.

Bob Buege grew up in Milwaukee during the Braves' glorious run, which he captured in his exhaustive and fascinating history of his beloved team in the aforementioned *Baseball Eulogy*. He said it was a different and better era for baseball.

"I probably got to 15 games a year and listened to the rest on the radio," said Buege, who attended his first game at age seven. "You would walk down the street and at every house there was somebody sitting out on the porch listening to the game. It was a much simpler time, and that's what they did. People in Milwaukee really supported the Braves, and baseball was America's pastime. Kids in my generation played baseball all day. Today, except for Little League, you can't find a game of baseball going on. Baseball was king, and Milwaukee was king of baseball."

Bud Selig can attest to that. "I was a freshman in college when the Braves came to town," Selig recalled via phone. "I had seen a lot of games by that point, but I couldn't believe that Milwaukee had a major league team. I remember driving over there just to watch them build County Stadium. It went way beyond excitement."

Teammates mob Henry Aaron after he clubbed a game-winning homer in the 11th inning against Saint Louis on September 23, 1957, sending the Braves to the World Series.

1953

Veteran right-hander Max Surkont got the call as the Braves opened their first season representing Beertown on Monday, April 13, in Cincinnati. He led Milwaukee to a 2–0, three-hit triumph at Crosley Field, in which Billy Bruton was the defensive standout and scored the team's first run.

Milwaukee's home-opening lineup at County Stadium the next day featured Joe Adcock at first base, Jack Dittmer at second, Johnny Logan at short-stop, and Eddie Mathews at third. Sid Gordon, Bruton, and Andy Pafko manned the outfield spots from left to right. Warren Spahn got the starting pitching assignment, while Del Crandall was his battery mate.

Fans started showing up at 7:30 a.m., and a standing-room-only crowd of 34,357 attended the showdown with Stan Musial's Saint Louis Cardinals. Bruton won it, 3–2, with a 10th-inning homer off Gerry Staley that ricocheted off the glove of Enos Slaughter in right, capping a whirlwind honeymoon that had started only a few days earlier when the Braves arrived in Milwaukee from spring training in Florida.

The 1953 Braves pulled an about-face from the disappointed and demoralized bunch that left Massachusetts, improving by 27 ½ games to finish 92–62, the most victories since the 1914 unit won 94 times. The team's magical first season in Milwaukee earned them second place, still a whopping 13 games behind the mighty Brooklyn Dodgers. Manager Charlie Grimm reveled in his team's success, his second stop in Milwaukee and his first full season at the helm after replacing Tommy Holmes during the forgettable 1952 campaign.

Several factors combined to reverse the team's fortunes. The Braves had obtained Pafko from Brooklyn and Adcock from Cincinnati and called Bruton up from the minors. Crandall and pitchers Johnny Antonelli and Bob Buhl returned from military duty to give the Braves a huge boost. Adcock finished with 18 homers and 80 RBIs while hitting .285, Bruton led the league with 26 stolen bases, Crandall chipped in 15 round-trippers and 51 RBIs, while Pafko was even better with 17 and 72, respectively.

Mathews led the big leagues with 47 homers and knocked in a team-record 135 runs while topping the Braves with a .302 average. Logan (11 HRs and 73 RBIs) and Gordon (19 and 75) made key contributions for the explosive Braves' attack.

Milwaukee's booming bats set a loop standard of 12 homers in a double-header sweep of Pittsburgh at Forbes Field on August 30, including eight in the 19–4, first-game rout. Reserve outfielder Jim Pendleton smacked three of his seven HRs as the visitors' eight bombs tied the 1939 New York Yankees' single-game record. Pendleton joined Mathews as the only rookies to hit three out in a game. Mathews sent two more balls into the stands to finish with four for the day en route to 30 HRs on the road as the Braves established a franchise high of 156 homers.

Antonelli fashioned a 12–12 mark with 11 complete games and a 3.18 earned run average, while Buhl finished 13–8 with a 2.97 ERA. Holdovers Lew Burdette, Surkont, and Spahn turned in excellent efforts. Burdette won 15 of his 20 decisions with a 3.24 ERA and a team-leading eight saves, and Surkont was 11–5 after starting out 6–0 while striking out what was then a major league-record eight straight Reds on May 25. However, Spahn was the staff ace with a 23–7 mark; his fifth 20-win effort earned him the Cy Young Award. His numbers included 24 complete games and a sparkling 2.10 ERA. The Braves led the NL with a 3.30 ERA.

But the most important statistic was 1,826,297. The club's attendance set an NL record, and as Gary Caruso said in his 1995 book, *The Braves Encyclopedia*, tickets sold like bratwurst and beer. And it happened even though the organization had literally no off-season to devote to ticket sales and promotional efforts. Milwaukee passed its abysmal 1952 season attendance after only 13 home dates (May 20). The day before, the Dodgers won 4–1 in front of 36,439, the largest paid crowd for any sporting event in Beertown's history up to that point.

Brooklyn clinched the pennant with a 5–2 verdict against the Braves on September 12, the earliest any team had accomplished the feat. However, the bond between the Braves and fans from throughout Wisconsin and the Midwest was only getting stronger every day.

"Many of the players lived in the community, so they were more like ordinary people," Bob Buege said. "Today's athletes think they're above society with all of their millions. In the old days, you'd see the players at neighborhood bars such as Ray Jackson's. Any kind of meeting such as the Rotary, Lion's Club, churches, high schools, and the Braves had people there. You couldn't go into a store and not see a sign or something about the Braves."

1954

Milwaukee's fortunes for this season and the foreseeable future took a crucial turn on February 1, which is when the Braves shipped pitcher Johnny Antonelli to the New York Giants in a six-player trade that netted them left fielder Bobby Thomson, the same guy who had won the 1951 pennant for New York with his homer, the "shot heard 'round the world," that won a playoff against the Dodgers. The Braves eventually slipped to 89–65 and into third place, but they were only eight games behind the Giants, who won the World Series over Cleveland with the help of Antonelli's 1–0 mark and 0.84 ERA after he earned 21 victories and registered a league-leading 2.30 ERA during the regular season. Meanwhile, Thomson broke his ankle during an exhibition contest and missed action until midseason, which in turn prompted Milwaukee's promotion of a lanky, quiet kid named Hank Aaron.

Seating was increased to 43,340, and fans continued to pour into County

Stadium at an alarming rate as the Braves became the first National League organization to surpass two million in attendance for a single season. Milwaukee was struggling at the .500 mark at the All-Star break despite a 10-game winning streak in May. But the Braves got red hot, winning 41 of their next 54 games, including another 10-game winning string, to take over second place in early September. Warren Spahn had won 11 consecutive decisions, but luck turned sour for Milwaukee as Aaron broke his ankle September 5 and Joe Adcock's wrist was broken when Don Newcombe hit him with a pitch six days later, eliminating any realistic chance of the Braves catching or at least making things interesting for the Giants.

Despite those injury woes, Milwaukee sported one of the top offensive units in baseball again. Eddie Mathews belted 40 homers, knocked in 103 runs and scored a team-high 96 times while batting .290. Aaron hit .280 with 13 homers and 69 RBIs in his rookie campaign, while Del Crandall also reached the 20-homer plateau (21) and brought home 64. Andy Pafko chipped in 14 homers and 69 RBIs, and Billy Bruton again led the league in stolen bases with 34 and topped the team with 161 hits for a .284 average.

Adcock added 23 homers and 87 RBIs and hit at a .308 clip. He set a big-league mark with 18 total bases on four homers and a double against the Dodgers at Ebbets Field on July 31. Using a borrowed bat, Adcock carried Milwaukee to a 15–7 triumph and gave him a two-day tally of 25 total bases, which tied the standard that Ty Cobb had established. Second baseman Danny O'Connell contributed 28 doubles and a .279 average. His 151 hits were fourth-highest on the team.

The Braves weren't bad in other facets either, posting the NL's top defense (.981) and second-best staff ERA (.3.19) despite Bob Buhl's subpar, injury-riddled 2–7 showing and Lew Burdette's 15–14 mark, even though the latter had registered the second-best ERA in the league (2.76). Spahn finished 21–12 with a 3.14 ERA, and rookie Gene Conley, who stood six-foot-eight and played in the National Basketball Association, was 14–9 with a nifty 2.96 ERA, while Dave Jolly contributed 10 saves and an 11–6 record in a team-high 47 appearances.

The team's biggest pitching moment occurred June 12, when Jim Wilson, who ended up 8–2 with a 3.52 ERA, fired a no-hitter against Robin Roberts and the Philadelphia Phillies at County Stadium. It was Wilson's first starting assignment after he had allowed seven runs in just 8 2/3 innings of relief work. Ironically, Milwaukee had placed him on waivers two weeks earlier. Luckily for Braves fans, there were no takers for the 32-year-old right-hander. Wilson baffled the Phillies, 2–0, in front of 28,218. It was the eighth such gem in franchise history and first since Vern Bickford's masterpiece in 1950. Roberts absorbed his first loss after nine straight wins over the Braves.

1955

Milwaukee was a top contender again, but its 85–69 mark was good only for runner-up status. The Braves couldn't catch the unbelievable Dodgers, who won 10 in a row to start the spring and 22 of their first 24 en route to a whopping 13 ½–game margin, assuring themselves of the top spot September 8. The Braves clubbed a team-record 182 homers, featuring 41 from Eddie Mathews, who knocked in 101 runs and hit .289 despite missing two weeks of action after undergoing an appendectomy. That gave him 40 or more dingers for the third season in a row.

Mathews's injury was only one downfall as Bobby Thomson banged up his shoulder and played in just 101 games; Gene Conley hurt his shoulder and didn't pitch much after the All-Star game; and Joe Adcock broke his wrist July 31, finishing with 15 homers and 45 RBIs.

Hank Aaron produced a .314 average while smacking 27 homers and bringing home 106. He shared league-high honors of doubles (37) with teammate Johnny Logan, while Billy Bruton made it three titles in a row with 25 of the team's 42 steals. First baseman George Crowe filled in admirably for Adcock with a .281 average, 15 homers, and 55 RBIs, while Logan contributed career highs in average (.297) and RBIs (83) and was 12 behind Aaron with 177 base hits. Second sacker Danny O'Connell knocked in 40 and Del Crandall belted 26 homers and had 62 RBIs despite hitting .225 and .236, respectively.

However, the team's pitching performance fell off despite a league-high 61 complete games as it finished with a 3.85 ERA. Warren Spahn was 17–14 and 3.26, and Bob Buhl was 13–11 with a 3.21 ERA. Lew Burdette finished 13–8 and Conley was 11–7, but both registered ERAs above 4.00. Ray Crone chipped in a 10–9 mark, splitting time between starting and relieving.

Despite watching the team come up short, Braves backers filled the seats and Lou Perini's pockets, pushing attendance over the two million figure for the second of what would become four consecutive seasons. This strong showing featured an NL-record opening day gathering of 43,640 as Cincinnati visited County Stadium.

1956

No matter how hard they tried, this version of the Braves unfortunately settled for the role as bridesmaid for the second consecutive season and the third time in four years in Milwaukee. The Braves captured the middle spot in a three-team chase for the National League pennant, finishing one game behind the Dodgers and one game ahead of Cincinnati with a 92–62 record. Milwaukee controlled the race at several points during the season but couldn't hang on. The Braves probably would have won going away if not for a sluggish start in which they sat at only 24–22 on June 16. That prompted management to replace Charlie Grimm as skipper with one of his coaches, Fred Haney, who had led losing efforts with Saint Louis and Pittsburgh.

Milwaukee responded magnificently, claiming victories in its first 11 contests under Haney's guidance to move into first place. The Braves won 15 of 17 after the All-Star break to lead the Reds by 5 ½ games and Los Angeles by 6. The Braves fell out of first place September 15 but entered a season-ending series at Saint Louis with a one-game cushion over the defending champion Dodgers. The host Braves lost the opener, 5–4, and Warren Spahn then suffered a 2–1 setback in 12 innings as Milwaukee fell one game back. Lew Burdette defeated the Cardinals on the final day, 4–2, but Los Angeles completed a sweep of the Pirates to claim the crown again.

Burdette (19–10), who tossed six of the Braves' 12 shutouts to lead the league, and Spahn (20–11) registered the best ERAs in the circuit at 2.70 and 2.78, respectively, as Milwaukee was the stingiest staff in that category at 3.11. Spahn completed 20 games and surpassed 200 wins at age 35. Bob Buhl bounced back with a fine 18–8 record and 3.32 ERA, but he was hit on his pitching hand by a line drive and was much less effective down the homestretch, while the team received 11 wins from Ray Crone in completing 64 games as a staff.

Gene Conley finished only 8–9 but compiled a fine 3.13 ERA, while the bullpen was awesome at times with the likes of Dave Jolly (3.74 and seven saves), Ernie Johnson (3.71 and six), Lou Sleater (2–2 and 3.15), Taylor Phillips (5–3 and 2.26), and Bob Trowbridge (3–2 and 2.66) doing their part. Milwaukee, which was third in defense, again fielded one of the most potent hitting lineups as it finished number three in homers, batting average, and runs scored.

Aaron won the batting championship with a .328 average and led the league with 200 hits and 34 doubles, adding 26 homers and 92 RBIs. He received plenty of help as Joe Adcock swatted 38 homers and Eddie Mathews added 37 while knocking in 103 and 95 runs, respectively. Bobby Thomson (20), Del Crandall (16), and Johnny Logan (15) contributed mightily as the Braves sent 177 souvenirs out of the park. Billy Bruton smacked a league-leading 15 triples. However, Crandall hit only .238 and Thomson finished at a .235 clip.

Attendance topped two million again, with a Monday, September 3, contest one of many ways that fans showed they were still nuts about their Braves. Milwaukee drew a home record for an evening date as 47,604 checked out a doubleheader against the Reds, which the teams split.

1957

Several injuries almost derailed Milwaukee's attempts at finally getting over the hump and claiming its first pennant, but unexpected contributions and a key acquisition helped the Braves end four years of near misses.

Starting on July 16, Milwaukee posted wins in 17 of 19 outings and 24 of 29 to grab what appeared to be an insurmountable 8 1/2–game advantage. However, the Braves teetered from their lofty position, dropping 8 of 11 as Saint Louis shaved six games off Milwaukee's margin by September 15.

Milwaukee then responded like a champion, ripping off seven consecutive triumphs, capped by a history-making 4–2 decision over its top pursuers September 23. The highlight came when Hank Aaron belted the first pitch he saw from the Cards' Billy Muffett over the center-field fence for a two-run homer in the 11th inning. Bedlam ensued as the Braves and their fans cele-

Young Milwaukee fans Michael Rodell and Thomas Greiner were disappointed at not being able to see their favorite Braves play on this day.

brated Milwaukee's first pennant after Aaron's 43rd of a league-topping 44 dingers for the season.

It occurred on what normally would have been an obscure blast, Aaron's 109th career HR. But to this day, Aaron calls it his most memorable of all, despite his clubbing 646 more during his illustrious career. He finished with league highs in RBIs (132) and runs scored (118), and he eventually was named the NL's most valuable player after contributing 198 hits, a .322 average and 27 doubles.

Bud Selig remembers homer number 109 like it was yesterday, and he said during a phone conversation that he was lucky to have witnessed it. "I was out of college and the service, but I was taking an accounting class at UW-M because my father wanted me to," Selig said. "I was driving to class and noticed the Braves were in town. I pulled into the parking lot, went up to the ticket window, and got one for a seat in the upper deck. I was all by myself. When Hank hit that homer, I couldn't believe it. I just sat and cried."

But these Braves were more than a one-man show, reaching the seats for a franchise record 199 homers, including 32 from Eddie Mathews to go with 94 RBIs and .292 average and 21 from Wes Covington, who hit .284 and knocked in 65 runs, most after being recalled from the minors to fill the hole left when Bobby Thomson was traded.

Milwaukee general manager John Quinn also shipped Danny O'Connell and Ray Crone to New York for second baseman Red Schoendienst at the June 15 deadline. The veteran batted .310 with 23 doubles and 56 runs scored in only 93 games. Schoendienst solidified the team's most obvious weakness defensively in the infield.

That maneuver definitely helped ease the pain of two crucial injuries. Joe Adcock broke his leg June 23 and was lost until September, limiting him to 12 homers and 38 RBIs. Then on July 11, leadoff batter Billy Bruton injured knee ligaments after colliding with shortstop Felix Mantilla while chasing a pop fly. Bruton missed the remainder of the season as the Braves combined for only 35 stolen bases, 11 of them from him to go with his nine triples in 79 games.

However, the Braves weren't to be denied as Aaron moved from right to center and an unknown player named Bob Hazle more than earned his nickname of "Hurricane" after being recruited from Wichita, ripping opposing pitchers for 54 hits in only 134 at-bats for a resounding .403 average while drilling seven of his career nine homers.

A prime example of Milwaukee's immense firepower and depth took place September 2 at Wrigley Field, as the Braves whipped Chicago, 23–10, in the first game of a doubleheader sweep. Hazle smacked four hits, while Frank

Torre, subbing for Adcock, scored six runs to tie a major league record. Those kinds of efforts helped Milwaukee lead the league in runs and triples while finishing with a .269 team batting average.

Another guy who had never worn a Braves uniform was 27-year-old hurler Don McMahon, who joined the parent club in late June. He promptly became Milwaukee's number-one closer before the term became popular, registering nine saves, two victories, and a sparkling 1.54 ERA.

Milwaukee's starting rotation was magnificent again despite Bob Buhl's late-season shoulder troubles. He posted a 2.74 ERA, while his 18-7 record gave him a loop-best .722 winning percentage. Warren Spahn topped the NL with 21 victories, including his 41st career shutout (a league mark for lefties) as he whitewashed the Cubs, 8–0, on September 3, en route to the Cy Young award. Spahn had 18 complete games and a 2.69 ERA. Lew Burdette finished 17–9 as the Braves were number two with a 3.47 ERA. Gene Conley added nine wins, while Ernie Johnson finished 7–3 with four saves, and Bob Trowbridge was 7–5.

Attendance reached an astounding 2,215,404, a number surpassed only twice in Milwaukee, first by the 1983 defending AL champion Brewers and second by the staggering 2.8 million who visited Miller Park during its inaugural season of 2001. If that wasn't enough excitement, October was even better for "Bushville" as Milwaukee hosted the Fall Classic, but that story awaits in chapter 3.

1958

Fred Haney's crew was tested early and often, more so by a wide array of injuries than any of Milwaukee's opponents, making this repeat performance as kings of the National League that much more impressive. The Braves didn't take control of the race until grabbing first place for good July 30th with a victory over the Dodgers. They then polished off the Giants, who along with the Dodgers had moved to the West Coast, in four straight contests at County Stadium during the first week of August. Milwaukee more or less cruised from there, holding off Pittsburgh by eight games and clinching the franchise's first back-to-back pennants since 1897-98.

Milwaukee, which finished 92–62, still unleashed enough offensive clout, with 167 homers, 675 runs and a league-best .266 average. However, the Braves defended their trophy behind a patchwork mound corps that finished as the senior circuit's best group by far.

Warren Spahn continued to dominate opposing lineups, turning in a 22–11 campaign. He led the NL in wins, complete games (23), and innings pitched (290). His 3.07 ERA helped the team finish number one at 3.21. The masterful veteran became the first southpaw to win 20 or more games for a ninth time, beating Saint Louis, 8–2, on September 13 to break a tie with Hall of Famers Eddie Plank and Lefty Grove. He then got credit for win number 21 as Milwaukee sewed up the crown with a 6–5 decision at Cincinnati on September 21.

He received plenty of help from buddy Lew Burdette, who finished 20–10 with a 2.91 ERA and won seven games in August as the Braves began to pull away, and Don McMahon, who was 7–2 and notched eight saves. Arm woes plagued Bob Buhl (5–2) and Gene Conley (0–6), but Milwaukee couldn't have asked for more from several newcomers, especially youngsters Juan Pizarro (6–4, 2.70), Joey Jay (7–5, 2.14), and rookie Carlton Willey (9–7, 2.70). Willey led the league with four shutouts after being plucked from Wichita in late May, while veteran Bob Rush (10–6, 3.42) provided stability after being acquired from the Cubs the previous December. By season's end, Milwaukee had recorded 15 shutouts.

Red Schoendienst was a steadying influence again, but he was limited to 106 games and lacked his usual offensive presence because of what was later discovered as the early stages of tuberculosis. Mel Roach hit .309 as his fill-in.

Wes Covington crunched 24 homers and knocked in 74 despite being limited to 90 games because of a knee injury he suffered in spring training. Billy Bruton didn't return to regular duty until late May after his injury from '57 but still hit .280. And Bob Hazle never rekindled the spark that had earned him unsung hero laurels the previous season, hitting only .179 in 20 games. He was beaned and carried off the field May 6 and was sold to the Detroit Tigers 18 days later.

Eddie Mathews swatted 31 homers despite watching his average plummet to .251 and knocked in only 77 runs, his lowest totals since his 1952 rookie season in Boston. Hank Aaron picked up the slack with 109 runs, 196 hits, 30 homers, 95 RBIs, and a .326 average. Joe Adcock banged 19 homers, Del Crandall chipped in 18, and Johnny Logan added 11.

Milwaukee's attendance dropped below the 2 million mark for the first time in five years, but the Braves took their rowdy supporters on another wonderful seven-game World Series ride. Unlike a year earlier, the Braves fell short this time around, as you'll find out in chapter 3.

1959

The expectations inside and outside the clubhouse couldn't have been higher after winning back-to-back pennants, but the Braves finished only 86–70 in

1959. And, as in 1956, it was a three-team free-for-all that went down to the final day of the season. San Francisco dropped both games of a doubleheader against Saint Louis on the last day, while Milwaukee and Los Angeles won their outings to force a two-way tie and a best-of-three playoff series.

John Roseboro's solo shot in the sixth inning decided a 3–2 L.A. victory in the opener at drizzly County Stadium. Dodgers' rookie Larry Sherry pitched 7 2/3 innings in relief for the victory. In Game 2 at the Memorial Coliseum, Lew Burdette was outpitching Don Drysdale as the Braves grabbed a 4–2 cushion in the sixth. That's when shortstop Johnny Logan was injured, which proved to be crucial. Milwaukee led 5–2 entering the ninth, but the Dodgers knotted the score against four Braves pitchers and then won the game and the NL pennant in the 12th on Felix Mantilla's off-balance throwing error with runners on first and second with two outs. He had moved over from second base to replace Logan.

Despite the disappointing ending, several Braves turned in commendable campaigns as they hit the most homers in the league and allowed the fewest. The mound corps recorded 69 complete games and 18 shutouts as Warren Spahn and Burdette shared the league lead in victories as both went 21–15. Spahn completed 21 games and Burdette 20, while Bob Buhl (15–9) was third in ERA at 2.86 and Don McMahon topped the circuit with 15 saves. Juan Pizarro won six of his eight decisions with a 3.77 ERA. However, several others suffered losing records, including Joey Jay at 6–11 and 4.09, Carlton Willey at 5–9 and 4.15, and Bob Rush at 5–6 despite a 2.40 ERA.

The Braves sorely missed second baseman Red Schoendienst, who batted only three times before tuberculosis sidelined him for the season. They could have used Gene Conley but had traded him to the Phillies.

Eddie Mathews topped the usual Milwaukee power surge with 46 homers, a league high. He added 114 RBIs and hit a career-best .306. Hank Aaron was sensational again, ripping NL pitchers for a league- and career-best .355 average (223 hits) to go with his 39 homers, 46 doubles, 116 runs and 123 RBIs. Del Crandall (21 HRs and 72 RBIs) and Joe Adcock (25 and 76) also helped the cause, while Logan chipped in 13 HRs and 50 RBIs, Billy Bruton hit .289 with 41 RBIs, and Wes Covington chipped in a .279 mark and brought home 45.

The Braves had won more games than anybody else in Major League Baseball during manager Fred Haney's three-plus seasons. With two or three more wins, Milwaukee could have won four straight pennants under his tutelage. Despite the team's success, the five-foot-six skipper nicknamed "Pudge" was called conservative by many and roundly criticized, retiring five days after the team's playoff series setback.

Logan was one who aired his feelings to members of the press after the announcement. "We should have won by 10 games without any question," the fiercely competitive Logan said. "When they announced Haney was out, you can bet very few of the players were sorry." Attendance dropped for a second consecutive season (1.75 million), which pretty much marked the beginning of the end of a terrific run as the team never finished closer than five games out of first place during its final six seasons in Milwaukee.

1960

Charlie Dressen, who had formerly managed the Dodgers and the Washington Senators, grabbed the team's reins as manager, and he rubbed even more people the wrong way than Fred Haney had, including some of his players. He was arrogant, and his disciplinarian style didn't sit well with many of the freewheeling, fun-loving characters on the Braves roster.

Milwaukee finished a respectable 88–66, which would have won the pennant a year earlier but wasn't nearly enough. The Braves never really caught fire despite holding first place late in July, finishing seven games behind eventual World Series winner Pittsburgh.

Eddie Mathews (40) and Hank Aaron (39) finished behind Chicago's Ernie Banks in the home run derby and were second and first, respectively, with 124 and 126 RBIs as the Braves' 170 round-trippers led the league. Joe Adcock contributed 25 HRs, knocked in 91, and batted .298; Del Crandall chipped in 19, 77, and .294; and Billy Bruton topped the league with 13 triples and reached double digits in homers (12) for the first time while hitting .286.

It still didn't catapult the Braves to the top because holes in left field and at second base weren't adequately filled. Wes Covington hit 10 homers in an injury-plagued campaign, while Red Schoendienst had recovered from his fight against TB but never returned to the form that had made him an integral cog during the 1957 championship season.

But even more disappointing was the pitching, which registered its highest ERA since '55. The big three did their jobs as Warren Spahn led the league with 21 wins and 18 complete games. He and Lew Burdette (19–13) each tossed four shutouts and notched no-hitters, while Bob Buhl finished 16–9 with a 3.09 ERA despite a league-high 103 walks. However, the depth that Milwaukee had enjoyed during the past several years was gone, and the other starting candidates were erratic. Reliever Don McMahon also struggled (5.94 ERA) despite 10 saves.

Milwaukee also didn't have much room for error later in the season because it had gotten off to a slow start, entering June at only 16–16. The

Braves had played only 32 games in a month and a half because bad weather had postponed 12 contests, thus adding to their already inconsistent play and poor bullpen.

Carlton Willey and Juan Pizarro both finished with 6–7 marks and high ERAs at 4.35 and 4.55, respectively. McMahon was 3–6 and Ron Piche wound up 3–5 but had a respectable 3.56 ERA and nine saves. Joey Jay was 9–8 and 3.24.

The highlights definitely were the two no-hitters, which took place less than a month apart at County Stadium. On August 18, Burdette downed former teammate Gene Conley and the lowly Phillies, who succumbed during a 1–0 masterpiece. The only runner Burdette allowed was Tony Gonzalez, whom he hit with a pitch in the fifth inning but erased on a double-play ball. Burdette also scored the only run of the contest. Five days later at the Coliseum in L.A., Burdette and the Braves whipped the Dodgers 7–0, as the visitors drilled five homers. Burdette's scoreless streak ended at 32 $2/3$ innings.

Meanwhile, Philadelphia also was Spahn's victim on September 16, this time against starter John Buzhardt. Spahn notched his 11th 20-win season and fifth in a row, 4–0, registering a Milwaukee club record with 15 strikeouts in slapping the last-place Phils with their 90th loss of the year.

Soon after gaining first place, the Braves dropped 11 of 15 contests to fall into fourth place. They never recovered, suffering the indignity of having the Pirates clinch the pennant at County Stadium on September 25 despite sweeping a three-game series from Pittsburgh, which was headed to the World Series for the first time since facing the mighty Yankees in 1927.

A big difference was the teams' season series. Milwaukee had won 15 of 22 showdowns in 1959, including a 5–0 mark from Spahn. A year later, Pittsburgh turned the tables, winning 13 of 22 overall and five of six decisions against the Braves' ace lefty.

Mathews, 28, had become the second-youngest player after Jimmie Foxx to reach 300 home runs. But attendance again faltered, dipping below the 1.5 million mark for the first time since the move and marking a Milwaukee low for the second consecutive season.

1961

The unraveling continued under Charlie Dressen. Several roster moves before and after the season started to take their toll, as did the patchwork and mostly substandard pitching performances, with the exception of Warren Spahn and Lew Burdette. Evidence occurred early and often as Milwaukee, which finished with 33 one-run losses (it won 30), gave up leads and homers at an alarming rate.

The Braves climbed two games above .500 only once until July 22.

The Braves finished with their poorest record (83–71) since coming to Beertown, which knocked them down to fourth, 10 games behind Cincinnati. Their undoing led to Dressen's short, tumultuous run as skipper when executive vice president Birdie Tebbetts took over on September 2.

Fans, who had hung Dressen in effigy (they'd done the same with Fred Haney despite the team's success), showed their displeasure with another decline in attendance. Only 1.1 million, half of the high-water mark from four years earlier, showed up—despite the fact that the Braves led the NL in homers for a third straight season with 188, including Joe Adcock's 35, 34 from Hank Aaron, and another 32 from Eddie Mathews. Frank Thomas filled in for Wes Covington in left field and belted 25 HRs; Frank Bolling took over at second base and added 15; outfielder Lee Maye contributed 14 long balls; and Joe Torre, who replaced injured Del Crandall at catcher, added 10.

However, proof as to why Milwaukee struggled was evident at Crosley Field on June 8. Mathews, Aaron, Adcock, and Thomas smacked consecutive homers against two Cincinnati pitchers, setting a major league record. But somehow the Reds won the game, 10–8.

Spahn, who had turned 40 in April, was masterful again. He led league hurlers with 21 victories, 21 complete games, and a 3.02 ERA. Two major career highlights occurred, the first on April 28, when he threw a no-hitter, his second in his last six starts spanning the past two seasons. Five days past his 40th birthday, Spahn outdueled the Giants' Sam Jones to become the second-oldest major league pitcher (after Cy Young) to hurl a no-no. It was Spahn's 290th career triumph and his 52nd shutout. Meanwhile, Aaron knocked in the only run against Jones, who finished with 10 strikeouts. Then in August, Spahn became a 300-game winner with a 2–1 triumph over the Cubs.

Even his sidekick Burdette's performance was pedestrian in some ways as his ERA ballooned to 4.00 despite his 18–11 mark. But Bob Buhl was even more ineffective, finishing 9–10 with a 4.11 ERA. Tony Cloninger won seven of nine decisions but posted a whopping 5.25 ERA, while Don McMahon rebounded with a 6–4 mark, eight saves, and a 2.84 ERA.

The Braves got tired of waiting for Joey Jay and Juan Pizarro to find consistency, trading them to Cincy and the Chicago White Sox, respectively. But as Milwaukee's luck would have it, they both excelled in new environments. Jay's 21 wins helped the Reds claim the pennant, while Pizarro was 14–7. Milwaukee, which had traded Billy Bruton to Detroit in the off-season, shipped mainstay Johnny Logan to Pittsburgh after having obtained weak-hitting Roy McMillan (.220 and seven HRs) in the Pizarro deal.

Baseball in Beertown

The Braves won 20 of 29 outings during August to reach third place and climb to within 6 ½ games of first place with 27 contests remaining. However, they couldn't sustain their momentum. Much of the magic was gone, and the situation didn't improve during the next several months.

Fans show their New York counterparts who's the champion of Major League Baseball after the Braves downed the Yankees in Game 7 of the 1957 World Series.

1962

The Braves continued their spiral downward in the standings as more remnants from their recent glorious past piled up. Milwaukee lost eight of its first 10 games and never recovered, finishing 86–76 for fifth place, the team's lowest spot and winning percentage since its days in Boston. The Braves never challenged the first-place Giants and ended up 15 ½ games back, grabbing an upper-division position only because the league had added expansion teams in New York and Houston.

Hitting home runs wasn't a problem, as the Braves' 181 clouts were second to San Francisco. However, they were inconsistent and finished ahead of only the Mets and Colt 45s (who changed their name to the Astros) in batting average at .252.

Hank Aaron was phenomenal again, belting 45 homers, knocking in 128, scoring 127, and hitting .323 with 191 hits and 15 stolen bases. Joe Adcock crunched 29 HRs, but his .248 mark was his lowest average since 1951, while Eddie Mathews equaled Adcock's long ball total, the first time he hadn't reached 30 since his rookie season. Roy McMillan (12), Mack Jones (10), and Lee Maye (10) also reached double figures in long balls.

Two of the many disappointing moments that signaled just how far the team had slipped occurred in May. The lowly Mets swept a doubleheader at the Polo Grounds, both on ninth-inning homers. Making matters worse was the fact that Craig Anderson won both games, the last of his career. He went on to lose his next 19 decisions before retiring two years later. The misfits, who went on to lose 120 games that season, inexplicably turned the trick again at County Stadium eight days later in games that the Braves had led.

A big part of the problem was that Milwaukee had shipped ace reliever Don McMahon to Houston four days before the first doubleheader because manager Birdie Tebbetts thought that McMahon had lost zip on his fastball. McMahon went on to win five games, saved eight, and led the majors with a 1.53 ERA.

Warren Spahn won 18 games and posted a 3.04 ERA, but like most of the staff he suffered from a lack of consistent run support and a makeshift relief corps. Lew Burdette had become a part-time starter and finished only 10–9 with a 4.89 ERA, while Bob Hendley (11–13) moved into the rotation, as did Bob Shaw, who had been picked up from the Kansas City A's. Shaw was a surprising 15–9 and finished second to Los Angeles's Sandy Koufax in ERA at 2.80. However, he didn't fare as well as a starter again. Tony Cloninger added an 8–3 record.

Bob Buhl pitched only two innings and was traded to the Cubs, where he won 12 times, including four against Milwaukee. The Braves also lacked depth and offensive firepower in left and right fields and in the middle infield. They could have used Frank Thomas but had sent him to the New York Mets, where he swatted 34 HRs and knocked in 94 for Casey Stengel's bunch.

The results coincided with a precipitous decline in attendance. Only 766,921 showed up at County Stadium, including the smallest-ever opening-day crowd, 30,001, and the lowest figure ever up to that point: 2,746 souls on May 10. A host of promotional efforts didn't help, and neither did the county board's gesture of lifting the ban on beer carry-ins June 8. And as if what was happening on the field and wasn't happening in the stands weren't bad enough, Tebbetts resigned five days after the season ended to become skipper in Cleveland.

But November 16 proved to be the most ominous day in Milwaukee baseball history. Lou Perini and the Perini Corporation, which had held a controlling interest in the Braves since 1944, sold it to the LaSalle Corporation, a syndicate of Chicago businessmen, for $5.5 million. William Bartholomay headed the syndicate, a group later to be known as "the Carpetbaggers."

Then, on November 27, the Braves sent aging slugger Adcock to the Indians in a five-player deal.

1963

The news didn't get any better before the 1963 season started. On April 7, a public stock offering of 115,000 shares in the team was withdrawn after only 13,000 shares were sold to 1,600 new investors. A "Go to Bat for the Braves" effort late in the season to appease owners, sell tickets, and obtain sponsorships fell short of expectations.

So there were only two good things about the Braves' 11th season in Beertown: Warren Spahn and Hank Aaron. Spahn, 42, despite elbow trouble that affected him through much of July and early August, turned in arguably his best performance. He went 23–7 with 22 complete games, a 3.04 ERA, and seven shutouts. His first victory of the year, number 328, made him the winningest left-hander in history. He pitched so well most of the time that even in defeat he couldn't be faulted. On July 2, he lost a 1–0 battle against the Giants' Juan Marichal in which Willie Mays's homer in the bottom of the 16th decided the outcome.

While Spahn continued to set records, Aaron, at 29, kept piling up huge numbers. He tied Willie McCovey for the HR title with 44, led the league in RBIs with 130 and runs scored with 121, and missed Triple Crown honors by seven percentage points with his .319 average. He also contributed 31 of the team's 75 stolen bases.

Power numbers were down throughout the NL, and it was particularly evident in Milwaukee, which hit only 139 homers while batting just .244. Four players hit 11 to 14 homers, but Eddie Mathews (23) was the only other real threat.

Milwaukee still couldn't find anybody to complement Aaron in the outfield. Joe Torre had relegated Del Crandall to backup duty at catcher, hitting 14 homers, knocking in 71, and batting .293. The infield was missing another key weapon after Adcock received his ticket out of town.

The Braves received promising help from young arms Tony Cloninger (9–11), Denny Lemaster (11–14), and Bob Sadowski (5–7), but they suffered from the team's often anemic offense. Bob Shaw was 7–11 but spent most of his time in the bullpen, where he registered 13 saves. Also gone was Lew Burdette, who was 6–5 before being traded to Saint Louis at the June 15 deadline.

Under Bobby Bragan, Milwaukee (84–78) mustered a sixth-place effort, its only second-division finish, which placed them 15 games behind the pitching-rich Dodgers. But the front-office politics going on behind the scenes upset fans the most, as only 773, 000 visited County Stadium. On July 21, *St. Louis Post-Dispatch* sports editor Bob Broeg had said the team would head for Atlanta if attendance didn't improve, and rumors were more common than victories.

And so were the denials, as chairman of the board William Bartholomay quickly contradicted Broeg's prediction: "We didn't buy the Milwaukee franchise to move it to Atlanta. How do these things get started?" On September 13, Bartholomay reiterated his point, saying, "I can't imagine the Braves anywhere but in Milwaukee." Braves president John McHale backed up those statements when he announced September 23, "The Braves will be in Milwaukee today, tomorrow, next year, and as long as we are welcome."

Milwaukee's management team continued the shuffling process. On December 3, the Braves sent Crandall, Shaw, and Bob Hendley to San Francisco for outfielder Felipe Alou, catcher Ed Bailey, and former Oshkosh high school pitching phenom Billy Hoeft.

1964

Under a cloud of uncertainty and gloom, the Braves were one of the most entertaining squads in Milwaukee's run, at least offensively. Five players reached the 20-homer plateau: Hank Aaron (24), Eddie Mathews (23), Rico Carty (22), Denis Menke (20), and Joe Torre (20). The team tied for first with its highest batting average (.272) since the '48 pennant winners and led the NL with 803 runs, 274 doubles, and 755 RBIs.

Carty batted .330 with 88 RBIs, Aaron .328, and Torre .321, and Lee Maye had his best season at .304 with 10 HRs, 74 RBIs, and a league-leading 44 doubles. Torre led the way with 109 RBIs. Aaron was the only player with steals in double digits (22) while finishing second with 95 RBIs. The team led the NL with 274 doubles, including 36 from Torre and 30 from Aaron.

However, Milwaukee never seriously challenged in a tight chase for the championship, finishing 88–74 and in fifth place, despite being only five games back. That was possible because the Braves won 14 of their last 17 outings and gained nine games on the champion Cardinals.

Pitching was the team's downfall as the staff posted a 4.12 ERA, worse than everybody except the Mets. The Braves had only 45 complete games, the lowest in franchise history up to that point. The club also lost 12 of 18 decisions to Houston.

Warren Spahn was no longer the number-one guy, and his days were numbered after he fashioned a 6–13 mark and 5.29 ERA. He was sold to the Mets in November. The constantly shuffling group featured Tony Cloninger (19–14) and Denny Lemaster (17–11), while Bobby Tiefenauer recorded 13 saves. Hank Fischer posted an 11–10 mark, Billy Hoeft was 4–0, and Wade Blasingame finished 9–5.

It was quite a season considering that Atlanta mayor Ivan Allen Jr. had said on March 5 that an unnamed team had committed to moving to the city in 1965 if a new stadium was built. An $18 million facility was approved the next day, and construction began April 15.

Still, Milwaukee fans pulled an about-face of sorts as almost 911,000 fans visited the ballpark. But on October 14, Braves officials admitted they had a lease offer and that they had Georgia on their minds.

Meanwhile, Milwaukee aldermen and congressman Henry Reuss suggested that the city take legal action. County board chairman Eugene Grobschmidt and Braves president John McHale led the war of words. Finally, on November 7, the NL gave the team permission to move to Atlanta, but not until 1966.

1965

On February 3, 1965, Braves officials proposed a $500,000 payment to the county in hopes that the club's lease to play in Milwaukee could be terminated a year early. The offer was refused. Eight days later, management said it would contribute five cents from each ticket sold to a fund for the purpose of bringing a new major league franchise to the city. Teams, Inc., a civic group headed by Bud Selig, accepted the offer, bought out the park for opening day, and staged a "Stand Up for Milwaukee" day.

Still, animosity and ill will filtered throughout the team and community. Some people, even players such as Warren Spahn and Billy Hoeft, had charged that management, including skipper Bobby Bragan, wasn't trying to win games. They pointed to Bragan's dozens of lineup changes as ample evidence that something was askew.

Their lame-duck status notwithstanding, the Braves embarked on a roller coaster of a season in Bragan's third year, one that ended at 86–76, 11 games behind the Dodgers and in fifth place. That's where Milwaukee sat, only two games over .500, at the All-Star break. However, the Braves' explosive bats carried them to 10 straight victories and into first place on August 18. They fell to fourth place after losing nine of 11 but bounced back to within 2 1/2 games before faltering down the stretch, dropping 14 of their final 21 contests at County Stadium. Only 12,577 bothered to attend the team's final game there September 22, a 7–6 loss to Los Angeles after it blew a 6–1 lead against Sandy Koufax.

Unfortunately, action outside the white lines often overshadowed exciting play on the diamond. Milwaukee and the state of Wisconsin filed antitrust suits against the team and the National League in August. The team was already playing in Fulton County Stadium when the issue was resolved the next year. On August 12, Selig applied for a National League franchise and followed the same procedure for an American League team on October 12.

Players couldn't blame the fans for not showing up, although 555,584 did, averaging 7,610 per game, almost twice as many as in the final season in Boston but a far cry from the recent past. The low point occurred when only 812 showed up for the Monday, September 20, 4–1 loss against Philadelphia.

Still, the Braves soldiered on, especially their offense, which topped the league with 196 homers as an NL-record six batters blasted 20 or more dingers. Hank Aaron and Eddie Mathews said goodbye to Milwaukee by sharing the top spot with 32 each, while surprising Mack Jones smacked 31, Joe Torre contributed 27, and Gene Oliver added 21.

Aaron topped the league with 40 doubles and had 181 hits and 24 steals. He and Mathews passed the tandem of Duke Snider and Gil Hodges for the most HRs by NL teammates and then rolled past the Babe Ruth-Lou Gehrig combination for the major league lead later in their careers. The high-powered squad also featured Felipe Alou with a .297 average, 23 HRs, and 78 RBIs; Frank Bolling's 50 RBIs; Oliver's 58 RBIs; and Rico Carty's .310 average and 10 homers.

After the shambles of the past couple of years, the pitching actually improved, finishing with a 3.52 ERA behind the likes of starters Tony Cloninger

(24–11), Wade Blasingame (16–10), and Ken Johnson (13–8) and reliever Billy O'Dell (10–6 and 18 saves). However, Denny Lemaster slipped to 7–13.

It didn't matter, as words such as acrimony and litigation echoed more often than "play ball." The relationship between the club and local and state parties grew increasingly ugly.

The court case went to trial March 1, 1966, and Judge Elmer W. Roller ruled that the Braves and the National League had violated antitrust laws and must either offer Milwaukee an expansion franchise for 1967 or bring the Braves back to County Stadium. The Wisconsin Supreme Court, by a 4–3 vote, overturned Roller's decision. And on December 13, the ruling stood when the U.S. Supreme Court refused to review the case.

Bragan didn't mince words when he had this to say after the team had moved to Atlanta: "I'll tell you how I feel about Milwaukee. It's a two-bit town, a short beer town. I've had it out there—from the public, the politicians, and the press. I wouldn't go back there for all the cheese in Wisconsin."

And Milwaukee cared even less about Bragan.

Remember that girl at George Devine's Million Dollar Ballroom, the one who had become a sex symbol? Well, she was just another girl again. Some may say that 1959, the Braves' most legitimate chance at a third pennant, was their last hurrah. But Robert W. Wells later wrote in *This Is Milwaukee*, the fall began right after the team reached its pinnacle of winning the 1957 World Series.

"It was not immediately apparent, but that was the night the honeymoon ended," Wells wrote. "The love affair had been consummated, with the customary result. It was a marriage now, not a romance, and when the Braves won a second pennant in 1958 but lost the Series, then settled down to being just another pretty good baseball team, the fans started noticing flaws.

"When a player popped up with the bases loaded, he was no longer a figure of heroic tragedy but a bum," Wells continued. "With triumph as well as aspiration behind them, the team's followers began to be like baseball fans elsewhere. The plump ladies with cowbells and baseball caps started missing games. When it looked like rain, people who had considered going to the stadium decided to stay home. The attendance was still good, but it wasn't breaking records anymore, and in 1962 [Lou] Perini sold 90 percent of the stock to suburbanites from—of all places—Chicago."

Mathews, in his 1994 collaboration with Bob Buege, *Eddie Mathews and the National Pastime*, contended that the Braves would never have left Milwaukee if Fred Miller, president of Miller Brewing Company, hadn't died in a plane crash in December 1954. He, his son Fred Jr., and two pilots were killed when an engine failed and the craft crashed upon leaving Mitchell Field for a trip to Miller's hunting cabin in Canada. In his book, Mathews wrote, "Miller also received an agreement from [Lou] Perini, as I understood it—although I can't prove it—that if Perini ever sold the Braves, Fred would have the first shot at buying them."

Buege agreed, saying in a phone interview that the powerful civic leader would have found a way, and the team and the city wouldn't have had to suffer through such a nasty divorce. "Fred Miller had a huge impact and was the one who really lobbied Lou Perini to come to Milwaukee," Buege said. "I'm sure he would not have allowed them to leave, and I'm guessing he would have bought the team."

Nobody will know for sure. The only certainty about America's pastime in Milwaukee was: Good-bye Braves. Good-bye baseball.

Buege said a combination of factors led to the team's rise and subsequent fall from grace, even though most franchises would kill to enjoy the success that Milwaukee attained for such a long stretch. "It had been a national phenomenon, really," he said. "They exceeded everybody's expectations from the start. They got lucky on some trades and brought in the right minor league players. With a couple of more wins here and there they could have won five, six, or even seven straight championships. They built an exciting, star-filled team, a collection of players that I don't think will ever be equaled again, what with the way baseball is structured and free agency and everything.

"Just start with the pitching," Buege added. "Warren Spahn was the best left-handed pitcher ever, Lew Burdette was almost his equal from the right side, and Bob Buhl was great when he didn't have arm problems, and so was Gene Conley. They had some of the legendary hitters in Mathews and Aaron, the leading home run hitters any one team has produced. Then you add in Joe Adcock and a lot of really good players such as Wes Covington."

However, the small, almost invisible cracks slowly widened and became gaping holes that couldn't be filled, as they always do. "In the 1960s, the novelty wore off," Buege said. "The team got older and the organization didn't replace those players soon enough. They had a good minor league system, but they didn't develop their young pitchers or gave up on them too soon, such as Juan Pizarro, who pitched sparingly in Milwaukee but did very well for a couple of other teams, and Joey Jay, who they signed as a bonus baby as a teenager. He went to Cincinnati and helped them win the pennant in 1961. Part of the blame goes to the front office, but judging ballplayers is an inexact science.

"They didn't hire the right managers, including Birdie Tebbetts and Bobby Bragan," Buege added. "Bragan was brash and outspoken, but most fans thought he was a clown. They also didn't do a good job of publicity and marketing. Milwaukee always had a great core of fans, if the team had been promoted better."

Chapter Three

"Bushville" No More: In the World Series (1957 and 1958)

1957: "THE MOST POPULAR VICTORY IN THE HISTORY OF BASEBALL"

Milwaukee right-hander Lew Burdette exacted sweet revenge against the organization and manager that had given up on him before his career had a chance to get off the ground. The West Virginia native baffled Casey Stengel's New York Yankees three times during the 1957 World Series.

Burdette finished with three complete-game victories, including back-to-back shutouts in Games 5 and 7, as the Braves claimed their first and only world championship in Beertown, downing the heavily favored Bronx Bombers in seven games. So he richly deserved the series' most valuable player award.

National League MVP Hank Aaron, who had clinched the pennant with a dramatic home run in September, was the hitting star of the Fall Classic, leading players on both teams with a .393 average, three homers, and seven RBIs. And then Johnny Logan's game-tying double and Eddie Mathews's game-winning homer in the 10th inning of the series-turning Game 4 were highlights few Braves fans have ever forgotten. However, two players who are often afterthoughts played monumental roles in allowing Milwaukee to upset the defending champions and formidable foes who had earned six of the past eight World Series titles.

Wes Covington came up through Milwaukee's farm system and played for the Braves from 1956 to 1961, fighting off injuries much of the time. The left-handed hitter clubbed 64 homers, 45 of them during the team's two pennant-winning campaigns. Not known for his defensive prowess in the outfield, he made two game-saving catches that arguably kept the Braves' hopes alive.

Pitcher Lew Burdette, center, celebrates with teammates after one of his three complete-game victories in the '57 Series.

The first occurred in Game 2 with the score knotted at 1-all in the second inning, when he snared a sinking liner off the bat of pitcher Bobby Shantz that could have scored two runs. Burdette and the Braves went on to even the series with a 4–2 win. In Game 5, Covington saved Burdette again, grabbing Gil McDougald's drive that would have gone for extra bases or maybe a home run, crashing into the wall in the fourth inning of a scoreless contest that Milwaukee eventually won, 1–0, to take the upper hand again heading back to Yankee Stadium.

And then there was the unusual but wonderful story of Nippy Jones, who recorded only 79 regular-season at-bats with the team, all after being called up July 6, 1957. But he was the lead character in perhaps the most crucial sequence of plays in the Series that the Braves trailed 2–1.

Jones hadn't played in the major leagues since 1952, when a back injury sidetracked his career with Saint Louis. He was called upon to pinch-hit for Warren Spahn to lead off the bottom of the 10th, with Milwaukee losing 5–4 after blowing a 4–1 lead in the 9th. Umpire Augie Donatelli called a ball on Tommy Byrne's first pitch that appeared to bounce in the dirt. But Jones argued that he had been hit on the foot, and the shoe polish on the baseball confirmed his argument.

Felix Mantilla ran for Jones, moved to second base on Red Schoendienst's sacrifice bunt, and scored the tying run on Logan's smash double down the left-field line. Then Mathews, hitting only 1-for-11 (.091) in the Series to that point, belted Bob Grim's 2–2 offering over the right-field fence for a 7–5 decision.

Those were only a handful of the big plays that huge crowds enjoyed in this matchup that featured future Hall of Famers such as Spahn, Aaron, Mathews, and Schoendienst for Milwaukee and Mickey Mantle, Whitey Ford, and Yogi Berra for New York. The Braves had won the NL race by eight games over the Cardinals, and opened the biggest series in their lives in front of a capacity crowd of 69,476 at Yankee Stadium on October 2 against a Yankees team that had outrun the White Sox by the same distance in the American League standings.

Milwaukee's first obstacle: ace lefty Ford, who was making his fifth of what would become 11 World Series trips. Ford was superb in allowing five hits, two of them from Covington, who scored the visitors' lone run on Schoendienst's single in the seventh. Ford struck out six as the Yanks claimed a 3–1 triumph over Spahn and gained a head start toward what most observers figured would be their 18th world championship. Hank Bauer brought home Gerry Coleman for a 1–0 New York lead in the fifth, and New York made it 3–0 in knocking Spahn out in the sixth on RBI singles from Andy Carey and Coleman, the latter's being a bunt.

In what started out as an offensive show, Burdette and the Braves settled down in Game 2 the next day, winning 4–2 with 65,202 on hand. Joe Adcock put the Braves on the board with a single that scored Aaron, who had tripled over Mantle's head to start the second. Enos Slaughter had walked and raced to third on Milwaukee native Tony Kubek's single. He tied the contest on Coleman's roller to third. But Covington's nifty catch snuffed out any chance of the Yankees' putting this one out of reach early.

In the third, Logan drilled Milwaukee's first homer of the Series for a short-lived 2–1 Braves' advantage as Bauer did the same in the hosts' half of the inning. In the fourth, Adcock, Andy Pafko, and Covington hit consecutive singles for a 3–2 Milwaukee lead, while Pafko came around when Slaughter's throw got by Kubek at third.

Burdette made the two-run cushion hold up, finishing with a seven-hit, three-walk performance. Kubek was the only Yankee with more than one hit, going 2-for-4 as New York stranded eight runners. Adcock and Covington each contributed two hits for the victors, who headed back to Milwaukee feeling good about the split.

However, Kubek and the Yankees wrestled the momentum right back with a 12–3 whipping in Game 3 in front of 45,804 followers in Milwaukee's first-ever taste of the postseason. Kubek became only the second rookie in Series history to smack two homers in a game, capping his three-hit outing with four RBIs and three runs scored. Mantle chipped in two hits, one of them a two-run shot in the fourth against Gene Conley to make it 7–1 before the Yanks tacked on five insurance runs with two outs in the seventh. Don Larsen, he of perfect game fame from the '56 Series, earned the victory with 7 1/3 innings of relief, while Milwaukee starter Bob Buhl was pulled after giving up two hits, two walks, and three runs in two-thirds of an inning. Milwaukee's six pitchers issued 11 free passes, but Larsen and Yankee starter Bob Turley combined for eight themselves as the Braves left a Series record-tying 14 runners on base.

Game Four had several plot twists and provided what many say was the turning point in the series as 45,804 more rowdies showed up at County Stadium for this key Sunday encounter. Spahn, as he did many times during his fantastic career, battled all the way despite not having his best stuff. He went 10 innings and was credited with the victory after allowing all five runs on 11 hits, including two apiece from Kubek, Berra, and McDougald.

McDougald brought in Mantle for a 1–0 margin in the first, and Yankee hurler Tom Sturdivant, who led the team with 16 victories, had the raucous home folks worried until the fourth. Logan coaxed a walk, Mathews doubled, and Aaron crunched a three-run homer into the left-field bleachers. One out later, Frank Torre padded the lead with another long ball, this one to right.

Milwaukee turned two double plays as Spahn faced the minimum of 18 Yankee batters from the second through seventh innings and entered the ninth hanging onto a 4–1 lead. Trouble began with two outs as Berra and McDougald singled, and fans who were heading toward the exits had to scurry back when first baseman Elston Howard crunched a three-run blast to tie the game.

New York again rallied with two down in the 10th. This time Kubek got things going with an infield single. Bauer then laced a triple over Aaron and off the center-field wall to make it 5–4. Then fate intervened on the Braves' behalf.

But before Logan and Mathews could deliver their big blows, it came down to Jones. He didn't register a hit or score a run, and he didn't play in the field, but he sure as heck made sure his footwear was well shined.

"Byrne started me off with a curveball," Jones said in a 1978 interview. "The ball hit me on the foot, and I dropped my bat and started toward first base. But [umpire] Augie Donatelli said, 'Come back here. That's ball one.' I couldn't believe it. I went right for the ball, and [catcher] Yogi Berra was pretty smart, so he did the same thing. I got there first, and there was a spot of shoe polish about a half-inch in diameter.

"The kids in the clubhouse shined the shoes after every game, and they were spotless," added Jones, who had been toiling in the Pacific Coast League when the Braves purchased the then 32-year-old's contract. "There was no question about the shoe polish, so I took the ball over to Donatelli and showed it to him. Just then Casey Stengel came out and said, 'What the hell is going on here?' Donatelli told him and I went to first base. Yogi said something or other, but he knew it had hit me."

Mantilla ran for the man whose given name was Vernal. One batter and out later, Logan, who was hobbling on a sore ankle, cracked a 2–0 pitch to the corner in left and trotted across on Mathews's game-winning blast.

Mathews had struggled before his game winner, although his first hit had been the two-bagger during the four-run uprising in the fourth. The smooth-swinging third baseman was using one of Adcock's bats because the knob of his had given him a blister.

"I was pretty sure it was going over, but I was worried for a second when I saw Bauer up against the fence pounding his hand into his glove," Mathews said after the game. "How did I feel? I felt about 10 feet tall." So did the rest of the team and its fans, because the win prevented the Braves from falling into a 3–1 hole that in all likelihood would have been too deep to dig out of.

The next day, Burdette returned to stifle the Yanks on another seven-hitter to beat Ford, 1–0. Mathews scored the only run after beating out an infield hit with two outs. Aaron and Adcock followed with singles.

"If the second baseman didn't back up on Mathews's ball to play it on the big hop, it's hard to tell how long it would have gone," Burdette said. "Jerry Coleman didn't know Eddie was the second-fastest guy on the club."

The Series headed east again, and New York staved off elimination with a 3–2 verdict, scoring the deciding run on Bauer's shot that bounced off the left-field foul pole in the seventh inning of a game in which every run scored via the long ball. The difference was Berra's two-run shot in the third against Buhl, one of his three hits in the game and his 10th Series homer. Torre and Aaron led off the fifth and seventh frames with solo round-trippers off Turley to make it 2-all. Turley finished with a four-hitter while striking out eight. Meanwhile, Bauer hooked his seventh hit of the Series just fair enough with one out against Ernie Johnson, who struck out five and gave up only two hits in 4 1/3 innings after replacing Buhl.

A crowd of 61,207, the smallest of the four contests in the Big Apple, witnessed another masterpiece from Burdette in the finale, a 5–0 triumph that was supposed to feature Spahn on the mound. However, the latter was out with the flu, prompting Milwaukee skipper Fred Haney to go with Burdette instead of Gene Conley, Bob Trowbridge, or Juan Pizarro in hopes that he still had enough left in his tank after only two days of rest. "It was nothing special for me," Burdette said later. "I had pitched three complete games in eight days before."

The victory gave him 24 consecutive scoreless innings, three short of Christy Mathewson's single-series mark and five from Babe Ruth's all-time Fall Classic standard. Burdette became the 10th three-game Series winner—three pitchers did it during an eight-game series—and the first since Harry Brecheen in 1946. He was the first to throw three complete-game victories since Stan Coveleski of Cleveland in 1920.

Burdette allowed merely 21 hits in his 27 innings of work, striking out 13 and walking four in posting a miniscule 0.67 ERA. "Let's face it," Burdette said. "I was trying my darnedest to beat 'em and I know they were trying like mad to get me out of there," he said after Game 7. "They kept yelling at me from the dugout all game. I couldn't hear what they were yelling about."

Milwaukee catcher Del Crandall marveled at his battery mate's dominance over the powerful Yankees. "I don't think he was as fast as he was in the first two games he won," Crandall said in the victorious Braves' locker room. "But he never had better control. He was keeping that ball low all afternoon. Everything he threw—sliders, screwballs, sinkers—he had them all in there where he wanted them and where the batters didn't want them."

Burdette didn't need much help, but the Braves gave him the support anyway.

Kubek's error opened the door for the Braves' four-run third inning. Mathews doubled into the right-field corner to score Bob Hazle and Logan for the first runs against Larsen. Aaron greeted Shantz with an RBI single for a 3–0 margin and scored the fourth run on Torre's grounder. Crandall belted a solo homer in the eighth to complete the scoring.

The Braves' defense also sparkled throughout the seven games, turning 10 double plays to five for New York, and the outfielders made several excellent catches. A prime example was in the ninth inning of Game 7. The Yankees loaded the bases on three singles. Mathews gloved a smash down the left-field line off the bat of Bill Skowron and stepped on third base as the Braves started the victory celebration in the House that Ruth Built.

It proved to be special for Burdette, who in 1951 had been sent to the minors despite enjoying a great spring training in the Yankees' camp. Then, in '52, Stengel made up his mind that he needed Johnny Sain from Boston and threw Burdette in for good measure. Braves fans couldn't have been happier with the way things turned out.

"I wasn't as sharp as in Milwaukee," Burdette said. "I couldn't reach back and get something extra in a pinch. But I did have good control and could get the ball where I wanted."

While it was far from the only factor, one reason the Yankees sputtered offensively was the lack of firepower from Mantle. He had ripped AL pitching for a .365 average, 34 home runs, and 146 RBIs, numbers that would earn him his second straight MVP award later that fall.

Mantle delivered two infield hits in the Series opener. He was 0 for 3 in Game 2 but finished with two hits, including a home run, at County Stadium in Game 3. However, a play that occurred in that game had a major effect on Mantle's career.

After Kubek homered with one out, Buhl walked Mantle and Berra. With Mantle on second, Buhl made a wild pickoff attempt. Second baseman Schoendienst leaped to catch the throw and fell on top of Mantle.

The Mick suited up in Game 4 but went hitless in five at-bats. The sore shoulder kept him out of the starting lineup in Game 5, although he entered as a pinch runner in the eighth inning. He sat out Game 6 and finished 1-for-4 in the deciding showdown. The injury turned out to be torn ligaments, and Mantle had problems batting left-handed for the rest of his career.

Still, Milwaukee deserved the accolades. The Braves were the feel-good story and the toast of baseball. As National League president Warren Giles said, "This is the most popular victory in the history of baseball. Fans everywhere wanted Milwaukee to win."

Stengel gave credit where it was due after his club fell to 6–2 in the World Series under his guidance. "You ran your team good all the way," he told Haney. "If we couldn't win it, there's no one I'd rather see do it than Milwaukee. That town deserves it."

And there was no bigger hitting star for Milwaukee in an otherwise pitching-dominated series than Aaron, who ended up 11-for-28 as the Braves hit only .209 overall. But eight of the team's 47 hits left the ballpark. The Yankees batted .248 with seven long balls and outscored the Braves 25–23. "Those Yankees were there almost every year," Mathews said. "We were not picked to win because of that, but we had a good team."

That they did. But what would have happened if Jones, who died in 1995, hadn't reached base in Game 4? "It's funny," Jones said in the 1978 interview. "The importance of the event seemed to grow as time went on. The main thing to me was winning, and I didn't care how we did it."

Five days after the Series ended, the Braves shipped Jones to Wichita in the American Association. He refused to report, was released, and returned to the Pacific Coast League, where he played through 1960, never seeing big-league action again.

As for Milwaukee, hundreds of thousands of people were still celebrating, which was oh, so sweet because they finally felt like they had shed the label of being a minor league city. This feeling was symbolized by the famous photo of a fan carrying a "Bushville Wins" sign through a throng of well-wishers.

Many believe that Stengel made the "bush league" comment, although coach Charlie Keller and trainer Gus Mauch became the two leading suspects. The true culprit didn't matter, as it became the fans' rallying cry throughout the '57 Series.

1958: WOULDA, COULDA, SHOULDA

The year after Milwaukee had rallied twice from one-game deficits to win the World Series title in 1957, the team was well on its way to a second consecutive crown when everything they had built fell apart.

There haven't been many better Fall Classic confrontations, at least on paper, than this rematch between the unquestioned top teams from their respective leagues. Both franchises had remarkably similar regular-season records. Both went 92–62 for the year, with the Braves winning the National League pennant by eight games and the Yankees claiming the American League flag by 10.

Each team featured a wonderful one-two, righty-lefty pitching combination as Milwaukee got 20 wins from Lew Burdette and 22 from Warren Spahn, while New York's Bob Turley led the AL with 21 victories and Whitey Ford added 14 and a league-leading 2.01 ERA. Hank Aaron and Eddie Mathews combined for 61 homers for the Braves, while Mickey Mantle (42) and Yogi Berra clubbed 64.

Milwaukee hit 167 homers and batted .266, while New York's totals were

164 and .268, respectively. The Braves' mound corps turned in a 3.21 ERA to the Yanks' 3.22.

However, it all came down to the fact that Milwaukee couldn't deal with prosperity after grabbing a commanding edge, as New York became the first team since the 1925 Pittsburgh Pirates to overcome a 3–1 deficit to take home the World Series trophy. And the biggest reason for this was that the Yankees' hurlers turned things around after getting shelled in the first two games, with the Bronx Bombers outscoring Milwaukee 17–5 during the final three contests. That didn't seem possible after the Braves exploded for 25 hits in the first two games in front of identical crowds of 46,367 at County Stadium.

New York's Bill Skowron scored the first run of Game 1 on his two-out solo homer just inside the left-field foul pole that gave Ford the upper hand against Spahn in the fourth. However, Milwaukee came right back with two tallies of its own in the bottom half. Aaron walked and scored two outs later on Del Crandall's single. The latter circled the bases on singles from Andy Pafko and Spahn.

Hank Bauer then planted a tater in the seats, with Ford aboard via a walk, to put the Yankees back on top, 3–2, in the fifth. Milwaukee drew even in the eighth when Mathews walked, Aaron doubled, and Wes Covington lifted a sacrifice fly.

It stayed that way until Milwaukee registered three singles (Joe Adcock, Crandall, and Billy Bruton), the last two with two outs, in the 10th to grab a 1–0 Series lead. Milwaukee did its damage against New York's bullpen ace Ryne Duren, a native of Cazenovia, Wisconsin.

The Braves didn't wait nearly as long in Game 2, battering Turley and Duke Maas for six hits and seven runs in the first inning, which Bruton, who had missed the previous World Series because of a knee injury, ignited with a leadoff homer. Burdette capped the uprising with a three-run homer, the first by a pitcher in the Series since 1940, finishing off the largest first inning in Series history. Milwaukee added a run in the second and then combined for five more in the seventh and eighth innings for a 13–5 triumph. No team had scored more against the Yankees in any postseason contest.

Burdette wasn't as sharp as during his fantastic '57 postseason run but still improved to 4–0 in Series competition. He went the distance, allowing seven hits and one walk. A key juncture occurred in the first, when New York scored only one run after loading the bases with no outs. Burdette coaxed two ground balls, including Berra's, which his defense turned into an inning-ending double play.

Milwaukee didn't have the services of Bob Buhl, who had missed most of the season because of arm trouble, so it went with Bob Rush. Rush had finished 10–6 during the regular season but couldn't match veteran Don Larsen. Rush allowed only three hits but walked five during his six-inning stint, while Larsen scattered six hits and combined with AL rookie pitcher of the year Duren on a 4–0 win.

Rush's wildness gave the Yankees all the offense they needed as the hosts broke open a scoreless duel in front of 71,599. Rush loaded the bases on free passes, the final two with two outs, and Bauer's single made it 2–0. Bauer again did the damage in the seventh after Enos Slaughter had walked with one out, belting a homer off Braves' reliever Don McMahon for the final margin.

Spahn put Milwaukee on the threshold of back-to-back crowns with a magnificent two-hit shutout in Game 4, contributing one of the Braves' nine hits in their 3–0 decision, outperforming Ford in the process. The Braves lefty issued his only walks in the first and third and didn't give up a hit until Mantle rocketed a triple off the scoreboard in left-center. Spahn forced Bill Skowron to hit a grounder back to the mound, while Red Schoendienst knocked down Berra's smash and barely threw him out at first. Skowron's one-out single in the seventh was all New York could muster after that. Spahn ended Bauer's 17-game Series hitting streak, a run that had gone back to 1956.

The Braves finally dented Ford for runs in the sixth, seventh, and eighth. Schoendienst started the sixth with a fly ball that Norm Siebern, subbing for Elston Howard in left, and Mantle let drop for a triple. Then Johnny Logan's grounder went through Tony Kubek's legs at shortstop for the 1–0 margin. In the seventh, Del Crandall walked, moved to third on Andy Pafko's double, and scored on Spahn's bloop single to left to make it 2–0. Siebern lost Logan's fly ball in the sun and it bounced over the fence for a two-bagger, and Mathews doubled to close the scoring.

Turley rebounded in Game 5, while New York showed that Burdette indeed was human, breaking open a 1–0 contest with a six-run sixth to stay alive. However, as with Wes Covington for Milwaukee the year before, the Yankees' fortunes turned on their left fielder's crucial play in the top of that inning. Bruton led off with a single and Schoendienst sliced a sinking liner that Howard corralled with a diving catch. Bruton had already rounded second base and was easily doubled off to end what could have been a big inning.

Turley finished with a five-hitter and struck out 10 in front of 65,279. Bruton had two of the Braves' hits.

Despite the letdown, faithful followers knew that Milwaukee needed to win only one of the final two games at home to secure another title. They didn't accomplish it, mainly because of squandered opportunities.

In Game 6, Bauer cranked his fourth homer of the Series to give the Yanks a 1–0 lead over Spahn. However, Milwaukee evened things on Aaron's two-out RBI single in its half. The Braves jumped on top, 2–1, in the second as Covington, Pafko, and Spahn registered consecutive one-out singles. Schoendienst then walked to reload the bases, prompting Casey Stengel to replace Ford with Art Ditmar. Logan flew out to shallow left and Pafko was thrown out at the plate for a double play.

Bruton then muffed a grounder in center that helped put Yankee runners on the corners in the sixth, one of four Milwaukee errors in the game. Berra's sacrifice fly knotted the score at 2.

Ditmar hurled 3 2/3 scoreless innings and Duren allowed only one run in 4 2/3 to get the win. Meanwhile, Spahn rolled along until the 10th, when McDougal smoked a leadoff homer, and with two outs and two runners on, Skowron brought home another tally against Don McMahon to make it 4–2.

Milwaukee fought back as Logan walked and took second as Mathews struck out. Aaron made it 4–3 with his single and advanced to third on Adcock's hit. But Turley came on to register the final out, getting pinch hitter Frank Torre to pop up.

Suddenly the Braves' comfort zone had evaporated as they faced a do-or-die situation in Game 7. Milwaukee's hopes again rested with Burdette, who fans hoped could repeat his stupendous outing in the same pressure-packed setting as a year earlier. It wasn't meant to be.

Larsen also got the call for New York, but he didn't stick around nearly as long. Schoendienst opened the first with a single and Bruton walked. Frank Torre sacrificed them to second and third, and Stengel ordered Larsen to intentionally walk Aaron. Schoendienst scored on Covington's grounder and Stengel followed the same strategy, putting Mathews aboard with another free pass. Crandall had a chance to break the game open, but he took a called third strike. The Braves led, 1–0, but it was a hollow victory and a crucial juncture that could have carried them to a big inning and maybe eventual triumph.

In the second, Burdette walked Berra to start the inning and Howard bunted to first baseman Torre. Burdette covered first, but Torre's throw was behind Burdette and went off his glove, putting runners on first and third. Jerry Lumpe then grounded to Torre, who held Berra at third but again made a throw that Burdette couldn't hold. Torre was charged with his second error and the bases were loaded. Berra scored when Skowron hit into a force play, and Kubek drove in the visitors' second run with a fly ball.

"I don't think I deserved the errors," said Torre, the NL's top-fielding first baseman during the regular season, after the game, "but if you want to have a goat, it might as well be me." Burdette took as much of the blame: "I deserved 'em as much as Torre did."

Still, Milwaukee could have taken control again in the third. Bruton and Aaron singled, ending Larsen's day. Stengel made what proved to be the most important decision of the game, banking his money on Turley, who got Covington to ground out. Stengel then ordered Mathews walked intentionally for a second time. Crandall again strolled to the plate with the bags juiced, but he grounded out.

Crandall homered off Turley in the sixth, but it wasn't enough as New York finally broke loose. Burdette registered two outs in the eighth, but Berra doubled off the right-field wall. Howard bounced a single up the middle and just beyond Logan's reach for a 3–2 lead. Haney stuck with Burdette, and Andy Carey singled off Mathews's glove at third. Skowron then smashed a Burdette offering, along with the Braves' spirits, with a three-run homer to left-center for a 6–2 lead that stood up.

Mathews led off the Braves' final chance in the ninth with a walk, but Crandall and Logan flied out. Adcock singled before Schoendienst lined out to Mantle as the Yankees savored Stengel's seventh title in 10 years as manager, which tied him with Joe McCarthy for the all-time lead. "This was the greatest Series we ever won," Stengel said.

In the opposite clubhouse, the difference was easy to explain. "The turning point was in our bats," Haney said. "We got eight runs in [the last] five games. . . . Instead of moaning, let's just say how good their pitching was."

The numbers didn't lie, as Mathews struck out 11 times, a dubious mark that stood until Kansas City's Willie Wilson broke it with 12 whiffs in the 1980 Series. The Braves' 53 whiffs also established a Series record.

"I was in a slump," Mathews said years later. "After we clinched the pennant, I tried to take a couple of days off, but the manager [Haney] wouldn't let me because the team we were playing was in a race for second place. So I went into the Series in a slump and I stayed in it. I fell on my face. If I had done anything, we'd have won that year, too."

Despite his efforts (.160), the Braves had seized a 3–1 lead and several players failed to produce in the clutch. Logan hit only .120 and Crandall finished at .240. But an even more telling statistic was in the RBI category, where Spahn and Burdette (three each) trailed only Covington's four. And Milwaukee managed only three homers compared to the Yankees' 10.

Chapter Four

Bud Brings Back Baseball (1966–77)

"There is no lonelier place than an empty ballpark," Gregg Hoffmann said in his book *Down in the Valley*. Nothing could have described the situation better after the Braves left Milwaukee without a major league team.

Hoffmann, who covered the Brewers from 1978 to 2004 for several publications, continued: "I often have gotten to assignments hours before games to watch the stadium come to life, as first the grounds crew, then the ushers, players, and finally the fans arrive. For several years, that process was halted at County Stadium. The White Sox played exhibition games there. The Packers played football games there. Other events were staged. But the ballpark was without baseball. The daily game that gives it life was missing. It was a lonely, sad place." Hoffmann's 2000 work is aptly subtitled *The History of Milwaukee County Stadium: The People, the Promise, the Passion.*

No one understands those words or believes in those ideals more than Bud Selig, the man most responsible for bringing baseball back to Milwaukee. To his credit, he accomplished this feat during a tumultuous time in our country's history and against a backdrop that focused on the bitter breakup of the Braves and Milwaukee fresh on people's minds and in their hearts.

In an interview conducted a few days before the Brewers' final game at County Stadium in September 2000, Selig said that the Braves' departure didn't sink in until the spring of 1966, on an evening when he had pulled into a gas station to listen to a radio broadcast of the Braves' first game in Georgia. "I tuned in to Bob Prince out of Pittsburgh and he opened by saying, 'Greetings from Atlanta's Fulton County Stadium. We're a long ways from Milwaukee, Wisconsin,'" Selig recalled. "I had tears in my eyes. I remember a guy came over and asked if I was all right. It was very heartbreaking. Except for the games the Packers played there, the stadium was empty the next four years. There was many a day I sat there staring out at the field."

On July 28, 1965, corporation papers were filed in Madison for the Milwaukee Brewers Baseball Club, and thus the search for another tenant for County Stadium had begun. Selig had loyal support from such visible city businessmen as Ed Fitzgerald, Bob Uihlein, Irv Maier, and Ben Barkin, but Selig considered it his duty to see that a Major League Baseball team in Milwaukee became a reality, and he never wavered from that mission.

The group had ammunition in the fact that a record 51,144 baseball-starved fans attended a Minnesota Twins-Chicago White Sox exhibition game at County Stadium in 1967, the first contest between major league teams in Milwaukee since the Braves left after the 1965 season. The largest crowd ever to attend a Braves game was 48,642 in 1959.

However, efforts such as those by Selig and Teams, Inc. were shot down time after time because of Milwaukee's court challenges to keep the Braves, and many major league executives considered Selig's bunch public enemy number one. "There was so much anger towards us," Selig said in a *Milwaukee Journal Sentinel* article. "I'd go to meetings and people wouldn't even talk to us. It was like we had leprosy. They hated Milwaukee, hated Wisconsin. It was probably the toughest five years of my life in terms of frustration and disappointment, but it was a great teacher for me, too. It taught me to be tenacious and have patience." The latter virtue was tested repeatedly.

Milwaukee sat and watched during an owners' meeting in Chicago as the National League awarded expansion franchises to Montreal and San Diego in 1968, after which Selig walked the streets of the Windy City for hours. He next attempted to buy the White Sox and thought he had a deal worked out, but Art Allyn recanted, instead selling the team to his brother. "When that deal went up in smoke, my heart sank," Selig recalled. "I knew we were coming to the end and that I couldn't hold this group together much longer."

But resolve is one thing Selig has always had in huge supply, and as the calendar flipped to 1970, Selig and his group confronted one final opportunity, a second chance at buying the Seattle Pilots, who had filed for bankruptcy after one miserable season. No local owner could be found to keep the team in the Pacific Northwest, so on March 31, the baseball gods smiled down on Selig as the federal court accepted his offer of $10.5 million. Milwaukee prepared to welcome another moribund team of youngsters and washed-up veterans, this time from the left coast and in the American League.

"It was 10:15 at night," Selig said in Chuck Carlson's 1993 book *True*

Brew: A Quarter Century with the Milwaukee Brewers. "Lloyd Larson, the *Milwaukee Sentinel* sports editor at the time, called to tell me. But I sort of knew from my lawyers."

To this day, Selig says there haven't been any bigger moments in his baseball life. "Of all the marvelous things that have happened to me, including becoming commissioner of baseball, that will always be my proudest accomplishment because the odds were stacked up tremendously against Milwaukee," Selig said in the *Journal Sentinel* interview.

Now, instead of religious revivals, tractor pulls, music concerts, and boxing matches, Wisconsin fans would once again get to see real baseball, although on many occasions during those lean early years fans may have thought they were witnessing the same exhibition contests that the White Sox and Minnesota Twins had played there. As happened 17 years earlier with the Braves, the Brewers had precious little time to get uniforms ready—they switched *Pilots* to *Brewers* on their jerseys and the S to an M on their caps—sell tickets, or throw together a roster before the April 7 season and home opener against California.

An estimated 8,000 well-wishers showed up at Mitchell Field to greet manager Dave Bristol and his band of mostly nondescript ballplayers, while another 200 or so were on hand at the hotel. Also similar to the Braves' experience in leaving Boston, the Pilots couldn't believe the support that was showered upon them in Milwaukee after what they'd seen in Seattle.

The first Milwaukee Brewers roster included slugging outfielder Danny Walton, who, like Andy Pafko before him, became a fan favorite. Tommy Harper was there, as were Ted Kubiak, Bob Bolin, Ken Sanders, Lew Krausse, Skip Lockwood, and Marty Pattin.

But no one on the team was happier than Black Earth, Wisconsin, native Gene Brabender, who had made a bold prediction years earlier, after his uncle took the then 12-year-old to a Braves game: "I told my dad that someday I was going to play in County Stadium," he said in *True Brew.*

Bob Uecker had played sparingly for the Braves in 1962–63, but he said this new cast of characters fit the city like their predecessors and those talented guys who would come along a decade later. I guess it takes a character to know one. "They were blue-collar," said Uecker, who became a permanent member of the Brewers' broadcasting team that first season. "Milwaukee was hungry and fans here didn't expect any greatness. They respected and cheered the players who worked hard, and they showed the fans that they really were trying. The fans liked that."

At the 1970 home opener, a crowd of 37,237 watched the Angels whip the Crew, 12–0, but most of those in attendance were happy to be rooting for a team again, regardless of how hapless it was. The Brewers didn't register their first home victory until a 4–3 decision May 6 against, of all teams, the one from Boston. The win snapped a nine-game losing streak as Bolin struck out seven Red Sox batters in a row and 10 total in eight innings, while John Kennedy hit a three-run homer and Kubiak's solo shot in the eighth decided the outcome and gave the home folks their first taste of victory in five years.

For the season, the Brewers drew 933,690 fans, a paltry figure compared to the Braves' inaugural season. However, it was better than attendance for those heavy-hitting lineups that circled the bases from 1962 to 1965. The team's ineptness on the field didn't help, but many fans refused to return to County Stadium, still angered at the previous franchise's painful exodus.

"The one miscalculation that I made in the '60s, along with everybody, was the number of people who were so bitter toward baseball over what happened," Selig said in 2000. "We paid a tough price for that for a while."

Some consolation could be taken from the fact that the Braves didn't fare much better in Atlanta. They recorded four winning seasons from 1966 to 1977, claiming the West title in 1969. However, they didn't earn a pennant until 1991, whereas the Brewers did it in '82. It also should be noted that it wasn't until their 18th season in Atlanta (1983) that the Braves cracked the two million mark in attendance.

1970

The supply of beer and bratwurst was never a point of contention at County Stadium, even for this collection of diamond misfits. However, in the Brewers' inaugural season, crowds were spotty at best, and Milt Mason decided to try to rekindle the party-type atmosphere that had endeared the old Braves to their fans in the 1950s.

The 69-year-old former aviation engineer put his aeronautical skills to the test in hopes of getting more people through the turnstiles, so he took a seat above the scoreboard in right field. Well, he actually took more than a seat. His publicity stunt featured a trailer that included a stove, a color television, a refrigerator, and two telephones.

Milwaukee's first "Bernie Brewer" began his vigil July 6, vowing to remain on his perch until the team drew a sellout crowd. Despite his national celebrity status, local fans weren't very accommodating, so he lowered his expectations and said he'd come down if 40,000 attended. It took 40 days and a Bat Day promotion on August 16 to draw 44,387.

Mason suffered burns on his hands and legs while descending too quickly on a rope, but his antics may well have offered evidence that followers were ready to embrace the Brewers. His chalet and his entertaining slides into a giant beer mug after homers and victories eventually made Bernie the most recognizable mascot in the land when he became a regular in 1973.

Despite dropping 20 of their first 25 games, the Brewers provided a few exciting moments for the fans, including a trip to Boston's Fenway Park in mid-July. Second baseman Ted Kubiak knocked in seven runs with a single, double, and grand slam to carry Milwaukee to a 10–5 win over the Red Sox, who blew a 5–1 advantage after Carl Yastrzemski and Reggie Smith had homered.

As expected, there were long dry spells between highlights, although Tommy Harper became the fifth player in baseball history to join the 30–30 club with 31 HRs and 38 stolen bases. Milwaukee finished 65–97, which tied them for fourth place in the Western Division with the Kansas City Royals.

For the season, first baseman Mike Hegan (11), Danny Walton (17), catcher Phil Roof (13), and Ted Savage (12) joined Harper with double-digit homer totals. On the mound, Marty Pattin was a bright spot on a staff dominated by right-handers, finishing with a 14–12 mark and an excellent 3.39 ERA. Lew Krausse (13–18) was the only other hurler to crack the 10-win plateau, as Skip Lockwood (5–12), Gene Brabender (6–15), Bob Bolin (5–11), and lefty Al Downing (2–10 despite a 3.34 ERA) took their lumps. In the bullpen, Ken Sanders showed signs of a brighter future with a 5–2 record, a 1.75 ERA, and 13 saves, while John Gelnar finished 4–3 with four saves.

1971

The club ended the next season in the Western Division cellar with a 69–92 record, and attendance reflected the performance, dropping to 731,000. Pitching was not the problem. The team recorded a team-high 23 shutouts, and reliever Ken Sanders posted seven triumphs

During the 1970s, Bonnie Brewer swept the bases between innings and was known to swat an opposing player.

and 31 saves, the latter total standing as a team mark until Dan Plesac reached 33 in 1989. But the Brewer batters hit an anemic, major-league-worst .229, so Ted Kubiak's propensity for late-game heroics and Danny Walton's power surges weren't nearly enough to make a big difference in this offense.

Johnny Briggs took over as the regular first baseman, hitting .276 with 21 homers and 59 RBIs; at second, Ron Theobald hit .276; third baseman Tommy Harper belted 14 homers and brought home 52; outfielder Dave May batted .277 with 16 round-trippers and 65 RBIs; and Andy Kosco, obtained from Los Angeles for Al Downing, contributed 10 homers. Milwaukee just couldn't muster enough offense, and it shipped Walton to the Yankees for prospects Bobby Mitchell and Frank Tepedino on June 7. Walton had banged 17 HRs a year earlier but was hitting just .203 when the move was announced.

As luck would have it, Downing posted 20 wins for the Dodgers, something Milwaukee could have obviously used. Marty Pattin was the ace again, registering a 14–14 mark, 3.13 ERA, and five shutouts. Bill Parsons joined the rotation and finished 13–17 with a nice 3.20 ERA. Lockwood wasn't bad either, with a 3.30 ERA despite a 10–15 record. Jim Slaton (10–8) and Lew Krausse (8–12) also kept the Brewers in many ball games with ERAs of 3.78 and 2.94, respectively.

On December 3, the Brewers traded reserve outfielder Jose Cardenal to the Cubs for pitcher Jim Colborn and two other players. Colborn would become the new ace within two years.

1972

The team's woes continued into 1972, even though the Brewers were now in the AL's Eastern Division. With a season total of a little more than 600,000, attendance took another dive, which may have been affected by a players' strike and surely was hampered by poor weather.

General manager Frank "Trader" Lane had acquired Johnny Briggs in 1971 and then pulled off a 10-player deal with Boston during that year's Fall Classic that yielded Milwaukee a man they called "Boomer" (George Scott). But Lane and skipper Dave Bristol were jettisoned and replaced with Roland Hemond and Del Crandall, respectively, as the Brewers stumbled to a 65–91 mark.

The flamboyant Scott hit only .266 but was the club's top run producer with 20 homers and 88 RBIs. Briggs equaled Scott's batting average and his own homer total from the previous season (21) while knocking in 65. Outfielders Joe Lahoud and Dave May combined for 21 homers but hit only .238 and .237, respectively, while young catcher Ellie Rodriguez showed promise with a .285 mark.

Jim Lonborg, obtained in the Scott deal that sent Marty Pattin eastward, compiled a 14–12 record and 2.83 ERA, Bill Parsons finished at .500 (13–13), and Skip Lockwood suffered another hard-luck season (8–15) despite his 3.60 ERA. Lockwood was involved in three one-hitters, two of his own and a combined effort with Ken Sanders in June. Ken Brett was 7–12 and fellow lefty Gary Ryerson was 3–8. Sanders had a decent 3.12 ERA and 17 saves but lost 9 of 11 decisions in relief. Frank Linzy chipped in 12 saves, while Jim Colborn was 7–7. Milwaukee added a little pop and an excellent glove October 31 when it obtained infielder Don Money in a seven-player transaction that sent four pitchers to Philadelphia, including Lonborg and Brett.

1973

It was only one season, but 1973 gave the faithful reason for hope—that is, after the team recovered from a 13-inch snowfall that canceled the first four games of the home schedule. Milwaukee ripped off a 10-game winning streak, including the first nine on the road, and sat one game from .500 as late as August 31 before the upstarts faltered during the final month. Although short-lived, optimism had returned after the 74–88 finish.

Jim Colborn became the club's first 20-game winner; Scott pounded 24 homers, drove in 107, and batted .306; and Dave May contributed a .303 average, 23 HRs, and a 24-game hitting streak. Youngsters Darrell Porter, Pedro Garcia, and Bobby Coluccio combined for 46 homers, while attendance broke the one million mark for the first time. And, unbeknownst at the time to Milwaukee's brain trust, the best thing it did was draft a California kid named Robin Yount.

Second baseman Garcia hit .245 with 15 homers and 54 RBIs, Money played third base and hit .284 with 11 HRs and 61 RBIs, and Johnny Briggs contributed 18 long balls and 57 RBIs. Although Briggs hit only .246, his season featured a 6-for-6 effort during an August victory over Cleveland. Outfielder Coluccio struggled at .224 but managed 15 HRs and 58 RBIs, while catcher Porter rattled off a .254 average with 16 taters while bringing in 67 runs.

Jim Slaton provided a nice complement to Colborn with his 13–15 mark and 3.71 ERA. Jerry Bell was a nice addition with a 9–9 finish, but Bill Parsons slipped to 3–6 and Skip Lockwood was 5–12. In the pen, Frank Linzy saved 13 games and Eduardo Rodriguez added five. Billy Champion was 5–8 with a 3.70 ERA.

Milwaukee was active again during the off-season, pulling off another 10-player blockbuster trade October 22 with California. The key components included pitcher Clyde Wright and outfielder Ken Berry changing into

Brewer uniforms, while the Angels received Lockwood, Ellie Rodriguez, and reserve Ollie Brown in a deal that did very little to help either team.

1974

The team improved in 1974—but barely—to 76–86, the best record yet but short of heightened expectations after what many thought was a break-through campaign.

Several of the guys who had shown so much promise a year earlier didn't repeat those performances, so management reached into its past, shipping Dave May and pitcher Roger Alexander to Atlanta for Hank Aaron on November 2. Although his skills had diminished considerably, Aaron had set the all-time home run record the year before and was obtained more for his leadership and owner Bud Selig's goodwill gesture of giving the city back one of its favorite players.

Selig recalled his rationale for the trade in Aaron's book *I Had a Hammer*:

The fact is, I had talked to [William] Bartholomay about purchasing Hank as early as 1972. I knew how popular he was in Milwaukee. Beyond that, when we had brought the Brewers to Milwaukee in 1970, we had underestimated the bitterness of Milwaukee people over the loss of the Braves. They felt rejected by the Braves leaving, and to a lesser degree, they feel it even today. In some quarters, people were still calling us the Braves. It was a hard thing to overcome in a town like Milwaukee, and we had gotten to the point that we needed to do something dramatic. I said at the time of the trade that there was nothing I was more proud of than bringing Hank Aaron back to Milwaukee, and that included giving the town a new franchise. Hank Aaron gave us credibility and momentum.

George Scott batted .281 but his power numbers declined to 17 homers and 82 RBIs. Pedro Garcia turned in almost identical stats (12 HRs and 54 RBIs), but his average plummeted to .199. Don Money was a model of consistency again, hitting .283 with 15 round-trippers and 65 RBIs. Briggs also provided some sting with 17 HRs and 73 RBIs, but Bobby Coluccio (.223), Dave May (.226), and Darrell Porter (.241) didn't offer enough offensive punch.

The year was noteworthy because it marked the debut of an 18-year-old shortstop named Robin Yount, whose first taste of the big leagues yielded three homers, 26 RBIs, and a .250 average. He slapped his first base hit against Baltimore's Dave McNally on April 12 and got his second the next day, smacking a game-winning homer off Ross Grimsley during a 3–2 victory over the Orioles.

Jim Slaton remained a mainstay on the pitching staff at 13–16 and 3.92, but Clyde Wright was a huge disappointment at 9–20 and 4.42. Jim Colborn slumped to 10–13 and 4.06, while Kevin Kobel was 6–14 with a 3.99 ERA. Billy Champion offered a lift, posting an 11–4 mark and a 3.62 ERA. Tom Murphy assumed Sanders's role as the best stopper, finishing 10–10 with a sparkling 1.90 ERA and 20 saves. Eduardo Rodriguez was 7–4, Bill Travers came on the scene at 2–3, and Ed Sprague was a nice addition at 7–2 and 2.39.

1975

The following year, a crowd of 48,160 filled the stands on April 11 to witness Hank Aaron's return to County Stadium. That proved to be one of the few shining moments during a dismal season. Aaron hit .234 with 12 homers, while Milwaukee lost 59 of its last 84 games after sitting in first place July 5. The team that finished 68–94 drew 1.2 million fans.

George Scott rebounded with his best season in Milwaukee, ripping American League pitchers for a .285 average, 36 homers, and a league-leading 109 RBIs. Don Money was tough again at .277 with 15 homers and 43 RBIs, but

In the 1975 home opener, Henry Aaron acknowledges a packed house in his first game as a Brewer at County Stadium.

Darrell Porter and Pedro Garcia struggled again. Garcia contributed only six homers and 38 RBIs with a .225 mark, while Porter slugged 18 homers and brought in 60 but hit just .232. Yount improved his numbers to .267 with eight homers and 52 RBIs. Sixto Lezcano joined the mix with 11 homers and 43 RBIs; Bill Sharp hit .255; and Gorman Thomas saw his first serious action, chipping in 10 homers while hitting a measly .179. Charlie Moore batted .290 with 29 RBIs, while Bobby Mitchell crunched nine homers and had 41 RBIs.

On the mound, Jim Slaton faltered to 11–18 and 4.52 and Bill Travers suffered growing pains at 6–11 and 4.29. Jim Colborn couldn't regain his 1973 form again at 11–13 and 4.27, while Billy Champion's ERA ballooned to 5.89 with his 6–6 record. Pete Broberg was a welcome addition with his 14–16 mark and 4.13 ERA. Tom Murphy also fell back considerably despite 20 saves, dropping 9 of 10 decisions. Eduardo Rodriguez picked up the slack with his 7–0 finish, 3.49 ERA, and seven saves, while Bill Castro came onto the scene with a 3–2 record and 2.52 ERA.

1976

Hank Aaron was asked to replace his old teammate, Del Crandall, as Milwaukee's manager for 1976, but he respectfully declined, instead rounding out his playing career with 10 homers and 35 RBIs under former Cincinnati coach Alex Grammas, who directed the Brewers to a disappointing 66–95 finish as attendance inched past the one million mark. Aaron batted only .229 and missed most of the final two months with a bum leg. However, 40,383 said goodbye to "the Hammer" on September 17.

George Scott and Darrell Porter failed to produce as expected in what proved to be their final season with the club. Scott was okay at .274 with 18 HRs and 77 RBIs but needed to be better, while Porter scuffled at .208 with five homers and 32 RBIs. The biggest problem was a lack of power, as Robin Yount (2 HRs) and Sixto Lezcano (7 HRs) went downhill from the previous season. Don Money ripped 12 homers and knocked in 62, while Von Joshua finished with the same .267 average. Gorman Thomas added eight HRs and 36 RBIs but failed to reach the .200 mark (.198) again.

Bill Travers turned in the best campaign among any of the pitchers with a 15–16 finish and 2.81 ERA. Jim Slaton again hovered around the .500 level with his 14–15 mark and improved ERA (3.44), while Wisconsin native Jerry Augustine played a prominent role at 9–12 and 3.30. Jim Colborn, despite a 3.71 ERA, finished 9–15 and was shown the door after the season, while Pete Broberg slipped mightily to 1–7 and 4.97 and was let loose.

Danny Frisella was a nice addition to the bullpen, posting a 5–2 record and 2.74 ERA with nine saves. Bill Castro was right behind with eight saves and a 4–6 mark. Lefty Ray Sadecki was 2–0, while Eduardo Rodriguez won five of six decisions and had eight saves.

Aaron reached two major milestones during his final season. On July 20, he connected on his 755th—and last—homer, a shot off Dick Drago during a 6–2 victory over the Angels at County Stadium. Then, on October 3, Aaron singled in his final major league at-bat, driving in his major league record 2,297th run in a 6–2 home setback against Detroit.

On December 6, Milwaukee made a vital maneuver in its push for respectability that would eventually come two years later, sending Scott and outfielder Bernie Carbo to the Red Sox in a trade that netted them left-handed hitting and slick fielding first baseman Cecil Cooper.

1977

Manager Alex Grammas lasted through the next season, one in which the team stumbled and bumbled its way to finishing 67–95 and 33 games out of first place as 1.1 million fans were forced to watch bad baseball again. However, the winds of change had started to blow, as Milwaukee outbid San Francisco for free agent third baseman and postseason veteran Sal Bando, brought in Cecil Cooper from Boston and added more pop with the arrival of Ben Oglivie from Detroit. The Brewers also traded with Cincinnati for Mike Caldwell, inked former Twin star Larry Hisle, and drafted a young up-and-comer from the University of Minnesota named Paul Molitor.

Bud Selig knew that drastic measures were necessary after eight seasons of futility, so he hired Harry Dalton as his general manager, who then tabbed George Bamberger as the new manager for 1978. "I knew that during the course of 1977 that our talent was better than what we were showing," Selig was quoted in *True Brew*. "There were a lot of things I didn't like, and the more I thought about it I knew we needed to make sweeping changes." That doesn't always lead to success, but Selig's intuition had served him well as Milwaukee teams embarked on six consecutive seasons of good fortune and good times at the old ball yard starting in 1978.

Cooper scratched the surface of what he would bring to this developing young team with a .300 average, 20 homers, and 78 RBIs; Money became a major cog with his customary .279 average plus 25 homers and 83 RBIs; while Sixto Lezcano continued his progress with 21 homers and .272 average. Robin Yount improved to .288 and knocked in 49, the same RBI total as Lezcano and Von Joshua. Charlie Moore chipped in five homers and 45 RBIs, while Bando showed he still had talent in his tank with 17 round-trippers and 82 RBIs.

Pitching was where the Brewers needed to make the most improvement, but several youngsters and newcomers earned valuable experience that would serve them well in the coming seasons. Jerry Augustine (12–18), Bill Travers (4–12), and Caldwell (5–8) gave the team a good left-handed arsenal to work with, while Jim Slaton marched along with a 10–14 mark and was joined on the right side by Moose Haas (10–12) and Lary Sorensen (7–10). Bill Castro was 8–6 with 13 saves, and Bob McClure finished 2–1 with six saves.

Caldwell had been picked up June 15 and started regaining his form after arm surgery. Milwaukee had to say goodbye to Slaton on December 9 to bring Oglivie's left-handed power potential to County Stadium, although the Brewers welcomed him back a year later to help them become a pennant-winning club.

Money said it was a struggle the first few seasons in Milwaukee, but eventually the team's fortunes turned around. "I was 25 and one of the older guys on the team, so most of the players were just kids getting their feet wet at the major league level," he said from his Beloit office in 2004, where he was managing the club's Class A affiliate in the Midwest League for a seventh and final season. "They were force-feeding these guys, so you knew they were going to make mistakes that would cost us ball games. But they started filling in the blanks with Robin, Gorman, Cooper, and Oglivie. Things started to jell, and then we got (Rollie) Fingers, (Pete) Vuckovich, and (Ted) Simmons and had the reliever who put us over the hump. For three or four years, we had the best record in baseball."

Dalton was the architect of that success from November 1977 to when he was released and replaced with Bando in 1991. The Brewers finished with nine winning records and had their last above-.500 mark in '92 with many of Dalton's acquisitions leading the way.

While the players and managers from the Brewers' postseason teams deserve the recognition, Dalton is often the forgotten man who brought those pieces together. He hired George Bamberger and Harvey Kuenn and later a little-known Tom Trebelhorn to lead from the bench.

And while the huge deal with St. Louis at the 1980 winter meetings was the biggest transaction in franchise history, he made moves and spearheaded drafts that had Milwaukee's farm system near the top of baseball during the final half of his tenure.

Chapter Five

The Brewers Turn It Around
(1978–89)

It was strictly a feeling, a feeling that life would be different and that good things were about to happen. But almost exactly as what hit town in 1953, the Brewers' immediate turnaround from basement dwellers to contenders couldn't have been predicted by anyone inside or outside of the organization.

Harry Dalton and his baseball people knew how to pull the trigger on trades, bringing in just the right pieces to fit into their puzzle. New manager George Bamberger had been on Earl Weaver's wonderful staff in Baltimore and had tutored one of the most talented pitching staffs ever assembled.

Milwaukee featured veterans with experience and ability such as Sal Bando, Don Money, and Larry Hisle. The team included guys who were coming into their own such as Robin Yount, Cecil Cooper, Bill Castro, Jerry Augustine, Bill Travers, and Moose Haas. Throw into the mix several players who had bounced around or hadn't gotten much of a chance to prove themselves regularly at the major league level such as Ben Oglivie, Sixto Lezcano, Jim Gantner, Bob McClure, and Charlie Moore. Then there were reclamation projects such as Gorman Thomas and Mike Caldwell. And spice things up with a rookie such as Paul Molitor, and Beertown had the makings of a perennial contender.

The Brewers gave opposing pitchers nightmares, unleashing some of the most awesome offensive displays ever, ones that would have made the old Braves proud. They became known as "Bambi's Bombers" and then "Harvey's Wallbangers," the most feared lineups in the majors during their run. Milwaukee also featured some of the game's best defensive players, which combined with a steadily improving collection of hurlers had succeeded in rekindling fond memories and community spirit.

Quality baseball was back, and with a vengeance.

1978

Milwaukee showed off its firepower from the start. In the season opener on April 7 in front of 47,824, Sixto Lezcano smacked a grand slam as the Brewers walloped the Baltimore Orioles, 11–3. Gorman Thomas duplicated the feat the next day as Milwaukee triumphed 16–3, and then Cecil Cooper followed suit in a 13–5 victory to complete the sweep while setting an American League mark and tying a big-league standard for grand slams in the first three games of a season.

The Brewers were the talk of the town again, finishing off the home stand with a 5–0 record. Moose Haas capped the string with 14 strikeouts against New York, including four whiffs of Reggie Jackson.

That set the tone for a wild ride the rest of the way. Milwaukee got hot during June, going 21–9, including a 10-game winning streak that pushed them from .500 toward a 93–69 finish, six games out of first and good enough for third place in the East behind New York and Boston, who decided the divisional crown in a three-game playoff that Bucky Dent won for the Yanks with his famous three-run homer off Mike Torres that sailed over the Green Monster at Fenway Park.

Mike Caldwell and Larry Hisle became Yankee killers and stamped the Brewers as legitimate threats for the postseason during the final two months. The highlight came during a series in early July. Caldwell, who ended up 6–0 against the Yankees, fashioned his third shutout versus the Bronx Bombers while Hisle knocked in four runs to help Milwaukee snap Ron Guidry's season-opening 13-game winning streak with a 6–0 decision in front of 40,210 at County Stadium. Hisle's eighth-inning home run gave the Crew a 6–5 win the next night.

Nobody was more excited about or deserved more accolades for the dramatic turnaround than Bud Selig, who started to believe that something special was in the works. "I was driving home on a Saturday night after Hisle had just beaten the Yankees and I'm thinking to myself, 'Goodness gracious, after all the dreams and hopes, we're good. We're really good,'" he said in *True Brew*.

And the people in the dugout were relishing the experience. "We could all feel it," Robin Yount said. "We knew we were getting better. It was like a gradual building process. We knew the pieces were fitting into place."

Caldwell finished 22–9 and earned Comeback Player of the Year honors, while Hisle took third in the voting for most valuable player with 34 homers and 115 RBIs. Molitor, who started at shortstop for the absent Yount to start the season, garnered rookie of the year laurels.

However, that was only the tip of the iceberg, as Milwaukee finished with the fourth-best record in the majors. The Brewers led the AL with 173 round-trippers and in six other offensive categories. And fans showed their appreciation, jumping on the bandwagon to the tune of 1.6 million in attendance, which was almost 500,000 more than the previous year. A prime example of their enthusiasm occurred during the August 4-6 series against Boston, which drew 153,974.

Milwaukee showed off its awesome power capabilities as seven players reached double digits in home runs, led by Hisle's 34 and Thomas's 32 to go with 86 RBIs. Ben Oglivie was next, with 18 to go along with his .303 average and 72 RBIs, while Sal Bando clubbed 17 to bring in 78 runs while hitting .285. Lezcano added 15 homers and a healthy .292 average, while Yount (71 RBIs) and Don Money (14 and 54) both batted .293. Cooper led the average charts at .312 and contributed 13 HRs and 54 RBIs. Molitor knocked in 45 and hit .273 in his inaugural journey through the American League, while Charlie Moore chipped in a .269 average.

The team's fortunes turned around because its pitching staff improved tremendously. Caldwell led the way with his franchise-record 22 wins to go with a 2.36 ERA, but he wasn't alone. Lary Sorensen finished 18–12 (3.21), Jerry Augustine was next at 13–12 (4.54), Bill Travers wasn't far behind with a 12–11 record (4.41), and Andy Replogle was 9–5 and 3.92 as a fifth starter. Bob McClure was only 2–6 but posted a team-high nine saves, while Bill Castro finished with eight saves, a 5–4 mark, and a 1.81 ERA.

1979

The following year, Milwaukee's hitting arsenal continued piling up staggering statistics, finishing second in the loop in homers (185), total bases (2,480), slugging percentage (.448), and doubles (291). The Brewers equaled or shattered 73 club records, which included 18 season marks and five single-game standards.

George Bamberger's hardworking, lovable bunch went 95–66 (.590), the best record in franchise history, a high-water mark for Milwaukee baseball since the Braves finished 95–59 in 1957. However, that squad wound up eight games ahead, while these Brewers ended up eight games behind division-winning Baltimore.

Still, contests at County Stadium were oh, so fun, with baseballs flying all over the place. Gorman Thomas led the way with 45 dingers, an AL high. He became the first Brewer to hit 12 homers in a month (August) and drove in 123 runs. Thomas also struck out 175 times and batted only .244, but he played a reckless center field and never met a wall he couldn't run into. That hell-bent style endeared him to hops and grains lovers across the Badger State.

Cecil Cooper, arguably the best pure hitter to don a Brewers uniform, assaulted opposing pitchers to the tune of a .308 average, 24 HRs, 106 RBIs, and a 16-game hitting streak. He also shared league-high honors with 44 doubles.

Gorman Thomas was a fan favorite, whacking 208 home runs in a Milwaukee uniform.

Ben Oglivie smacked 28 homers, drove in 81 runs, and hit .282; Paul Molitor laced a team-record 16 triples and batted .322; and Sixto Lezcano finished with a .573 slugging percentage to go with 28 homers and a .321 average. Robin Yount (.267) and Sal Bando (.246) slipped, but Charlie Moore (.300) and Dick Davis (12 HRs and 41 RBIs) more than proved their worth.

Milwaukee's offense wasn't stopped often, as Minnesota's Jerry Koosman became a 20-game winner on the final day of the season with a 5–0 victory in Minnesota, the only time the Brewers were shut out all year and ending a streak of 213 games. Had the Brewers scored, they would have shared a record with the 1932 Yankees.

Milwaukee's maturing mound corps also contributed mightily to the cause, reminding people of the Warren Spahn-Lew Burdette days with a major league-best 61 complete games, including a stretch of seven in a row during May. On the flip side, Brewers pitchers issued a major league low 381 walks. Mike Caldwell earned 16 wins, while Lary Sorensen and Jim Slaton, the latter having been reacquired from Detroit during the off-season, registered 15 apiece, which was a career best for Slaton in a Brewers uniform. Bill Travers improved to 14–8 and 3.89, while Moose Haas finished 11–11.

Bill Castro led the bullpen by committee with six saves, with Jerry Aug-

The Brewers Turn It Around (1978–89)

ustine and Bob McClure chipping in five each. Castro was 3–1, Augustine 9–6, and McClure 5–2.

Attendance rose to more than 1.9 million, and the team and its followers sensed that the Brewers were on the cusp of something great.

1980

A series of obstacles knocked the Brewers down a spot in the 1980 standings (86–76) as they ended up 17 games out of first. And the mediocre showing was reflected at the gate (1.86 million).

The first setback occurred when George Bamberger suffered a mild heart attack in early March and underwent surgery, returning June 6 with the Brewers sitting at 26–21. Buck Rodgers served as the interim manager as Milwaukee stayed within 5 1/2 games of New York. And as soon as the skipper returned, leadoff batter and sparkplug Paul Molitor, who was leading the circuit in hitting at .358, tore a rib cage muscle and was forced to miss 38 games. Somehow, the Brewers managed to hang around, trailing the Yankees by 7 1/2 at the All-Star break with a 43–34 mark.

Milwaukee again lit up the scoreboard as Cecil Cooper led the league in RBIs with 122 and finished second in batting (.352), trailing only George Brett of Kansas City, who finished with a .390 average after flirting with the elusive .400 mark much of the summer.

Cooper and Don Money crunched grand slams in the second inning, becoming the fourth teammates to turn the trick, as Milwaukee crushed Boston, 18–1, on April 12. That happened two days after Sixto Lezcano had cranked one with two outs in the ninth to win the home opener, 9–5, for 53,313 jubilant fans.

The Brewers established 65 more team marks and topped the league in home runs, RBIs, total bases, and slugging percentage, but again it wasn't enough. Rodgers took over for good when Bamberger retired September 5, but Harry Dalton's trip to Dallas for baseball's winter meetings proved to be the biggest one in franchise history. The Brewers needed an ace relief pitcher, and Dalton knew that Saint Louis couldn't find enough innings for both Bruce Sutter and Rollie Fingers.

Well, Dalton pulled the trigger on a blockbuster deal that brought him Fingers and veteran catcher Ted Simmons. And for good measure, the Cardinals threw in somebody named Pete Vuckovich in exchange for Dave LaPoint, Lary Sorensen, Lezcano, and minor league star David Green, whom many in the organization were reluctant to give up. Boy, were they ever wrong, and did the Brewers ever get the best of that transaction as their new

63

trio made huge impacts while none of those shipped to the Cardinals accomplished anything special in their new home.

Meanwhile, the Brewers continued to pound the ball. Ben Oglivie shared the league homer title with his 41 clouts. He knocked in 118 runs and hit .304, the same mark as Molitor. Gorman Thomas smacked 38 more HRs and brought home 105. Robin Yount had a big year, hitting .293 with 23 long balls and 87 RBIs, while Lezcano, despite his .229 average, had 18 homers. Don Money belted 17 round-trippers, while Jim Gantner (.282) and Charlie Moore (.291) were valuable contributors. Moore capped his season October 1, hitting for the cycle to lead the Brewers' 10–7 win over California.

1981

Milwaukee's upgraded lineup had started the 1981 schedule with a modest 9–7 record but was beginning to hit its stride when a players' strike began June 12, wiping out 53 games. New York won the first half of the season and would meet the winner of the second half in a playoff to determine the American League's East Division champion.

Milwaukee accepted the challenge, earning the top spot with a 31–22 record to finish 62–47 overall. The Brewers rode the arm of Rollie Fingers, who figured in 21 victories (16 saves and five wins) and posted a 0.72 ERA after action resumed. He wrapped up a postseason spot with a save in the crew's 2–1 triumph over Detroit on October 3. "Every bit of blood in my body rushed to my head," Fingers said after the franchise's biggest regular-season victory. "It was wonderful. I felt happiest for the other guys. They've never been through this."

One of them was Ted Simmons, who couldn't contain his emotions. "This is the greatest moment of my life," Simmons said. "I've always wondered what it would be like to hit .330 and win. I found out what it's like to hit .210 [actually .216] and win. I've played 12 years and I finally earned respect. I've done all the things that people can statistically do, but I've never won a division pennant. Now I feel that I've earned that respect."

The three newcomers obtained from Saint Louis played vital roles. Fingers won the Cy Young award and American League MVP trophy with a 6–3 record, 1.04 ERA, and league-high 28 saves. Pete Vuckovich was 14–4, while Simmons hit 14 homers and brought home 61 despite his subpar batting average.

Milwaukee received consistent production from a host of starters and role players.

Cecil Cooper led the charge with his .320 average, 12 homers, and 60

RBIs, while Charlie Moore backed up Simmons and hit .301. Robin Yount (10 HRs), Ben Oglivie (14), and Gorman Thomas (21) supplied enough power, while Jim Gantner, Don Money, Mark Brouhard, and Roy Howell made contributions. Injuries limited Paul Molitor (.267) to 64 games, while Larry Hisle played sparingly again.

Mike Caldwell and Moose Haas added 11 triumphs apiece, while Jim Slaton was 5–7. Slaton pitched eight innings of no-hit ball against Minnesota on September 5 before settling for a 5–3 win. Newcomer Randy Lerch finished 7–9, and fellow southpaw Jamie Easterly chipped in a 3–3 mark, a 3.19 ERA, and four saves.

Bitterness over the work stoppage lingered, meaning the first playoff game in club history was watched by only 35,064 on October 7. Milwaukee lost both games at County Stadium, 5–3 and 3–0, but rallied back to even the series at Yankee Stadium with 5–3 and 2–1 verdicts. However, their season ended with a 7–3 loss in Game 5 in New York. (See chapter 6 for more details about these playoff games.)

Despite the distractions and the disheartening setback to close out the campaign, Milwaukee was ripe for another run at a title.

1982

Regardless of any resentment remaining from the strike, the Brewers forced their followers to come back, although they sputtered out of the gates. Milwaukee was stuck at 23–24 on June 2 and heading nowhere under Buck Rodgers. Harry Dalton again waved his magic wand, canning Rodgers and promoting easygoing hitting coach Harvey Kuenn, a Milwaukee native and former American League batting champ with Detroit. The club responded like they were supposed to.

"I felt Buck didn't have a handle on it," Dalton said. "I thought he could manage, but I didn't think he was the man for that club at that time. I felt Harvey knew them all; they liked and respected him. He lifted a blanket off the club."

That he did as Milwaukee stormed to a 72–43 mark under Kuenn. "He was the nicest guy in the world, but when the game started he was out there to fight," Robin Yount said of Kuenn. The Brewers went 20–7 in June and won 11 of their first 15 outings in July to move into first place. And they did it behind the most powerful and balanced offensive juggernaut the franchise ever assembled.

Yount, later named the league's most valuable player for the first of two times and the squad's second in a row, accumulated career highs in runs

(129), hits (210), triples (12), homers (29), RBIs (114), and average (.331), spending most of his time batting second behind Paul Molitor, who hit .302, ripped 19 HRs, and added 71 RBIs. When they got on base, and that was often, number three batter Cecil Cooper usually sent them home. Cooper hit .313, crunched 32 round-trippers, and knocked in 121.

That wasn't all. Ben Oglivie hit just .244 but smacked 34 homers and had 102 RBIs; Gorman Thomas sent 39 out of the park with 112 RBIs; and Ted Simmons batted .269 with 23 taters and 97 RBIs. That meant the Brewers were only the second team since 1940 (the 1977 Red Sox were the other) to have four players top the 100-RBI plateau, and had Simmons added three more they would have been the only squad besides the 1936 Yankees to have five accomplish the feat.

Don Money proved to be one of the league's top utility players again, batting .284 with 16 HRs and 55 RBIs. Jim Gantner hit .295 and knocked in 43, while Charlie Moore brought home 45 more. Roy Howell, Marshall Edwards, Ed Romero, Mark Brouhard, and current Milwaukee skipper Ned Yost, a backup catcher, paid dividends in the field or at the plate.

The Brewers' pitching wasn't bad, either. Pete Vuckovich turned in an 18–6 mark and a 3.34 ERA and twice rattled off eight-game winning streaks, which earned the team its second consecutive Cy Young award recipient. Mike Caldwell didn't match his 1978 numbers, but he still won 17 games. Moose Haas (11–8), Bob McClure (12–7), Jim Slaton (10–6), Randy Lerch (8–7), and midseason pickup Doc Medich (5–4) posted winning marks. Rollie Fingers (5–6) was again one of the league's top relievers with a 2.60 ERA and 29 saves despite missing September with an injury that forced him to sit out the postseason. Right-hander Dwight Bernard helped fill the void with a 3–1 record and six saves.

Just a couple of days before Fingers went on the shelf, Dalton had pulled off another excellent move, trading three minor leaguers for veteran Don Sutton, who had won 13 games with Houston that season. All he did was win four out of five decisions with a 3.29 ERA.

The Brewers were 4 ½ games ahead of Boston at the time but couldn't put enough distance between themselves and their nearest pursuers, including hard-charging Baltimore. Sutton defeated Mike Flanagan and the Orioles on September 24 to give Milwaukee a four-game cushion, but Baltimore claimed 7–2 and 5–2 wins at County Stadium to shave the Brewers' margin in half. Milwaukee headed to Fenway Park to kick off a seven-game, season-ending road swing.

Medich got a big win in the opener, and McClure got the win in relief in Game 2 as Yost smacked his only homer of the season over the Green Monster in left field in the ninth inning for a 6–3 victory. That proved crucial as Boston won the finale to put Milwaukee ahead by three games with a four-game series at Baltimore's Memorial Stadium.

Milwaukee needed every inch of room. The Orioles whipped Vuckovich, 8–3, and Caldwell, 7–1, in a doubleheader to climb to within one game on October 1 with a crowd of 51,583 looking on. Game 3 proved just as easy for Baltimore, an 11–3 thrashing that left both teams sitting at 94–67.

That left Sunday's classic matchup of Sutton and Jim Palmer. A sea of broom-wielding fans greeted the Brewers' team bus on the way to the stadium. Sutton got the better of the duel, thanks in large part to Yount, who crunched two home runs, including a first-inning shot, and a triple as Milwaukee won easily, 10–2. Oglivie's sliding catch in the left-field corner with two runners on base and Milwaukee clinging to a 5–2 lead in the eighth was also one for the scrapbook.

Bud Selig said that the enormity of what the Brewers had accomplished didn't sink in until many hours later back in the Midwest. "We had flown back from Baltimore that Sunday and then were driving home on the freeway, and there was something going on, so much action," he said via phone interview. "I asked my wife what she thought and it finally dawned on me that the city was celebrating [our victory]."

However, that was nothing compared to the fervor that hit Milwaukee when the team won an even bigger prize about a week later. "It was fabulous," Selig said. "We had lost to the Yankees the year before in a series we should have won." He continued:

Then we lost the first two games out in California before winning the last three to win the pennant. Right then, that was the most emotion I'd ever seen at a Milwaukee sporting event, before or since. I got home that night about 10 or 10:30 and was reading and watching TV until right around 1 a.m. A CBS announcer, and I can still hear his voice, said 'In the 79th World Series, it will be the Saint Louis Cardinals against the Milwaukee Brewers.' That's when it hit me.

And the 1982 Brewers partied with the best of them. They tailgated with fans often and slept off their share of hangovers. But when it was time to lace up their cleats and put on their uniforms, they were all business.

"I never seen a bunch of horses go out there and put such numbers on the board," said Randy Lerch, a starting pitcher who won eight games before being traded late in the season. "I played for the Phillies when they won the World Series in 1980. That team had Pete Rose, Mike Schmidt, Garry Maddox,

Bob Boone, Greg Luzinksi, Bake McBride, and Manny Trillo. Then I came to Milwaukee, and those guys were every bit as good and maybe better." (For more about the Brewers' marvelous postseason, see chapter 6.)

1983

There's nothing more satisfying than reaching the top, and there's nothing more painful than coming down, as the organization found out in September after a rocky 1983 season. Pete Vuckovich and Rollie Fingers succumbed to the injury bug during spring training. It was discovered on March 15 that Vuckovich had a torn rotator cuff, forcing him to miss almost the entire season. The medical list only got longer as Robin Yount, Ben Oglivie, Moose Haas, and others missed playing time.

As a result, Milwaukee struggled to a 35–36 record through June. Among the fallouts of such a season are roster changes, and the one that hurt the most, even though on paper it may have been necessary, was when Harry Dalton sent Gorman Thomas to Cleveland on June 6. Dalton was an easy and frequent target for angry and loyal fans of Number 20.

Then the reigning AL champions responded, winning 40 of their next 61

Fans enjoy "The World's Largest Tailgate Party" during the 1983 season, an event that drew more than 3,400 revelers.

contests in July and August while surging into first place. However, the emotional and physical effects of climbing back into the hunt took a heavy toll. They never recovered from a 3–8 West Coast trip and lost 10 consecutive games in September, dropping 18 of their final 30 contests to plummet to fifth place at 87–75.

Cecil Cooper was a beacon during an otherwise dreary season. He batted .307 and tied for the league lead with 126 RBIs, still a team record, despite playing in only 106 games.

A then-record 2,397,131 fans, an average of 31,000 per game, crammed into County Stadium, the third-best attendance in baseball. The Brewers reached the two-million mark September 5, the earliest in Milwaukee history at the time.

It was the franchise's sixth straight winning record, but it wasn't enough to save Harvey Kuenn's job. He resigned October 2 and was replaced by 38-year-old Rene Lachemann, who had already been fired in 1983 (by Seattle).

The season wasn't a total loss as several individuals reached personal milestones: Robin Yount moved past the 1,500-hit mark and Ted Simmons registered his 2,000th. Don Sutton surpassed the 3,000-strikeout plateau, becoming the eighth pitcher in major league history to do so, during a 3–2 victory over Cleveland on June 24, a game that saw 46,037 fans welcome Thomas back to County Stadium as a member of the Indians.

Simmons enjoyed his best season as a Brewer, batting .308 with 13 HRs and 108 RBIs. Yount, Paul Molitor, and Ben Oglivie came down to earth somewhat. Yount hit .308 with 17 homers and 80 RBIs, Molitor batted .270 but hit 15 HRs, and Oglivie chimed in at .280 with 13 long balls and 66 RBIs. Jim Gantner had his best power numbers with 11 homers and 74 RBIs, while Charlie Moore chipped in a .284 average and knocked in 49.

Moose Haas led the staff with a wonderful 13–3 record and 3.27 ERA, but his buddies didn't fare as well. Mike Caldwell finished 12–11 but his ERA rose to 4.53, while Sutton dropped to 8–13 and Bob McClure to 9–9, and Chuck Porter was 7–9. Pete Ladd (3–4) filled in admirably for Fingers with a 2.55 ERA and 25 saves. Jim Slaton finished 14–6.

1984

The next year, attendance nose-dived by more than 700,000, and who could blame the fans? Rene Lachemann's first and only season at the controls was a disaster as the proud sweethearts of the baseball world from two years earlier hit the cellar, and they hit hard, finishing 36 ½ games behind the powerful Detroit Tigers. A 67–94 record said it all, and as with the franchise before them, age, decreasing skill levels, and injuries combined to bring the Brewers crashing down.

Rollie Fingers, who spent all of 1983 recuperating after elbow surgery from his late 1982 injury, returned to register 23 saves in his 33 outings and had a fine 1.96 ERA. However, misfortune struck again in the form of a herniated disk in his back, and he underwent surgery August 3.

Don Money had been released in January and played in Japan, while Jerry Augustine, Mike Caldwell, Roy Howell, and Don Sutton played their final games with the team. Cecil Cooper (.275), Jim Gantner (.282), Robin Yount (.298), and Ben Oglivie (.262) had good years, but it wasn't enough after several great ones. Yount led that bunch with 16 homers and 80 RBIs. Outfielder Dion James (.295) and backup catcher Bill Schroeder (14 homers) came onto the scene. A major factor in the crash was the absence of Paul Molitor, who missed all but 13 games because of injury.

Sutton rebounded to finish 14–12, including a 3–2 decision at Kansas City on August 8 that stopped the team's 10-game losing streak and pushed him past the 100-strikeout standard for a major league-record 19th straight season. However, his counterparts struggled at best. Moose Haas was 9–11, newcomer Jaime Cocanower went 8–16, and Caldwell said good-bye after going 6–13. Pete Ladd (4–9) and Bob McClure (4–8) had their troubles, although Chuck Porter (6–4) and Tom Tellmann (6–3 and 2.78) did well in the bullpen.

It seemed only fitting that Detroit clinched the AL East crown with a 3–0 triumph over the Brewers at Tiger Stadium on September 18. Randy O'Neal registered his first big-league win as the Tigers joined the 1923 Giants, the 1927 Yankees, and the 1955 Dodgers as the only teams in the 20th century to be in first place every day of the season.

1985

Brewer stalwarts such as Robin Yount, Paul Molitor, and Jim Gantner were still going strong, but the transition period shifted into high gear as 1985 proved to be the last season for Ted Simmons, Rollie Fingers, Moose Haas, Mark Brouhard, and Pete Ladd, who had all played major roles on the postseason teams. In his final hurrah, Fingers returned to record his 341st and final save against the White Sox, finishing the season with 17.

But a few newcomers—notably Teddy Higuera, Bill Wegman, Juan Nieves, and Mike Felder—from a good farm system were stepping in to take their place. Higuera especially sparkled, winning six straight decisions to go 15–8. He set a Brewers' rookie mark of 12 strikeouts in a 3–2 win over Texas en route to being selected the *Sporting News'* top first-year player.

Milwaukee wound up in sixth place with a 71–90 showing under George Bamberger, back for his second go-round as attendance slipped to 1.36 million. Cecil Cooper led the RBI brigade with 99 to go with his .293 average and 16 homers, while Simmons hit .273 with 76 RBIs. Molitor bounced back with a .297 campaign, and Yount hit .277 with 68 RBIs. Ben Oglivie turned in a .290 average, while Ernest Riles became the regular shortstop and hit .286. Paul Householder was another new face, batting .258 with 11 homers.

Higuera was the only regular starter or reliever to post a winning record as Danny Darwin lost 18 of 26 decisions despite a 3.80 ERA, Ray Burris finished 9–14, Pete Vuckovich wasn't his old self at 6–10 but earned his first wins since 1982, Jaime Cocanower was 6–8, and Moose Haas ended up 8–8. Fingers ended on a down note with a 1–6 mark and 5.04 ERA, while Bob Gibson contributed a 6–7 record and 11 saves.

1986

The transformation begun the year before was almost complete in 1986 as names such as Chris Bosio, Rob Deer, Dan Plesac, Dale Sveum, and Glenn Braggs filled the lineup card instead of Bob McClure, Charlie Moore, and Pete Vuckovich. The Brewers also continued another slow climb toward respectability, improving to 77–84, although George Bamberger retired again, to be replaced by third-base coach Tom Trebelhorn.

It was a nice recovery after tragedy struck during spring training. Coaches Tony Muser and Herm Starrette, players Bill Schroeder and Bill Wegman, Bamberger, and Harry Dalton were hurt when a natural gas explosion rocked the team's facility in Chandler, Arizona.

Robin Yount pushed across the 2,000 hit marker September 6, while Teddy Higuera notched his 20th victory in a 9–3 win against Baltimore on September 25. Cecil Cooper's last hurrah featured a .258 average, 12 homers, and 75 RBIs; Moore closed out his Milwaukee career with a .260 mark and 39 RBIs; and Ben Oglivie's swan song turned out a .283 average, five dingers, and 53 RBIs.

Jim Gantner (.274 and 38 RBIs), Yount (.312 and 46 RBIs), and Paul Molitor (.281 and 55 RBIs) soldiered on, while Deer burst on the scene with 33 homers and 86 RBIs, although he hit .232. Ernest Riles contributed nine homers and 47 RBIs, while Sveum and Bill Schroeder chipped in seven homers apiece and Rick Manning had eight.

Higuera finished 20–11 with a splendid 2.79 ERA, but Tim Leary (12–12) was the only other starter to reach the .500 level. Wegman (5–12), Danny Darwin (6–8), and Juan Nieves (11–12) had their moments. In the bullpen, Mark Clear was 5–5 with 16 saves and Plesac was 10–7 with 14 saves.

Although the on-field record was slightly better than in 1985, attendance slipped to 1.26 million.

1987

The final major connection to the glory years was severed when the team said good-bye to Cecil Cooper after the 1987 season, formally silencing the chants of "Coop, Coop" that used to echo through County Stadium. Otherwise, the season was a thrill-a-minute ride as this bunch became known as "Team Streak," aided by the addition of such players as B. J. Surhoff, Chuck Crim, and Greg Brock. The squad featured 14 players with one year or less of major league experience. Maybe that raw enthusiasm, led by an untested manager, made the difference. But whatever it was, these Brewers were up and down from the get-go, finishing with a solid and surprising 91–71 campaign. Fans began to return, as 1.9 million hopped on for what became perhaps the franchise's most roller-coaster of seasons.

Milwaukee kicked off the season with what became a major league-tying and American League record-setting 13-game winning streak. It started with a three-game home sweep of the defending league champion Red Sox, including an opener in front of 52,585. Rob Deer's pair of three-run homers and Surhoff's eighth-inning shot pulled out a 12–11 win and 3–0 record. Milwaukee then mowed down the Rangers in Texas as the team exploded for eight-run innings in the first two tilts and got Surhoff's game-winning hit in the 12th of the finale to improve to 6–0.

The Brewers took their show to Baltimore, where Brock and Deer led the way with three hits apiece in the opener at Memorial Stadium. Then five Brewers slugged homers to make it eight straight. On the rainy evening of April 15, Milwaukee got its first and only no-hitter in franchise history as Juan Nieves struck out seven and walked five in a 7–0 contest. And Robin Yount put an exclamation point on win number nine with a spectacular diving catch of Eddie Murray's liner in right-center field.

"My stuff was awful," said Nieves afterward about his early trouble. "I felt bad. I couldn't throw a slider. My changeup was up. I felt like a pregnant lady. I just kept throwing and all of a sudden, everything just turned around." He won 14 games that year, but unfortunately for the lefty, injuries piled up quickly and he was out of baseball a couple of years later at age 25.

But the Brewers' fortunes that spring couldn't have been better. They returned to County Stadium to 42,000 patrons after 20,000 had greeted them at the airport the night before. Teddy Higuera got his fourth victory as

Milwaukee thrashed Texas. The crew made it 11–0, setting up one of the most talked about contests in team annals.

It was Easter Sunday and 29,357 were on hand. The Brewers' prayers were answered. Trailing the Rangers 4–1 going into the bottom of the ninth, Milwaukee found its magic. With two men on, Deer smashed an 0–1 curveball with one out from Greg Harris into the bleachers in left to knot the score. With two outs, Jim Gantner walked. Then Dale Sveum drilled Harris's 3–2 fastball over the fence in right, causing bedlam. Singing and dancing to the Monkees' "I'm a Believer" continued through the wee hours.

That win pushed the Brewers past the 1981 Oakland A's string of 11, and the next game took thousands of fans south to Chicago's Comiskey Park. Yount and Paul Molitor contributed RBI singles in a 5–4 victory, tying the Brewers with the 1982 Atlanta Braves' achievement.

Chicago's Joel Davis silenced Milwaukee's bats the next night, but the Brewers surged onward to a record-tying 17–1 record and finished April at 18–3. Then it became May and they headed in the opposite direction, finding ways to lose games, including a then-club record 12 straight setbacks.

Dan Plesac recorded 18 saves to become the team's lone All-Star representative, but the Brewers were stuck in neutral at 42–43. But the fans, if they had learned anything, should have known that another streak was on the way.

Molitor had missed 44 games before the break, but he got a hit in his first game back on July 16 and kept on hitting, and the Brewers went along for the ride. Molitor didn't stop until August 16, a string of 39 consecutive games that captured the imagination of baseball fans nationwide. His became the fifth-longest string in the century and the seventh-longest of all time. Cleveland's John Farrell ended the glorious run, and Brewers' outfielder Rick Manning was roundly booed for driving in the winning run against future Milwaukee reliever Doug Jones with Molitor kneeling in the on-deck circle and one out in the 10th.

"It was definitely a highlight for me," said the *Journal Sentinel*'s Tom Haudricourt in a phone interview. "It was remarkable to watch and created a buzz around the ballpark during a memorable season."

Higuera also established a team mark with 32 straight scoreless innings, while Molitor finished with a .353 average, 16 homers, and 75 RBIs. But it wasn't enough, even though the Brewers shared first place with Toronto at one point in September.

Brock proved to be a fine addition, producing a .299 average, 13 homers, and 85 RBIs. Sveum was a pleasant surprise, clubbing 25 HRs and knocking in 95 runs. Yount was a bright spot again, batting .312 with 21 homers and a team-high 103 RBIs. Deer cracked 28 homers and brought home 80, while Glenn Braggs and Surhoff added 77 and 68 RBIs, respectively. Cooper chipped in 36 RBIs. Jim Gantner batted .272, while Bill Schroeder was extremely productive in a reserve role, hitting .332 with 14 homers and 42 RBIs.

Higuera wound up 18–10, while Nieves finished 14–8 and Bill Wegman turned in a 12–11 mark. Plesac notched 23 saves and five victories, Mark Clear added eight wins and six saves, and Crim won six times and saved 12 others. Chris Bosio had a high ERA (5.24) but won 11 games.

1988

The Brewers settled for a tie for third place with Toronto in 1988, only one game behind Detroit and two steps below Boston despite an 87–75 record. But unlike a year earlier, this group got off to an 0–6 start after losing 7–1 to the Yankees in front of a record 55,887 fans on April 15.

Milwaukee got back into the race with a 10-game winning streak in May, highlighted by Bill Wegman's four-hitter and 9–1 win over Texas. In June, Teddy Higuera tossed a no-hitter through seven innings before giving up a solo homer in the eighth, while Mark Clear, Chuck Crim, and Dan Plesac finished off the one-hitter against Seattle.

The Brewers suffered a blow when shortstop Dale Sveum broke his leg when he collided with outfielder Darryl Hamilton. That issued in the big-league career of Gary Sheffield and his tumultuous stay in Milwaukee that ended after the 1991 season.

Paul Molitor (.312) and Robin Yount (.306) led the Brewers' offense, chipping in 13 homers each as Yount drove home 91 and Molitor 60. Molitor was fourth in the AL in runs with 115 and his average was fifth, while he and Yount shared the number-four spot in base hits (190). On June 12, Yount became the third of what currently stands at five Brewers to hit for the cycle as Milwaukee whipped the White Sox, 16–2, at Comiskey Park. He also shared the league lead with 11 triples.

Rob Deer blasted 23 homers to lead the club for a third straight season while finishing with 85 RBIs and a .252 average. Jim Gantner hit his usual .276 and added 47 RBIs. Sveum had nine homers and 51 RBIs before his injury.

Higuera sparkled again, fashioning a 16–9 mark and 2.45 ERA. The latter figure tied him with Minnesota's Allan Anderson for the American League's lowest, while Higuera tied for fourth with his 192 strikeouts. Wegman finished 13–13, Mike Birkbeck was 10–8, and Don August enjoyed an excellent season with a 13–7 record and 3.09 ERA. Chris Bosio didn't get enough run support, sporting a 7–15 mark despite a 3.36 ERA. Dan Plesac won only once but had a

2.41 ERA and saved 30 games, while Chuck Crim finished 7–6 with a 2.91 ERA and nine saves. Crim's 70 appearances topped the league as Milwaukee's team ERA of 3.45 was second to Oakland.

1989

The next year, new guys Jaime Navarro, Bill Spiers, and Greg Vaughn arrived on the scene, giving the Brewers another influx of youth that they hoped would raise them up a couple of notches in the AL East pecking order. However, it was the old man, Robin Yount, who stole most of the thunder. His 276-game playing streak was snapped June 14, but he contributed a 19-game hitting streak during a campaign in which he registered his 2,500th career hit and 200th home run. "The Kid," as announcer Bob Uecker still called him, played a masterful center field and won his second most valuable player award. Yount batted .318, which tied him for fourth in the league, with 21 homers and 103 RBIs. He also finished third in slugging percentage at .511, was third in runs scored at 101, and fourth in hits with 195.

It wasn't enough, as Milwaukee slipped to .500 and eight games out of first in Tom Trebelhorn's third full season as manager. Paul Molitor batted .315 with 11 homers and 56 RBIs, but besides Jim Gantner's .274 and Greg Brock's .265, most of the Brewers struggled at the plate. Spiers hit .255; Glenn Braggs was at .247 despite hitting 15 HRs and driving in 66; while Rob Deer slumped to .210 and brought home only 65 runs despite cracking 26 homers, a team high for the fourth time in a row. B. J. Surhoff had 55 RBIs but hit .248, while Joey Meyer, used mostly as a designated hitter, finished at .224.

Chris Bosio turned in a 15–10 campaign with a 2.95 ERA and tied for fourth with 173 strikeouts, but the rest of the rotation took its lumps, especially Don August, whose ERA skyrocketed to 5.31 despite a 12–12 record. Teddy Higuera's injury woes started, limiting him to a 9–6 finish. Navarro was only 7–8 but registered a 3.12 ERA. Dan Plesac was great in the closer's role again, posting 33 saves, which tied him for third in the league. Chuck Crim was 9–7 with seven saves and a 2.83 ERA and topped the circuit again with 76 appearances. Tony Fossas won twice, while Mark Knudson won 8 of 13 decisions with a 3.35 ERA.

The Brewers' biggest off-season move occurred December 3, when they signed 38-year-old slugger Dave Parker, who had hit 22 homers and knocked in 97 for the world champion Oakland A's.

Chapter Six

Suds Flow Again: Postseason Play (1981 and 1982)

Harry Dalton had built a winner in Baltimore, but most onlookers probably thought that one of baseball's best architects had taken on too big a reclamation project when he was named general manager of the Brewers in 1977. However, he quickly added pieces to a youthful foundation, and the franchise enjoyed success almost overnight. Dalton continued to tinker with what he'd built, but it wasn't until December 1980 that his blueprint was completed with the blockbuster deal that brought the relief pitcher the team so desperately needed to take the final, and toughest, steps toward the top.

Rollie Fingers brought talent, experience, and name recognition, and Milwaukee went from being a good team to being a legitimate title contender. The Brewers finally had a well-rounded pitching staff to complement their formidable offensive machine, and everything came together with back-to-back postseason appearances in 1981 and 1982.

1981: UP AGAINST THE YANKEES

The Brewers entered their final three-game regular-season series against Detroit with a half-game lead over the runner-up Tigers at County Stadium. Moose Haas fired a five-hitter as Milwaukee won the opener, 8–2, striking out eight batters. The right-hander had limited his foes from Motown to one hit through five innings in front of a crowd of only 23,540 on a Friday night.

Left fielder Ben Oglivie belted a two-run homer, and Robin Yount and Paul Molitor added two RBIs each as Milwaukee moved to within one victory of clinching the East. Yount wound up 3-for-4 and improved his current hot spell to 22-for-52 while extending his hitting streak to 10 games. The crew sewed up the city's first postseason spot since 1958 when Rollie Fingers saved a 2–1 victory the next day, October 3.

Only 28,330 bothered to show up at County Stadium to watch that clinching game, maybe because many folks were still ticked off about the strike that had shut down baseball for two months and the split-season format, and maybe others weren't convinced the Brewers really had a shot at doing much damage. Most of the celebration occurred in the stadium as hardly any revelers were witnessed along Wisconsin Avenue or elsewhere in the city.

Meanwhile, Buck Rodgers's players turned their attention toward the first-half-winning Yankees. Haas said the Brewers were prepared to face the more experienced and battle-tested New Yorkers. "They're a quality team like we are," Haas told reporters as the Brewers prepared for Game 1, which he was scheduled to start. "The only difference is they've been through the playoffs and we haven't. But I think we've grown up a lot. We had to win this series with Detroit, and we did."

Veteran third baseman and captain Sal Bando was accustomed to handling the pressures of playoff baseball from his years with Fingers in Oakland. "It can be a big factor," Bando said. "The first year we won our division in Oakland was 1971, and we lost three straight to Baltimore because we were in awe of them. You have to be through it once. But this team has matured a lot in the last two or three weeks. Every game was important, and we did what we had to do. We didn't back-door into the playoffs. I think the pressure we've already handled will be equal to the pressure we'll face against the Yankees."

Fingers accounted for 55 percent of the Brewers' regular-season victories, accumulating 28 saves and six wins. But he didn't get as many chances in the Eastern Division playoffs against the defending American League champions.

In the first postseason contest played on Wisconsin soil since Game 7 of the 1958 World Series, Charlie Moore's single and Cecil Cooper's sacrifice fly staked the hosts to a 2–0 cushion after three innings. However, New York rallied for four runs in the fourth and added an insurance run in the ninth for a 5–3 victory October 7.

Oscar Gamble's two-run homer against Haas was the big blow in the fourth. Gamble was scuffling in an 0-for-27 slump and hadn't registered a base hit since September 11. He finished 3-for-4 as his two-run dinger tied the game during his team's big uprising. Rick Cerone smacked a two-run double during the crucial inning.

The left-handed-hitting Gamble said he was due and wanted only a chance to redeem himself. "I felt if I could get in the lineup, I could get a big hit," Gamble said.

Haas said it was strictly a matter of Gamble doing his job and winning the one-on-one confrontation. "I thought the pitch to Gamble was a good one," Haas said. "Five of the eight hits off me were off their fists. They were fighting the pitches off."

New York also received excellent work from its bullpen as winning pitcher Ron Davis and Rich "Goose" Gossage closed the door with 4 ²/₃ combined innings of one-hit ball after Milwaukee had recorded seven hits against starter Ron Guidry in front of 35,064 fans.

Bando and Molitor said that Milwaukee's hitters never caught up to the heat from the Yankee hurlers. "With Davis and Gossage throwing that hard, they've got enough fuel to light a furnace," said Bando. "Guidry was throwing about 93 mph," Molitor added. "Then the second guy comes in and throws 95, and the third throws 99. You just climb the ladder." Another critical juncture occurred in the third inning, when New York third baseman Graig Nettles robbed Ted Simmons of a hit and the Brewers of at least one run with a leaping, back-handed snare of a line drive with two runners on base.

Pitching and power again led the Yankees, who were making their 34th trip to the postseason, in Game 2 the next evening as only 26,295 showed up at County Stadium. Lou Piniella crunched a homer in the fourth off starter and loser Mike Caldwell, and Reggie Jackson swatted one during a two-run ninth, while left-hander Dave Righetti and the righty combination of Davis and Gossage whitewashed the Brewers, 3–0.

Both teams finished with seven hits, but the Yanks mustered enough offense to put the game away as the Brewers' hitters struggled again, striking out 14 times. Gossage pitched out of a bases-loaded, one-out jam in the seventh as New York grabbed a 2–0 series lead. Righetti, a rookie, allowed four hits and struck out 10 in six innings. Pete Vuckovich was supposed to start for Milwaukee but was sent to Mount Sinai Hospital with a 102-degree temperature and laryngitis/tonsillitis.

Action shifted to the Big Apple for the rest of the series. Trailing, 1–0, in Game 3 and having been held scoreless for 19 straight innings, Milwaukee broke out of its offensive slump. Simmons's two-run round-tripper keyed a three-run seventh, and Molitor's solo homer ignited a two-run eighth as the Brewers handed Tommy John a 5–3 defeat at Yankee Stadium. Fingers became the beneficiary and got the victory in relief of Randy Lerch, who tossed six solid innings in front of the series' biggest crowd (56,411).

Milwaukee staved off elimination after the Yankees had tied the score at 3 in the seventh against Fingers. Simmons's long ball in the top half of the inning had helped the visitors grab a 3–1 lead. Molitor's solo shot pushed the

Brewers back on top, 4–3, and they tacked on an insurance run. Fingers then shut the door in the eighth and ninth innings.

With New York leading, 1–0, and Brewer Cecil Cooper aboard with a single in the seventh, a fan jumped out of the stands and tackled umpire Mike Reilly. Both benches cleared. The unusual goings-on may have unnerved John as Simmons then drilled a hanging forkball into the left-field stands for a 2–1 Milwaukee advantage. Bando's single made it 3–1. Lerch had allowed only three hits and one run in six innings. Milwaukee was outhit, 8–5, but made the most of its opportunities.

Milwaukee again staved off elimination in Game 4, which belonged to feisty right-hander Vuckovich, the third piece of the puzzle from Harry Dalton's monster trade with Saint Louis. Vuckovich pitched five innings, shaking off the flu and a fever while outdueling former Cubs veteran Rick Reuschel. The Brewers tallied twice in the fourth on Ben Oglivie's double, and Vuckovich and Fingers made it stand up with a 2–1 triumph that evened the series and forced a deciding fifth game. Milwaukee finished with only four hits, while the Yankees mustered just five.

New York's potential collapse after taking a 2–0 cushion didn't sit well with Yankees owner George Steinbrenner, who exchanged heated words with a few players, including Cerone. That must have helped to fire up the Yankees as the series came down to Sunday, October 11, to see which team would advance to the Championship Series, where the Oakland A's, who had swept Kansas City, awaited. The Brewers scored single runs in the second and third, including Gorman Thomas's homer, but New York chased Haas, who lasted 3 1/3 innings, for the second time in claiming a 7–3 decision.

Gamble and Jackson crunched their second homers and Cerone clubbed his first. New York scored four times in the fourth—the Yankees tallied 10 times in that inning during the series—and then put things out of reach with a run in the seventh and two in the eighth. The Yankees finished with 13 hits to support Righetti's second win.

Yount led Brewers hitters with a .316 average, going 6-for-19 while scoring four runs. Bando was 5-for-17 (.294), but the rest of Milwaukee's vaunted attack was shut down. The Brewers batted only .222 while striking out 39 times, including nine by Thomas and seven by Oglivie.

Milwaukee's pitchers finished with a respectable 3.48 ERA, although Haas was roughed up to the tune of seven runs and 13 hits in 6 2/3 innings. Brewers hurlers finished with a 22–9 strikeout-to-walk ratio.

Jackson's solo homer, his 16th in postseason play, ignited the hosts' key outburst to erase their 2–0 deficit. Gamble laced a liner over the fence in right. Milwaukee closed to 4–3 in the seventh, but Cerone's solo blast restored order, and the Yankees added two runs in the eighth.

The victory gave New York the series, 3–2, and offered it a chance to face former skipper Billy Martin. Yount had three hits and Oglivie chipped in two in front of 47,505. Haas suffered his second loss of the series, allowing five hits and three runs in 3 1/3 innings.

"It was a good year for us," Cooper said afterward. "People know who we are now. We just have to go out and do it again next year."

For Bando, it was his last game as a player. "We proved we were a playoff team and we gained a lot of valuable experience," he said. "We've certainly seen the value of pitching. That's the way the Yankees beat us. I know in the future you'll hear a lot from the Milwaukee Brewers."

Haas couldn't hide his disappointment, but he vowed to help get his team back to the playoffs. "Reggie beat me," Haas said. "After he hit it and went back to the dugout, I gave him a nod. He gave me a nod back. I was just saying, 'Hey, you beat me.' I don't think we have anything to be ashamed of. I think the big thing was to get here. To win this would have been icing on the cake. Losing the first games at home, that hurt. But we didn't quit. People have to know who the Milwaukee Brewers are."

Milwaukee players entered the off-season with a bitter taste in their

Ecstatic Milwaukee fans celebrate on the field after the Brewers downed California in a dramatic Game 5 rally to win the 1982 American League pennant.

mouths knowing how close they had come to reaching the ALCS, a hurdle they wouldn't stumble over the next time. It's something that players don't forget.

"That was our first taste," Don Money said during a 2004 interview. "I remember in Game 5, I think it was the seventh inning [actually it was the eighth]. I pinch-hit against Gossage and almost hit a home run that would have tied the game or put us ahead. [Dave] Winfield caught it at the fence." Gossage had walked Bando and Roy Howell with two out to set the stage for Money's near heroics.

Cooper said that the disappointing outcome was still a vital part of the Brewers' development at that stage. "It took us two or three years to grow together, but those playoffs were important for the organization to finally experience something like that," Cooper said during a 2004 phone conversation from his Indianapolis office, where he was finishing his second full year as manager of the Brewers' Class AAA squad. "Getting into the postseason and playing a big-time franchise like the Yankees was a big step. We grew from that. It helped us break through and get to the World Series the next year."

1982: A SEASON LIKE NONE SINCE

The Brewers had made it interesting and nerve-wracking for themselves and their fans, but after posting their 10–2 triumph on the final day of the season at Baltimore, all else was forgotten because Milwaukee had another playoff team. "This has been a club of character right along," Robin Yount stated after carrying the Brewers past the Orioles. "We were loose throughout this series. We approached every game with the same attitude, with a positive feeling. Today was no different."

Oh, yes it was. Milwaukee had erased memories of three consecutive setbacks to the Orioles by a combined 26–7 margin. Milwaukee pounded six extra-base hits, three of them from Yount as he clubbed two homers, including one to help the visitors jump to a 3–0 first-inning lead against Jim Palmer, and a triple to cap his most valuable player season. Cecil Cooper added a solo homer and a two-run double after going 7-for-47 against Baltimore without an RBI up to that point in the season. Ted Simmons hit a two-run shot in a five-run ninth that sealed the deal.

Winning pitcher Don Sutton was simply happy to be around for the amazing finish. "I knew all along this club was going to win, with or without me," Sutton said. "It's the best collection of talent I've ever played with. I'm glad to be along for the ride."

Ben Oglivie's sliding catch with two runners on in the eighth, while Milwaukee was protecting a 5–2 advantage, helped put a damper on what turned out to be Baltimore manager Earl Weaver's final game in the dugout. In the process, the Brewers almost became the first team since the 1930 Cardinals to have all four infielders hit .300 as Jim Gantner finished at .295.

The Brewers' most talented lineup and greatest season featured some of the game's biggest names. However, they wouldn't have won the division crown and surely wouldn't have advanced to the World Series without surprising contributions from guys such as Mark Brouhard, Pete Ladd, Charlie Moore, and Marshall Edwards.

Milwaukee had limped home after getting whipped 8–3 and 4–2 to open the American League Championship Series in California. The Angels had battered the Brewers' top two pitchers, Mike Caldwell and Pete Vuckovich, early and often in moving within one game of a sweep. Veterans Tommy John and Bruce Kison, the latter in particular, had stymied the most prolific offense in the big leagues, holding them to 12 hits in Anaheim.

In Game 1, California, which had clubbed 186 homers, battered Caldwell for seven hits and six runs in three-plus innings in posting an 8–3 win behind John. "I just didn't locate my pitches very well," Caldwell said. "Every time I made a mistake, they hit it hard. It was just their night, not mine. We'll be back." The largest American League playoff crowd of 64,406 attended as California erased a 3–1 hole with a four-run third, putting the game out of reach with three more runs in the next two innings.

Game 2 was closer, but the Brewers' missing offense sealed their fate again. Vuckovich entered the contest with a 3–0 mark versus the Angels in the regular season, but the hosts' Kison was better. He retired the final 13 Brewers he faced as California jumped out to a 2–0 series lead. Vuckovich allowed six hits, but none after the fourth inning. Molitor registered only the second inside-the-park homer in league playoff history.

The Brewers had shrugged off brooms before in winning the East after dropping the first three games of the deciding series. They used that resolve again in proving they were the best team the AL had to offer, and this time they did it in the friendly confines of County Stadium. And they accomplished the feat despite hitting just .219 as a team.

Sutton took the hill in Game 3 and showed why Milwaukee had made a wise investment, striking out nine, including Reggie Jackson three times, in 7 2/3 innings to lift the Brewers to a 5–3 win. Molitor's homer in the seventh provided what proved to be the difference maker after the hosts had scored three runs in the fourth.

Ladd, a former prison guard, recorded his first of two saves in the series. He relieved Sutton with the tying run at the plate in the eighth inning and retired the four batters he faced to preserve the win as the Brewers stayed alive for one more day.

Milwaukee jumped to a 3–0 advantage against Geoff Zahn in the fourth, and Molitor's two-run shot made it 5–0 in the seventh. Sutton took a four-hit, 5–0 lead into the Angels' eighth when Bob Boone lifted a controversial solo homer that Oglivie said he would have caught if a fan hadn't reached over the fence and grabbed it. The visitors added two runs before Ladd closed the door.

Game 4 belonged to Brouhard, a former Angels prospect. Subbing for an injured Oglivie, he went 3-for-4, scored an ALCS record four runs, and knocked in three more. He contributed a single and a double and then cemented the victory after California had shaved a six-run deficit to 7–5, blasting a two-run homer for a 9–5 win. Moose Haas, shelled in two outings the previous year in the divisional round against New York, got the win after surviving three rain delays and carrying a no-hitter into the sixth. Jim Slaton held on for the save.

That set up the finale in front of 54,968, and what a game it was. Vuckovich started but trailed 3–1 until Oglivie crunched a solo homer in the fourth. It stayed that way until the seventh, arguably the most exciting inning in team history.

Considering the fact that "Harvey's Wallbangers" had belted 216 homers during the regular season and scored 10 or more runs on 22 occasions, the rally of rallies started innocently, but controversially, enough with one out. Moore, who had gunned down Jackson trying to go from first to third to snuff out a fifth-inning uprising, cued a soft liner over the pitcher's mound. Two umpires said that Angels second baseman Bobby Grich had caught the ball, but the other two said he had trapped it. The latter judgment prevailed, and the home crowd went nuts. Gantner followed with a single, and one out later Robin Yount walked to load the bases. Up walked Cecil Cooper, struggling at 2-for-19 in the series. He redeemed himself with a single to left as Moore scored and Gantner slid across the plate with the eventual winning run. "I do know that I would have traded all 205 hits I got this year for that one," Cooper said in the victorious clubhouse. "This was, without a doubt, the greatest hit of all."

Bob McClure set the Angels down in the eighth, aided by a potentially game-saving, leaping grab of Don Baylor's drive in center field by reserve Edwards, who batted only once in the five contests. McClure allowed a leadoff single in the ninth, so Brewers skipper Harvey Kuenn called upon Ladd. The rookie retired the next three batters, including future Hall of Famer Rod Carew for the final out, a bouncer that Yount threw to Cooper to set off pandemonium.

"I still remember that play vividly," Yount said in later years. "You could usually hear the bat hit the ball. You can hear things going on during the game, but not this time. All you did was react to the sights. I remember catching it and when I threw it, it seemed like it took five minutes for the ball to get over there."

Cooper was one of the happiest guys in the victorious locker room after his gaffe in the fourth inning, a play in which he mishandled a bunt, had helped the Angels take a 3–1 advantage in a series in which Fred Lynn was named the most valuable player in a losing cause. "I could have been the goat of the series," Cooper said. "I made a bonehead play in the field. I'm just thankful I had a chance to redeem myself."

Kuenn didn't care how his team had arrived at this point; the main thing was that they deserved to be there. "This is the greatest thrill of my life," Kuenn said. "The guys couldn't have played any better. They came back all year and they did it again today."

Simmons said he tried to stay as calm as possible until the outcome had been determined. "I never got to the point where I thought this was going to happen until I saw Robin field the ball clean," Simmons said. "Then I knew we were going to the World Series."

In the other clubhouse, California's Reggie Jackson, a year removed from eliminating the Brewers from the postseason when he was a Yankee, gave Milwaukee its due. "Milwaukee's a damn good ball club," Mr. October said. "They played better than us the last two days, but we outplayed them in Anaheim. They did the same thing last year in New York [coming back], and it just shows how good a ball club they have."

It didn't matter, as the stadium and the streets of Milwaukee filled with revelers, soaking in the moment and starting another 10 days of jubilation. Art Spander of the *San Francisco Examiner* had this to say about Milwaukee's maiden appearance in the Fall Classic: "What Milwaukee has is a town and a team that were made for each other, blue collar and red-blooded, with sloppy mustaches and shaggy hairdos. But they're not concerned as much about appearances as they are by results."

Dave Kindred of the *Washington Post* chimed in this: "It's a war in Yankee Stadium, it's a beer jingle in Saint Louis, it's a movie in Los Angeles— and it's a pep rally in Milwaukee." Fans couldn't have been more jacked up than that after the opener of the "Suds Series" that started at Busch Stadium in Saint Louis.

Molitor, Yount, and the gang ripped Bob Forsch and the Cardinals' pitching staff for 17 hits in a 10–0 pasting that was almost too easy while producing the largest victory margin in a Series debut since 1959 and the second-largest ever. Molitor beat out three infield hits while going 5-for-6, a record for hits in a game. Yount was right behind with four base knocks as Milwaukee scored in four of its first six at-bats and then iced the rout with a four-run ninth.

Catcher Simmons and pitcher Caldwell were two other major players. Simmons had played with the Cardinals for 11 seasons and made a triumphant return with the only homer of the contest, while Caldwell, who had passed through Saint Louis during his big-league travels, allowed only three hits while registering 15 ground ball outs for the complete-game victory.

"That was an old-fashioned butt-kicking," colorful Saint Louis manager Whitey Herzog said. "I'm just glad we didn't have a doubleheader." Unfortunately for Milwaukee, it couldn't save any of those runs or hits for later.

In Game 2 the Brewers grabbed a 3–0 advantage but couldn't hold onto the lead despite Simmons's second homer in as many nights, dropping a heartbreaking 5–4 setback that many believe would have been reversed had relief ace Rollie Fingers not been on the shelf with an injury. The score was tied at 4 in the eighth when Ladd entered to face Lonnie Smith with runners on first and second. Ladd, Simmons, and even Smith, who turned toward the dugout, thought a 3–2 offering was strike three. But home plate umpire Bill Haller saw it otherwise, which loaded the bases for pinch hitter Steve Braun. Ladd lost his composure and issued another free pass on four pitches, sending the Series to Milwaukee all even.

Saint Louis rookie center fielder Willie McGee was the star of Game 3, the first Series game in Milwaukee since Dwight Eisenhower roamed the White House. McGee lifted two homers off Vuckovich and then climbed the fence to take a two-run shot away from Gorman Thomas that would have shaved the deficit to 6–4 in the ninth as 56,566 crazies were silenced. Smith also collected a double and a triple for the Cards, who had wrested home-field advantage back and assured that at least one more game would be played at Busch Stadium.

In Game 4, Milwaukee did it the hard away again, falling behind 5–1 through six innings. However, the no-quit crew dug deep and scored six times with two outs in the seventh for a 7–5 triumph. Gantner started it with an RBI double, Yount lined a two-run single, and Cooper brought in another to tie it. Then Thomas, who had fouled out for a second time to start the inning, smacked a two-run single to left.

Milwaukee took control again in Game 5. Although Caldwell struggled in giving up 14 hits, he earned his second victory. McClure notched his second straight save in the 6–4 decision. Yount homered to highlight his second four-hit effort, the first player to do that in one Series.

Like the opener, Game 6 was a lopsided affair, except this time it was the Cardinals who did the thumping, tattooing Sutton to the tune of 13–1, scoring 11 runs from the fourth through sixth innings. Former Brewer Darrell Porter and Keith Hernandez crashed homers, while youngster John Stuper baffled the Brewers on four hits to set up a Game 7 showdown.

Joaquin Andujar, who had won Game 3 but was knocked out in the seventh when hit in the knee by Simmons's one-hopper, recorded his second win with seven good innings. Vuckovich and the Brewers couldn't hold a 3–1 lead in the sixth, with McClure suffering his second loss in the 6–3 decision. Porter hit only .286 (8-for-28) but was named the Series MVP, while the Cardinals' Dane Iorg finished 9-for-17 (.529).

Despite the empty feeling, more than 150,000 faithful lined the downtown streets for a motorcade upon the team's return October 21. A rally at County Stadium drew an estimated 20,000 fans, who went wild with Yount's grand entrance, fist raised in the air, on his motorcycle.

Manager Harvey Kuenn and his wife, Audrey, greet fans in a motorcade through downtown Milwaukee after the Brewers lost the 1982 World Series to Saint Louis.

"I told the players after the final game that they were world champions in my eyes and they had nothing to hang their heads about," Kuenn said. "The reception the fans gave us showed us [that] you feel the same way. It's something that could only happen in Milwaukee."

Little did the Brewers and their fans realize how precious this Series was and how special it would have been to win, because they've never been back to the playoffs since. Yount (.414), Molitor (.355), Moore (.346), and Gantner (.333) enjoyed an excellent Series, as did Caldwell with his 2.04 ERA. However, Vuckovich (4.50), Haas (7.36), and Sutton (7.84) couldn't match the Saint Louis staff (3.39) and could only wonder what might have been.

Several players did just that in August 2002 as part of a 20th anniversary celebration of that team and season. "I don't know if I would have made a difference," Fingers said in a *Journal Sentinel* article. "But I will say this: I would have liked to have been there to try."

His former teammates agreed. Thomas, one of the team's biggest pranksters, also lamented the missed Series opportunities. "We did everything together," Thomas said. "We had a camaraderie that I don't think you'll ever see again. There will never be another team that has what we had. It's just sad we came up one game short."

Vuckovich, when he was pitching coach for the Pittsburgh Pirates in the 2002 season, recalled that many of the squad's veterans were banged up, and he himself was operating at far less than a hundred percent, which contributed to his not winning his starts in Games 3 and 7. "There were a bunch of hurt guys out there," Vuckovich said. "But they battled their tails off all year and became a close-knit bunch. Every one of them came to play. It's never enjoyable losing. You spend your whole life throwing baseballs off a wall, saying, 'It's the seventh game of the World Series and here's the pitch.' Then you get there and it doesn't work out the way you wanted it to. That's life."

Cooper said the 1981-82 playoff teams created memories he still cherishes, even if he's often too busy to reminisce. "Sometimes you play certain things over and over in your mind," he said via phone about his pennant-clinching single against California. "The thing was that I had failed in my first two chances, but I came through on my third. It was the biggest hit of my career.

"Without question that was a fun time," Cooper added. "I replaced George Scott, and the fans could have been negative. But they accepted me and were friendly. We had guys who were All-Stars, but they still weren't household names like a Reggie Jackson or somebody. We had a bunch of good guys who played hard and respected each other, and that's why we were successful."

Perhaps Gantner summed it up best: "When I think of '82, I think of Vukey wearing two different shoes, spitting and gagging on the mound. I wish we could turn back the clock, but we can't."

Oh, how their fans wish they could.

Don Money said in a 2004 interview that having Fingers available would have put Milwaukee over the top, but nothing can take away from what those teams accomplished.

"We had a great group of guys who did a lot of things together off the field," Money said. "Of the 25 guys on that team, I believe 15 to 18 of them are still in baseball, which shows you the kind of talent we had."

Chapter Seven

A Decade of Decline
(the 1990s)

The 1990s were a time of stability in the managerial ranks in Milwaukee, as Tom Trebelhorn's five-plus-year reign ended after the 1991 season and Phil Garner's run lasted until August 1999.

However, the two winningest skippers in franchise history mustered only two winning seasons during the decade, Trebelhorn's last and Garner's first. Milwaukee challenged in the American League's Eastern Division race both years, but 1992 was the only time that the Brewers finished closer than eight games out of first place. These two skippers combined to win 48 percent of their games, which was respectable but mostly mediocre.

Although they seldom moved high in the standings, the Brewers were moving. Realignment placed them in the Central Division starting in 1994, and then they switched to the National League beginning in 1998, where many old-timers and baseball purists felt Milwaukee's team belonged ever since the Braves left town 33 years earlier.

While the action on the field didn't always inspire, goings-on off the field made news, such as when owner Bud Selig became Major League Baseball's commissioner and the legislative and financial fight to build a new stadium garnered headlines. And then there was the work stoppage of 1994-95, when County Stadium was void of America's pastime again. Despite all of that turmoil and eight losing seasons during the decade, including the final seven, Milwaukee's attendance never dropped below the one million mark.

1990

In the first year of the decade, new blood arrived in the form of Dave Parker, who brought his designated hitting talents and championship ring from the

Bay Area, and youngster Gary Sheffield. Parker batted his customary .289 while driving 21 balls into the seats to go with a team-high 92 RBIs. Sheffield showed tons of potential with a team-best .294 average plus 10 homers and 67 RBIs.

They didn't get enough help, however. A 12–6 start in April quickly faded as the Brewers compiled only one other winning month. A 10–19 record in June proved to be the most damaging, with Milwaukee never recovering and finishing in sixth place at 74–88, 14 games behind Boston.

Paul Molitor hit .285 with 12 homers and 45 RBIs in 103 games, but the rest of the lineup provided little pop, although B. J. Surhoff batted .276 with 59 RBIs and Mike Felder hit .274. Jim Gantner was steady at .263, but Robin Yount hit a career-low .247 despite knocking in 77 runs with 17 homers. Greg Vaughn also slugged 17 HRs and knocked in 61 and Greg Brock brought home 50, but they hit .220 and .248, respectively. Rob Deer topped the club in long balls for a fifth consecutive season (27) but hit a feeble .209 in what proved to be his final year in Milwaukee.

The team's pitching staff enjoyed a few bright moments, but there were too many lows in between. Ron Robinson, formerly of Cincinnati, won a team-high 12 games against only five setbacks as he ended with a 2.91 ERA. Teddy Higuera was next with 11 victories, but he lost 10 times despite a credible 3.76 ERA. Mark Knudson was 10–9 and Jaime Navarro finished 8–7, while Chris Bosio faltered at 4–9. Dan Plesac began to show wear while recording 24 saves that overshadowed a 3–7 mark and 4.32 ERA. Chuck Crim was reliable again with three wins, a 3.47 ERA, and 11 saves.

1991

The following year, Milwaukee finished 40–22 from August to the end of the season. Unfortunately, the Brewers were 14 games under .500 before they caught fire, enabling them to tally an 83–79 record that gave them a fourth-place finish.

Several newcomers played prominent roles, especially veteran second baseman Willie Randolph, who didn't homer but knocked in 54 runs and batted .327 after a long career with the Yankees. First baseman Franklin Stubbs came over from the Dodgers and hit 11 homers but had only 38 RBIs and a .213 average. Dante Bichette (.238) joined the team from California in a trade that involved Dave Parker and contributed 15 homers and 59 RBIs. And Darryl Hamilton saw much more playing time in the outfield, hitting .311 while driving in 57.

Greg Vaughn became the number-one run producer with 27 dingers and 98 RBIs, but he managed only a .244 average. Robin Yount finished with 77

RBIs, while Paul Molitor hit .325 and added 75 RBIs and 17 HRs. On May 15, Molitor hit for the cycle, capping off Milwaukee's 4–2 win against Minnesota with a homer in the seventh inning. B. J. Surhoff got in the act with 68 RBIs and a .289 average, while Jim Gantner and Bill Spiers both hit .283 and combined for 101 RBIs.

Jaime Navarro (15–12) and Bill Wegman (15–7) shared team-high honors in victories, posting 3.92 and 2.84 ERAs, respectively. Chris Bosio bounced back with a 14–10 mark and 3.25 ERA, while Don August also had a winning record at 9–8, albeit with a lofty 5.47 ERA. However, the crew lost Teddy Higuera for the season, his first of a $13 million, four-year contract. The lefty had started the year on the disabled list and went on the DL again after a significant tear in his rotator cuff was discovered. Doug Henry came out of nowhere to become the team's closer with 15 saves and a 1.00 ERA. Chuck Crim was the key setup man again with an 8–5 mark.

1992

The year was marked by Milwaukee's inspired play under new skipper Phil "Scrap Iron" Garner, finishing above .500 during every month except May. They put a scare into Toronto's pennant hopes with a 22–9 effort in September and October. However, the Brewers' surprising run ended at 92–70, four games behind the Blue Jays and in second place. The West-winning A's eliminated the Brewers with a 10–3 triumph October 3 in Oakland.

The front office defused a possible cancerous clubhouse situation, sending discontented and outspoken Gary Sheffield to San Diego in a five-player trade March 27. The move netted the Brewers serviceable performers in pitcher Ricky Bones, shortstop Jose Valentin, and outfielder Matt Mieske.

Darryl Hamilton was an excellent defensive outfielder and twice hit above .300 in his six-plus seasons with the Brewers. He stands fourth in the team's record book with a .290 career average. (Photo by Joe Picciolo)

Whereas the long ball had been such a major weapon in Milwaukee baseball history, this group played from base to base and used its speed to cause havoc. Shortstop Pat Listach batted .290 and recorded what was then a team record 54 stolen bases to win rookie of the year honors. Darryl Hamilton recorded 41 thefts and Paul Molitor added 31 as the Brewers totaled a team record 256. The Brewers also received lifts from two veteran acquisitions, second baseman Scott Fletcher and third baseman Kevin Seitzer. Fletcher hit .275 and knocked in 51 runs, while Seitzer batted .270 and had 71 RBIs.

Molitor (.320) topped the team with 89 RBIs, while Greg Vaughn (23 homers) brought home 78 and Robin Yount added 77. B. J. Surhoff plated 62, as did Hamilton, who batted .298. Dante Bichette hit .287 in spot duty, while Jim Gantner bowed out at .246.

The team's offensive strategy was no more evident than on August 28, when it pasted front-running Toronto, 22–2, cracking an American League record 31 hits at the SkyDome. It was the most hits by a major league team in 91 years. Milwaukee's 26 singles set a league mark, with Seitzer and Fletcher rapping out five hits apiece while combining for eight RBIs and seven runs scored. It was also important in that it was the Brewers' first road win in their last 11 games.

But the season's brightest moment occurred during a 5–4 defeat to Cleveland on September 9, when Yount ripped his 3,000th hit, a single to right-center against Jose Mesa in the seventh inning. Who could forget that heartfelt moment when longtime teammates Molitor and Gantner greeted him at first base and the team carried him around on their shoulders? Yount became the 17th player—and third youngest after Ty Cobb and Henry Aaron—in history to reach the plateau as 47,589 fans at County Stadium roared. Yount would also become only the second player in history to record 200 home runs, 200 stolen bases, and 100 triples, duplicating Willie Mays' feat.

"There are a few moments in baseball I won't forget, and that's one of them," Gantner said in *True Brew.* "There wasn't too much said between the three of us because the emotional level was so high. But there was a lot of hugging. I was pretty choked up." Molitor agreed, adding, "The tears were flowing. I was pretty numb. He gave us the biggest bear hugs and on a normal day Robin would fight at being picked up."

Tom Haudricourt said it was one of a handful of the greatest moments he's witnessed since joining the *Milwaukee Journal Sentinel* in 1985. "His chase for 3,000, especially the last couple of days, created as much or more electricity as there's ever been at County Stadium," Haudricourt said.

Jaime Navarro won a personal best 17 times against 11 losses while posting a 3.33 ERA to lead the pitching staff. Chris Bosio won 16 of 22 decisions with a

3.62 ERA, while Bill Wegman finished 13–14 with a decent 3.20 ERA. Ricky Bones came on board with a 9–10 mark, but the Brewers got the biggest spark from rookie Cal Eldred, who was dominating at times with an 11–2 mark and miniscule 1.79 ERA. Meanwhile, Doug Henry registered 29 saves despite a high ERA (4.02). Darren Holmes chipped in six saves and a 2.55 ERA, while Jesse Orosco, Mike Fetters, and Jim Austin were wonderful in relief with a combined 13–4 record. Dan Plesac was 5–4 (2.96) in his final season with the team.

However, such a promising season couldn't prevent the future from taking a startling turn, unraveling before Christmas as the small-market Brewers began to feel the pinch of a changing economic landscape that sent the franchise into a downward spiral it hasn't recovered from. On December 3, the Seattle Mariners signed Bosio to a four-year contract. Molitor followed suit and headed for Toronto on December 7, a day that will live in infamy in Milwaukee baseball circles. Then the Cubs inked Plesac to a two-year deal.

1993

Those key free-agent losses were tough, but the fall occurred even faster than most people thought it would as the 1993 Brewers went from challenging for first to seventh—and last place—at 69–93, 26 games behind Paul Molitor and the world-champion Blue Jays. Milwaukee started and ended well enough, but it went a combined 19-36 in June and July, eliminating itself from contention early. Tons of veteran leadership left in the departures of Molitor, Jim Gantner, Kevin Seitzer, and Scott Fletcher, and the Brewers never put it together.

Yount played in 127 games, his fewest since 1985, in his 20th and final season, batting .258 with eight homers and 51 RBIs. He would announce his retirement in February 1994.

John Jaha was a nice addition at first base, hitting .264 with 19 homers and 70 RBIs, B. J. Surhoff adapted to third base with a .274 average and 79 RBIs, Darryl Hamilton smacked the ball around to the tune of a .310 average, Greg Vaughn hit .267 with 30 HRs and 97 RBIs, and Australian-born Dave Nilsson took over most of the catching duties while hitting .257 and knocking in 40 runs. However, Kevin Reimer, even though he hit 13 homers and drove in 60, didn't provide nearly enough to replace Molitor as the designated hitter.

Cal Eldred won a team-high 16 times but lost just as many. His 4.01 ERA was the lowest of the top four starters as Jaime Navarro (11–12), Ricky Bones (11–11), and Bill Wegman (4–14) were roughed up often, and the team never found another candidate to push for a spot in the rotation.

Doug Henry struggled again, but Milwaukee didn't have any alternatives for the closer's role. Henry netted 17 saves but had a 5.56 ERA. Jesse Orosco;

Graeme Lloyd, another Aussie; and Mike Fetters each won three games in relief, with Orosco notching eight saves.

1994

Take away a horrendous month of May, when the team suffered through a 7–21 record, and the Brewers were five games above .500 for the 1994 season. But they found themselves at 53–62 and in fifth place in their first season in the Central Division when owners and players called off the season. The owners pushed for some form of salary cap and revenue sharing, but the sides couldn't work through their problems. So the World Series was canceled for the first time since 1904.

Milwaukee sorely lacked power as John Jaha and Greg Vaughn were limited to 12 and 19 homers, respectively. Jose Valentin (11) and Dave Nilsson (12) contributed, but the outfield of Vaughn, Turner Ward, and Matt Mieske combined for only 38 round-trippers. Veteran Jody Reed hit .271 at second base, while Kevin Seitzer returned at third and was the most productive with a .314 average. Brian Harper took on most of the DH duties, hitting .291.

Meanwhile, the pitching staff was mostly a shambles. Cal Eldred posted his second consecutive .500 campaign (11–11), Bill Wegman rebounded with an 8–4 mark, and Ricky Bones was 10–9, but Teddy Higuera's long and arduous comeback attempt failed miserably as he finished 1–5 with a 7.06 ERA. Jaime Navarro also struggled, finishing 4–9 with a hefty 6.62 ERA. The bullpen was so-so with Mike Fetters recording 17 saves, but Graeme Lloyd, Jesse Orosco, and Doug Henry finished with losing marks and ERAs at 4.60 or higher.

On November 30, the Brewers traded Henry to the Mets in a deal that netted them second baseman Fernando Vina. That wasn't enough to erase another lost season, one in which the Brewers had established a team futility standard with a 14-game losing skid.

1995

The strike lingered through spring training the following year, ending one day before the regular season was originally supposed to start. Milwaukee played .500 baseball through August, but a dismal 7–21 mark the rest of the way left them at 65–79 and in fourth place in the Central Division.

The Brewers sported a fairly consistent offense that featured a good combination of experience and youth, but their pitching was woefully lacking in talent and depth. Ricky Bones finished 10–12 and led the team in victories. Steve Sparks was 9–11, and everybody else who was plugged into the rotation finished below .500: Brian Givens (5–7), Scott Karl (6–7), and Bob Scanlan (4–7). Bill Wegman sputtered at 5–7, as did Sid Roberson (6–4) and Angel Miranda (4–5), with all three posting ERAs of 5.23 or higher. Mike Fetters continued as the top closer with 22 saves, while Graeme Lloyd suffered through an 0–5 season and four saves.

B. J. Surhoff (.320), John Jaha (.313), and Kevin Seitzer (.311) led the hitting charge. Surhoff provided pop with 13 homers and 73 RBIs, as did Jaha with 20 and 65, respectively. Jose Valentin (11), Matt Mieske (12), Joe Oliver (12), Dave Nilsson (12), and Greg Vaughn (17) also reached double digits in long balls. Fernando Vina (.257) was steady at second and Jeff Cirillo (.277) took over at third.

Milwaukee, as usual, lost out during free agency. Darryl Hamilton headed to Texas on December 14, while Surhoff agreed to a three-year deal with Baltimore on December 20.

1996

The Brewers did their share of hitting, with and without bats, during the 1996 campaign. And it started in the season opener at Anaheim Stadium on April 2.

Milwaukee won the slugfest, 15–9, with Jose Valentin and Chuck Carr each contributing four hits to a 22-hit attack. Valentin and Greg Vaughn homered, and then Vaughn got plunked with a pitch during the eighth inning, prompting winning pitcher Kevin Wickander to retaliate against Garret Anderson in the bottom half. The benches cleared for the usual jousting match on the infield.

On May 31 at County Stadium, the powerful Indians came to town and laid a 10–4 decision on the Brewers. However, the biggest hit occurred when volatile Cleveland slugger Albert Belle, on board after being hit with a pitch and running from first to second, decked Fernando Vina with a forearm in the eighth to ignite a brawl. In the ninth, Milwaukee's Terry Burrows threw three inside offerings before finally drilling Belle again. Cleveland's Julian Tavarez then threw behind Brewer catcher Mike Matheny, who charged the mound. In the scrum, Tavarez slammed down umpire Joe Brinkman while Belle knocked down Steve Sparks. Belle, Tavarez, and Matheny were slapped with five-game suspensions. The teams scuffled again the next day when Indians leadoff hitter Kenny Lofton started the game with a double and shoved Vina. The dugouts cleared again, but the Brewers got revenge with a 2–1 victory.

Milwaukee's offense finally started producing, with John Jaha (.300), Jeff Cirillo (.325), Kevin Seitzer (.316), and Dave Nilsson (.331) having excellent seasons. Jaha finished with a team-high 34 homers and 118 RBIs after Vaughn (.280, 31 HRs, and 95 RBIs) was shipped to San Diego for outfielder Marc Newfield and pitchers Bryce Florie and Ron Villone in another cost-cutting maneuver July 31.

Jose Valentin powered 24 homers and knocked in 95, while Nilsson added 17 HRs and 84 RBIs and Cirillo chipped in 15 long balls and brought home 83. Nilsson became the first Brewer to homer twice in the same inning as Milwaukee scored 11 runs in the sixth to defeat the Twins, 12–1, in May. Matt Mieske improved to .278 and clubbed 14 HRs, while Seitzer added 12 dingers. Vina was a sparkplug with his .283 average.

If only the pitching could have matched the scoring. Ben McDonald (12–10) and Scott Karl (13–9) were the only reliable starters as Ricky Bones slipped to 7–14 with a 5.83 ERA. Jeff D'Amico showed promise at 6–6, while Cal Eldred (4–4) tried to overcome arm problems and Sparks's knuckleball didn't knuckle enough hitters as he finished 4–7 with a 6.60 ERA. Mike Fetters was excellent with three wins and 32 saves, and Graeme Lloyd had a nice year with a 2.82 ERA. Ramon Garcia won four times and Angel Miranda seven, but they struggled at 6.66 and 4.94, respectively.

Meanwhile, the Brewers stayed active in personnel matters. On August 23, they sent Lloyd and Pat Listach to the Yankees in exchange for outfielder Gerald Williams and UW-Whitewater graduate Bob Wickman. New York later filed a grievance with the league office that both players were damaged goods, but the complaint was ignored. However, the Brewers took Listach back and sent them Bones a week later. Milwaukee then traded Seitzer to their sparring partner, Cleveland, for outfielder Jeromy Burnitz. All of the activity resulted in an 80–82 mark and a third-place spot in the Central.

John Jaha played first base for the Brewers from 1992 to '98. His best season was '96, when he smashed 34 homers and finished with 118 RBIs. (Photo by Joe Picciolo).

1997

Milwaukee revamped its outfield and sported a new closer in 1997, but a 10–16 record during September put a damper on another ho-hum campaign, the team's fourth and final season in the Central Division and its last year in the American League. The Brewers never got too high or too low, playing within four games of .500 every month except September, producing a 78–83 record and another third-place finish, marks that were all that could be expected.

Jeromy Burnitz gave the Brewers another power source, belting 27 homers for 85 RBIs while hitting .281. Gerald Williams provided 10 homers but only a .253 average, while Darrin Jackson hit .272 and Matt Mieske finished at .249. Otherwise, Dave Nilsson (20 HRs and 81 RBIs) and Jose Valentin (17 and 58) were the only long-ball threats, although Jeff Cirillo hit .288, sent 10 into the seats, and knocked in 82. Fernando Vina hit .275, while Mark Loretta started seeing more playing time, providing a .287 average and 47 RBIs. John Jaha added 11 homers and 26 RBIs in limited duty, undergoing shoulder surgery June 3.

Grizzled veteran Doug Jones led the bullpen with a 6–6 record, 2.02 ERA, and then team record 36 saves, while Bob Wickman chipped in a 7–6 mark and 2.73 ERA. As for the starters, Cal Eldred resurfaced with a 13–15 showing, while Scott Karl was the only other double-digit winner at 10–13. Jose Mercedes (7–10) had a respectable 3.79 ERA, but Jeff D'Amico (9–7) and Ben McDonald (8–7) had their ups and downs.

In trades that did little to improve the team's fortunes, the Brewers obtained outfielder Marquis Grissom and pitcher Jeff Juden from the Indians for McDonald, Ron Villone, and Mike Fetters on December 8 and received pitcher Chad Fox from Atlanta for Williams on December 11.

1998

The following year, Milwaukee became the first team to switch leagues since 1901, but the historic move didn't mean much in the final standings as the Brewers faltered down the stretch to finish 74–88 and in fifth place in the National League's Central Division. Schedule makers saw fit to have the Brewers open the season March 31 at Turner Field in Atlanta. Bob Wickman was tagged with the loss as the Braves plated the winning run in a 2–1 verdict with two outs in the ninth inning. However, the visitors turned the tables in the next game two nights later as Jeromy Burnitz smacked two homers, including a grand slam in the 11th, to hold on for an 8–6 triumph.

Most of Milwaukee's hitters adjusted well enough to the new league and different strike zone, but its mound corps struggled. Reliever Al Reyes (5–1) was the only one among the team's top 11 hurlers to post a winning record, and Steve Woodard (10–12) and Scott Karl (10–11) were the only double-digit winners. Jeff Juden (7–11) finished with a porous 5.53 ERA, and Cal Eldred (4–8, 4.80), Brad Woodall (7–9, 4.96), and Bill Pulsipher (3–4, 4.66) weren't much better. Wickman took over as the closer, finishing 6–9 with 25 saves after Jones (12 saves) struggled with a 5.17 ERA. Mike Myers was a nice left-handed option at 2–2 and 2.70, but Chad Fox was 1–4 and 3.95.

Mark Loretta, Fernando Vina, and Jeff Cirillo gave the Brewers plenty of base runners, but they were stranded far too often by a lackluster run-producing group with the exception of Burnitz. Loretta hit .316 with six homers and 54 RBIs; Vina batted .311, chipped in seven HRs, and had 45 RBIs; and Cirillo led the way at .321 with 14 dingers and 68 RBIs. Burnitz whacked 38 homers and had 125 RBIs. However, Jose Valentin (.224), Marquis Grissom (.271 with 10 HRs), Mike Matheny (.237), and John Jaha (.208) didn't provide enough punch. Geoff Jenkins came on the scene with nine homers but sputtered at .229, the same average as young catcher Bobby Hughes, who also hit nine homers. Dave Nilsson contributed 12 homers and 56 RBIs.

Milwaukee won seven of its first nine contests en route to a 13–5 start, but it fell below .500 by May 23. The Brewers bounced back by improving to 43–37 on June 23 and hovered within a few games of the break-even mark until dropping below it for good on August 7. The only fan attraction left was to see how many homers Chicago's Sammy Sosa and Saint Louis's Mark McGuire could hit off Milwaukee pitchers.

On September 12 at Wrigley Field, Sosa became the fourth player in history to reach the 60-homer mark for a season after slugging number 60 off Valerio De Los Santos in the seventh inning of the Cubs' 15–12 win. The next day, Sosa crunched two more against the Brewers in an 11–10 win, tying him with Ralph Kiner (1947) for his 10th multihomer contest of the season. The dingers also moved him into a tie with McGuire.

McGuire clubbed number 64 in a 5–2 victory at County Stadium on September 18. Five days later, Sosa broke out of an 0-for-21 slump with numbers 64 and 65 to carry the Cubs to a 7–0 advantage. However, Milwaukee added a bit of uncharacteristic drama of its own as it rallied and won 8–7 when Brant Brown dropped a fly ball with two outs and the bases loaded in the ninth, and all three runners scored.

1999

Another halfway respectable season was ruined when the Brewers suffered through an 8–21 record during August, finishing the year in fifth place with a 74–87 mark. Many observers point to Wednesday, July 14, as the catalyst for the

Brewers' fall. That's the day three men died when a 567-foot crane nicknamed "Big Blue" collapsed while lifting a section of Miller Park's retractable roof. The accident postponed completion of the new park and delayed the team's move from County Stadium for a year, dampening the spirits of those inside and outside the organization during the time of mourning.

However, regardless of which side of the stadium debate people stood, a common resolve, buoyed by the announcement early in the reconstruction process that Miller Park would play host to the 2002 All-Star Game, carried the project forward. It helped solidify a sometimes teetering bond among the organization, the workers, and the team's fans.

While action on the field was substandard again, and the team and its supporters realized that their dream of seeing a new stadium become reality was dashed for another full season, they mourned for their lost comrades and soldiered ahead toward the ultimate goal.

Then, on August 12, Phil Garner was fired as manager with the team sitting at 52–60. Batting coach Jim Lefebvre took over for the remainder of the season.

Milwaukee provided numerous offensive thrills as Jeromy Burnitz clubbed 33 homers, Geoff Jenkins and Dave Nilsson smashed 21 apiece, Marquis Grissom belted 20, and Jeff Cirillo added 15. The latter led the average charts at .326, while Jenkins (.313), Nilsson (.309), and Alex Ochoa (.300) also were demons at the plate. Burnitz finished with 103 RBIs, with Cirillo (88), Grissom (83), and Jenkins (82) next in line. Mark Loretta contributed a .290 average and 67 RBIs, while rookie second baseman Ron Belliard chipped in at .295 and 58.

Pitching was another story. Hideo Nomo rejuvenated his career with a 12–8 record, and Scott Karl and Steve Woodard finished with 11 wins apiece. After that, Milwaukee couldn't find any solid starters as Bill Pulsipher finished 5–6 but with a 5.98 ERA. Cal Eldred (7.79) and Jim Abbott (6.91) were both 2–8. Bob Wickman saved 37 games but lost 8 of 11 decisions, while Mike Myers, Eric Plunk, and David Weathers posted ERAs of 4.65 or worse.

Changes were inevitable, and the first major one happened on November 4 when another former All-Star second baseman, Davey Lopes, was named the new manager. Myers was shipped to Colorado for Curtis Leskanic on November 17. Then, on December 13, in what was believed to be baseball's first four-team swap in 14 years, Milwaukee bid good-bye to Cirillo and Karl and said hello to Jamey Wright, Jimmy Haynes, and Henry Blanco. The Brewers weren't done, as they signed free agent Jose Hernandez to a three-year deal and then got Juan Acevedo and two minor leaguers for Fernando Vina.

Chapter Eight

Change and Uncertainty (2000 and Beyond)

As the world spun into the year 2000, construction on state-of-the-art Miller Park continued at a feverish pace, as did life in general once people discovered that time wouldn't stand still because of the Y2K scare. And in the Menomonee Valley, despite knowing that the team would have to make it through another year in storied but well-past-its-prime County Stadium, a quiet but determined resolve continued in light of a promising future.

Milwaukee's front office also continued to remodel its roster in hopes that a new manager, Davey Lopes, and his staff could start molding a winner to move into their new home. Unfortunately, many of those plans crumbled and forced another major renovation project on the baseball side of the equation within three years.

2000

General manager Dean Taylor and the Brewers' brass were active in January, but most of their wheeling and dealing yielded little between the white lines. On the 12th, Milwaukee got former Brewers starter Jaime Navarro and John Snyder from the White Sox for shortstop Jose Valentin and pitcher Cal Eldred. Navarro had lost more games (43) than anybody in the major leagues the previous three seasons and looked the part, dropping all five decisions while compiling an astronomical 12.54 ERA. Snyder was just as disappointing, finishing 3–10 and 6.17.

On the 14th, the Brewers traded Alex Ochoa, a serviceable hitter and good fielder, to Cincinnati for fellow outfielder Mark Sweeney, who promptly hit .219 in limited duty. Then, on the 21st, Hideo Nomo, whose agent had turned down a multiyear contract to stay with the Brewers, inked a one-year deal with Detroit.

Milwaukee dropped 20 of its first 30 games and never recovered, finishing 73–89 for third place in a talent-poor National League Central. A big reason for the team's troubles was the pitching staff. Jimmy Haynes and Jamey Wright had their moments but didn't provide the answers in the starting rotation, posting 12–13 (5.33) and 7–9 (4.10) records. Steve Woodard lost seven of eight decisions and allowed almost six runs per nine innings, while Everett Stull was 2–3 and 5.82. The only bright spots were reliever Curtis Leskanic—who won nine games and lost only three and took over the closer's role (12 saves) after Bob Wickman was shipped to Cleveland in the Richie Sexson trade July 28—and youngster Jeff D'Amico. The latter finished third in the ERA charts in the National League at 2.66 and ended up 12–7.

The offense also was inconsistent, hitting for power but suffering in the average department. Geoff Jenkins proved he could be a run producer and became a fan favorite with his Brett Favre looks and rugged style of play. He finished with a .303 average to go with his 34 homers and 94 RBIs. Mark Loretta became a steady influence with a .281 average and 40 RBIs, while Tyler Houston displayed some pop with 18 HRs. And Sexson showed awe-

Geoff Jenkins was the Brewers top draft pick in 1995 and despite several injuries has been one of the team's top run producers. (Photo by Scott Paulus)

some potential with 14 round-trippers, 47 RBIs, and a .296 average during the final two months.

However, Jeromy Burnitz, although he clubbed 31 homers and brought home 98, produced a .232 average under his $4.46 million contract. Jose Hernandez, largely because of his strikeouts, managed just a .244 average, 11 HRs, and 59 RBIs for his $3.3 million paycheck. Marquis Grissom, making a whopping $5 million, also hit .244 and finished with 14 homers and 62 RBIs. Ron Belliard's batting average slipped 32 points in his sophomore campaign.

Although their crystal ball was no better than anybody else's, Milwaukee made what proved to be another disastrous move when it signed outfielder Jeffrey Hammonds to a three-year, $21 million contract December 23. His injury-filled stay ended quietly with his release in 2003.

2001

After years of planning, controversy, construction delays, and general hoopla, Miller Park was ready for the new season. President George W. Bush was on hand for the festive opening day, as he was one of 42,024 in attendance April 6. The Brewers rallied behind Richie Sexson's two-run homer in the eighth inning to down Cincinnati, 5–4. But like Bush's ceremonial first pitch, which bounced well short of home plate, the Brewers were off-target much of the summer en route to a 68–94 record and fourth-place finish.

Milwaukee continued to ride an all-or-nothing offense that crunched a lot of home runs but shattered the 1996 Detroit squad's big-league season record for strikeouts during a loss to the Reds on September 21. Combine that with a pitching staff that opposing hitters feasted on and it was easy to see why they suffered an 11-game losing streak in July.

Sexson tied Gorman Thomas's club mark with 45 homers and came within one RBI of equaling Cecil Cooper's team standing of 126 while hitting .271. Jeromy Burnitz hit .251 and slammed 34 homers for 100 RBIs. Jose Hernandez chipped in 25 HRs and knocked in 78 but batted only .249. Ron Belliard (11), Tyler Houston (12), Devon White (14), and Raul Casanova (11) also registered double-digit home run totals. Geoff Jenkins slipped to .264 but walloped 20 long balls for 64 RBIs despite injury troubles. On April 28, Jenkins smacked three homers and drove in six runs in an 8–4 home win over Montreal. The next day, Jenkins drilled four hits, including two HRs and six more RBIs as Milwaukee won 10–0 over the Expos. His five homers in two games tied the major league record.

Sexson and Burnitz put on a long-ball exhibition September 25 against the Diamondbacks at Bank One Ballpark. They each blasted three homers in

Milwaukee's 9–4 triumph to become the first teammates to accomplish the feat in the same game. They belted back-to-back HRs twice, the second time that teammates did it that year.

Jamey Wright posted an 11–12 record and 4.90 ERA, and rookie Ben Sheets joined the rotation and finished 11–10 with a 4.76 ERA. Jimmy Haynes sputtered more times than not, losing 17 of 25 decisions for a 4.85 ERA. The rest of the starters struggled mightily, with Allen Levrault going 6–10 and 6.06 and Paul Rigdon winding up 3–5 and 5.79. Injuries started Jeff D'Amico's decline to 2–4 and 6.08. In the bullpen, Curtis Leskanic slipped to 2–6 and 3.63 but recorded 17 saves. Ray King was 0–4, but Mike DeJean (4–2 and 2.77), Chad Fox (5–2 and 1.89), and David Weathers (3–4 and 2.03) performed admirably.

Despite their woes, Milwaukee cruised past the two million mark in attendance on August 3, the earliest point and only the second time in franchise history. The Brewers won the game, 3–2, over Atlanta. Attendance ended up at more than 2.8 million, largely because people were more curious about Miller Park than the product on the field. That novelty wore off quickly; crowds dwindled during the next two seasons before rebounding in 2004.

At least the cash registers were ringing. On December 7, figures released by Major League Baseball showed that Milwaukee was its most profitable club, after revenue sharing, in 2001. Without revenue sharing, the Brewers were the fourth-most profitable.

2002

The prosperity didn't last long. The following year, supporters definitely didn't get their money's worth, and it cost skipper Davey Lopes his job early in the season and general manager Dean Taylor his in the fall. That's when the Brewers began a major housecleaning after a descent into oblivion that even the most pessimistic fans couldn't have predicted.

Jerry Royster replaced Lopes after Milwaukee's 3–12 start. The Brewers fell into a deep rut and stayed there, taking a 33–55 mark into the All-Star break en route to a Milwaukee baseball worst 56–106 finish. Royster also received his ticket out of town after the season.

The only excitement during the campaign occurred in July when Miller Park hosted the All-Star game. But things went awry at the time-honored event as both teams ran out of players, forcing Bud Selig, after consultation with the managers and umpires, to call the game with the score tied at 7-all in the 11th inning. To top the week off, the roof leaked during the home run derby, the party on the lakefront was a rain-soaked flop, and members of the national media bellyached about the city and its hotel accommodations, or lack thereof.

Richie Sexson hit .279 with 29 homers and 102 RBIs, Eric Young batted .280, Jose Hernandez improved to .288 with 24 homers and 73 RBIs, but he and the team were embarrassed when he sat out games late in the year to avoid setting a major league record for strikeouts. Tyler Houston hit .302 but got hurt, as did Geoff Jenkins, who managed 10 homers and 29 RBIs. Matt Stairs hit 16 homers but batted only .244, while Jeffrey Hammonds received enough playing time to hit nine homers and drive in 41 runs despite a .257 average.

Pitching featured Ben Sheets' 11–16 mark and 4.15 ERA after he won six of his last eight decisions. But his mates were poor at best: Glendon Rusch was 10–16 and 4.70, Ruben Quevedo finished 6–11 and 5.76, and Jamey Wright ended up 5–13 and 5.35. Mike DeJean became the closer with 27 saves and 3.12 ERA, while Ray King (3.05) and Luis Vizcaino (5–3, 2.99) were adequate.

The Brewers' dreary summer allowed them to join a group they'd just as soon not be a member of, becoming the fifth franchise since 1960 to finish below .500 for at least 10 consecutive seasons, the first since Seattle stopped its 14-year streak in 1991. Only the Montreal Expos have suffered a longer playoff drought than Milwaukee. Montreal last qualified in 1981, a year before the Brewers' last time, but even it was in first place when the players' strike occurred in '94. It also was the sixth year in a row that the Brewers hadn't improved their victory total.

Doug Melvin was brought in on September 29 to reverse the team's ugly situation, taking over as executive vice president and general manager. As GM in Texas, he had helped the Rangers earn their first playoff spot ever in his debut season of 1996, and they went on to win three division titles before he was done in 2001.

Still, Dennis Semrau of the Madison *Capital Times* wrote what most people across the state were feeling in October 2002:

> So a franchise that was once a source of state pride has become a national joke where reaching even a .500 record appears to be a pipe dream. At one time, the main concerns were beating the Yankees and having enough charcoal for the pregame tailgate party. Now, the club has to deal with worrying about losing 100 games and protecting its players from achieving such dubious accomplishments as [Jose] Hernandez's run at eclipsing Bobby Bonds' major league record for strikeouts in a season. Over the past two decades, there have been three general managers, soon to be eight managers, a slew of coaches, and a steady parade of players filing

through Milwaukee. The team even changed stadiums. The only constant
as memories of the glory days begin to fade is the losing beat that goes on.

Changing the team's sagging image and halting an atmosphere of losing wouldn't be easy, but Melvin's first order of business was finding a manager he thought could bring the Brewers out of their doldrums. On October 29, he brought back a name from the team's glory days of the early 1980s, Ned Yost, who had coached in baseball's most successful organization the past 12 seasons, Atlanta. A couple of days later, Melvin brought in Gord Ash as assistant GM. Ash had spent the past 25 years with Toronto.

Melvin had already been busy trying to improve the product on the field before those two developments, adding an unknown career minor league outfielder named Scott Podsednik, picking him up on waivers from Seattle on October 11. On November 8, he signed pitcher-pinch hitter Brooks Kieschnick as a minor league free agent. He obtained right-hander Matt Kinney in a deal with Minnesota on November 15, and he shipped Ray King to the Braves in a move that netted him third baseman Wes Helms on December 16. Little did anybody know how much these guys would contribute in their first seasons with the organization.

2003

All of the tinkering didn't prevent this young squad from starting 0–6 in 2003, but halfway through this tough opening week the team inked someone named Dan Kolb to a minor league contract. The Brewers rebounded to 8–11 but suffered losing streaks of six and five games to fall to 13–28. They won 12 of 18 but faltered again, entering the All-Star break at 37–56.

Milwaukee continued to struggle, falling 27 games below .500 at 48–75 on August 17. However, the scrappy Brewers ripped off 10 consecutive victories and won 12 of 13, which included three-game sweeps of Philadelphia and Pittsburgh at home and a four-game set at Cincinnati before taking two of three from the Cubs at Wrigley Field to improve to 60–76. They ran out of steam, dropping 18 of their final 26 outings to finish 68–94. Disappointing for sure, but it was a 12-game improvement compared to the 2002 debacle, and more importantly the team came to play every day, something that many people didn't see nearly enough the year before.

Kolb became another welcome surprise, joining the club June 18. He recorded his first save July 24 and became the closer the team desperately needed after the Brewers had shipped Mike DeJean to Saint Louis, accumulating 21 saves and a 1.96 ERA. Doug Davis was signed as a minor league free agent in July and was called up August 10, going 3–2 with a 2.58 ERA in eight starts. Ace Ben Sheets started 10–7 but finished 11–13 with a 4.45 ERA.

Otherwise, Milwaukee's inexperienced staff mostly took a beating. Kinney and Wayne Franklin were both 10–13 but posted ERAs of 5.19 and 5.50, while Glendon Rusch was terrible at 1–12 and 6.42 as the Brewers compiled a team ERA mark of 5.02.

Offensively, the team also was sporadic, hitting .256 with 196 homers but recording more than twice as many strikeouts as walks. Richie Sexson blasted 45 homers to tie the team record he holds with Gorman Thomas and knocked in 124. Geoff Jenkins clobbered 28 HRs and brought home 95 with a .296 average. Helms (23) and Keith Ginter (15) contributed some power, as did John Vander Wal (14) and Royce Clayton (11), but none of the four hit higher than .261.

Podsednik came out of nowhere after replacing Alex Sanchez, who was shipped to Detroit, in the starting lineup May 13. He was everybody's rookie of the year except the Baseball Writers of America, becoming only the fourth rookie since 1900 to hit .300 or higher, score at least 100 runs, and steal more than 40 bases. He topped NL rookies in average (.314), runs (100), hits (175), multihit games (55), triples (eight), total bases (247), stolen bases (43), walks (56), and on-base percentage (.379). His 47-game string of reaching base safely was second only to Barry Bonds's 58-game run.

But the team's biggest noise came during the off-season, when it had to decide what to do with Sexson and Jenkins, two sluggers who carried big contracts that would only become bigger when they hit the open market after the 2004 campaign. This was something management knew it couldn't afford when news started to circulate that the team was trimming its payroll from $40.6 million to closer to $30 million, perhaps the lowest in the major leagues. Arizona wanted Sexson badly, and Milwaukee obliged on December 1, sending him to the Diamondbacks in a nine-player blockbuster. In return, the Brewers obtained infielder Craig Counsell, second baseman Junior Spivey, first baseman Lyle Overbay, catcher Chad Moeller, and young pitchers Chris Capuano and Jorge De La Rosa.

"We were faced with the reality of maybe not having Richie Sexson back here next year," Melvin said about recouping the potential loss with an even better deal than many fans expected. "This is a tough deal for the fans, tough deal for the ball club and all of us up here. But we have to move on, and we feel we filled a lot of holes with this trade." It provided a nice mix of youth, experience, and talent while filling those holes, and the five players (besides De La Rosa) combined would earn about $3 million less than Sexson's $8.6 million.

Counsell, a graduate of Whitefish Bay High School, won World Series rings with Florida in 1997 and Arizona in 2001. He scored the winning run in Game 7 of the 1997 Fall Classic against Cleveland. Injuries limited Counsell to 89 games in '03. Versatility was his forte and gave the Brewers several options. Spivey batted .255 with 13 homers and 50 RBIs after being an All-Star in 2002. Overbay batted .276 but hit only four homers and had 28 RBIs before being demoted to the minors. Moeller played in 78 games, batting .268 with seven homers and 29 RBIs. Capuano appeared in nine games (five starts), going 2–4 with a 4.64 ERA after returning from elbow surgery. Arizona had acquired De La Rosa from Boston in the Curt Schilling deal. He went 6–3 with a 2.80 ERA in 22 games in Class AA and 1–2 with a 3.75 ERA in five Class A starts.

2004

Despite the front-office infighting and talks of selling the team, manager Ned Yost, his coaches, and their youthful roster went about their business in 2004, and in surprising fashion. Through July 1, the team sat alone in third place and had people actually uttering the words "wild card race."

The Sporting News and Baseball Digest named Scott Podsednik the National League's top rookie in 2003. (Photo by Scott Paulus)

In other good roster news, center fielder Scott Podsednik signed a deal that keeps him with the team through 2006, making him the fifth Brewers player to agree to a multiyear deal, joining third baseman Wes Helms (signed through 2005), infielder Keith Ginter (2006), left fielder Geoff Jenkins (2007 with a club option for '08), and minor-league infielder Enrique Cruz (2005). Left-handed pitcher Doug Davis added to that group later in the season.

Attendance proved that fans were pleased with what the scrappy and overachieving Brewers were doing, at least until their tailspin in August sent them spiraling out of control and back into the cellar. July series against Chicago and Cincinnati were major draws, as were many of the other contests, given that 28 of the 29 games for the month were Central Division showdowns. The 10 outings against the Cubs provided a big financial boost and pushed ticket sales well ahead of the team's preseason forecasts of around 1.4 million tickets sold.

Fans had to be impressed with the team's pitching for much of the season as Ben Sheets turned in several remarkable performances, including an 18-strikeout masterpiece against the Braves; he made the All-Star team along with relief ace Dan Kolb. Reclamation projects Davis (12–12 and 3.49 ERA) and Victor Santos (11–12, 4.97) also provided steady outings, Luis Vizcaino was a quality setup man for most of the campaign, and Mike Adams was a nice addition.

Sheets finished 12–14 because Milwaukee's hitters often failed to support his efforts, which included a sparkling 2.70 ERA and club record 264 strikeouts against only 32 walks. He allowed just 201 hits in his 237 innings that featured five of the team's six complete games. The right-hander underwent back surgery in October but was expected to be ready for spring training in 2005. Kolb struggled during the final few weeks of the season but registered a team standard with 39 saves in 44 opportunities and had a 2.98 ERA.

Despite a strong start, the offense sputtered and then went into the tank as the Brewers, with the exception of first baseman Lyle Overbay, stumbled to a 6–21 record for August (.222 winning percentage), the franchise's worst since the Pilots were 6–22 in their only season in Seattle in 1969. Ironically, their swoon also occurred in August. Milwaukee set the dubious major league mark of having the worst record (22–53) of any team with a winning record at the All-Star break (45–41).

Podsednik, who shattered Pat Listach's club record of 54 stolen bases with 70 thefts, saw his average plummet to around .250 for a good portion of the year, finishing at .244. Geoff Jenkins offered power (team-leading totals of 27 homers and 93 RBIs), but he also never got into a rhythm until late in the year and hit only .264. Helms was injured in a freak accident while the team was playing Montreal in Puerto Rico early in the season and was a shell of the player who had earned the third base job in 2003, losing a lot of playing time to mid-season acquisition Russell Branyan. Junior Spivey showed flashes early but was injured and missed most of the season. Milwaukee got little offensive firepower out of its right fielders, shortstop Craig Counsell, or the catching combination of Chad Moeller and Gary Bennett.

Milwaukee lost 34 of its first 45 contests after the All-Star break, so in September, Yost started throwing younger players brought up from Class AAA Indianapolis into the mix in order to see what they could do at the big-league level, slowly continuing the transition that the franchise hopes will lead to better days in the near future. One of them was pitcher Ben Hendrickson, who lost eight of nine decisions but showed glimpses of being a starter in Milwaukee's needy rotation.

There's reason for optimism. The minor league system, which was rated number 30 just a few years ago, earned *Baseball America*'s top ranking before the 2004 season. Big reasons for that come in the form of names such as Rickie Weeks, Prince Fielder, and Corey Hart, along with J. J. Hardy, David Krynzel, Mike Jones, Manny Parra, Brad Nelson, Dennis Sarfate, Chris Saenz, Dana Eveland, Tony Gwynn Jr., and Lou Palmisano. However, injuries have already cast doubt over the careers or progress of Jones and others, and, as always, the big bugaboo is turning potential into production. The June 2004 draft featured 32 pitchers out of 50 selections, starting with top pick Mark Rogers, who was followed by Yovani Gallardo, Josh Wahpepah, and Josh Baker in the first four rounds.

A CLOUDY FUTURE

To help our look into the Brewers' crystal ball, we need to return to late 2003, when plenty of turmoil was brewing within the organization leading up to the holidays. Ulice Payne Jr. had been the franchise's unofficial press secretary, the Brewers' public face, since replacing Wendy Selig-Prieb in September 2002. Thirteen-plus months later he had gone public with misgivings about where the financially strapped franchise was heading, thus prompting his buyout agreement with the team that left curious minds wondering if he was just trying to save face.

Payne left his cozy digs at One Brewers Way with his popularity and reputation apparently intact when people learned that he and the team's board of directors hadn't been the best of roommates and that he was on his way out. Thus, the media and many fans, at least most of those who initially vented on the Internet and on radio talk shows, laid the blame squarely on the Brewers. Who could fault them after 11 consecutive losing seasons (which eventually turned to 12) despite a fancy, taxpayer-financed stadium and a promise to field a competitive team?

"The taxpayers stepped up to the plate and built the team this new stadium," Andrew Yergens of Mukwonago told the *Milwaukee Journal Sentinel*. "Now it's time for the management to hold up their end of the deal. Don't ruin any chance we have at a winning season by trying to do it on the cheap." Don Stockhausen echoed those sentiments, saying, "You can't win with the current ownership. Ulice was a breath of fresh air. To lose him is to dump on the customers one more time."

Journal Sentinel columnist Dale Hofmann had this to say in one of his pieces:

The directors' stunning arrogance in calling for a 25-percent reduction in payroll is matched only by their bad timing. When the Brewers hired Ulice Payne last year to reverse more than a decade of self-defeating management, it made so much sense you wondered what they were thinking. Now you know. They must have figured they could always tie his hands next year. The Brewers president combined with Doug Melvin and Ned Yost last summer to produce a minor marketing miracle. They generated enough enthusiasm for a perennial last-place club to entice 1.7 million people to pay their way into Miller Park. The sound you just heard was the miracle swirling down the drain. If Melvin doesn't get the money he needs to build off last year's start, the fans will walk away and never come back. They've been double-crossed for the last time.

Some fans, such as Delafield's Dan Trzinski, were more forgiving and thought the team should receive the benefit of the doubt. "I, too, am frustrated with the 20-plus years of subpar performance of our Brewers, but we have to keep our eye on the ball," he said. "We are a small-market franchise with limited resources. Ten million dollars in payroll will not make a lot of difference in wins and losses in today's brand of baseball. Cutting payroll obviously has not made public relations sense, but it does make baseball sense." Regardless of who said or did what, an article on the Web site OnMilwaukee.com perhaps said it best: "It's amazing no one put an eye out with all the finger-pointing going on behind closed doors."

Journal Sentinel baseball writer Drew Olson brought up another side to the Payne fiasco, the fact that it was another blatant example of how someone was being paid not to work for the team. Injuries can't be avoided or predicted, but classic instances of big mistakes that resulted in huge sums of revenue being doled out to players and personnel members who no longer worked for the organization included the following:

1. Jeffrey Hammonds signing the richest contract in team annals in the winter of 2000, a three-year, $21.75 million deal. The return on investment read 187 games, 16 homers, and 65 RBIs.

2. Teddy Higuera inking a four-year, $13.1 million deal that he deserved in 1990 but couldn't stay healthy enough to earn. He pitched in 32 games after that.

3. Jaime Navarro finishing with an 0–5 record in 2000 and earning $1 million per loss.

4. Several other marginal performers pocketing serious cash they didn't earn: Franklin Stubbs got $1.5 million after his release in '93, Sean Berry got hundreds of thousands for his 32 contests, while Eric Young ($1 million), Glendon Rusch ($500,000), and Royce Clayton ($250,000) didn't deserve what they got. Throw in unlucky draft picks such as Ken Felder ($525,000), Antone Williamson ($895,000), Kyle Peterson ($1.4 million), and J. M. Gold ($1.675 million) and you have quite a mess.

5. Former general managers Sal Bando ($1 million) and Dean Taylor ($500,000) also receiving nice parting gifts.

Olson's assessment was right on when he noted that every team makes mistakes, but, as he added, "It's not a reach to say that one of the main reasons the Brewers can't afford to pay their current employees is that they have paid so much to former employees. Teams like the New York Yankees, who have the highest revenue in baseball, can obviously afford to make mistakes. Teams like the Brewers that are limited monetarily simply cannot afford too many."

While these episodes only added fire to fans' frustrations and provided ammunition for their contentions of severe mismanagement during the Seligs' reign, they also illustrated the point that simply spending money doesn't guarantee more wins than losses. These moves and big expenditures of dollars also proved what Bob Uecker, an employee at the time and longtime friend of the Selig family, had to say about the verbal tug-of-war taking place during this tumultuous period. "What bothers me is the way fans view the baseball operation in Milwaukee," Uecker told the *Journal Sentinel*. "The club isn't trying to lose. It's trying to do the best it can to put a good team in there. Nobody likes to lose. I hate to lose. I go to the ballpark every day expecting to win. When you look at what happened with the club last year [2003], I think the people of Milwaukee enjoyed watching that team play. And there's lots of good players in the system. They're our future. If they don't work out, you start over and try again. That's all you can do."

Meanwhile, the backlash only intensified as the public, rightfully so, wanted to know where all of the money was going. And, of course, politicians had their say as legislators called for the team to open its books. In the end, nobody emerged from this public-relations nightmare unscathed.

With the arrival of 2004, more troubles appeared on the horizon. Losing weight is perhaps the number-one New Year's resolution, and those on both sides of the Milwaukee baseball story felt like they'd shed more than their share after the January 16 announcement that the Brewers had been put up for sale. Bud Selig could breathe easier knowing that he and his family were no longer saddled with the responsibility of trying to feed such an enormous operation on table scraps during another year of financial belt-tightening, while those who had been calling for them to leave the baseball business got their wish, nourishing hopes that another prospective owner with deeper pockets could afford a much more nutritional shopping list to improve the team's fortunes.

Everyone also was assured that the franchise wouldn't and couldn't move away, at least for a long time, keeping alive ownership's legacy of securing the future of baseball in Milwaukee. Any individual or group would need the permission of the state and the Miller Park stadium district first, one of several legal hurdles in the team's lease agreement with the district. A separate non-relocation agreement was also in place.

Wendy Selig-Prieb, then chairman of the Brewers' board of directors, called the 30-year lease (which is scheduled to end December 31, 2030) iron-clad. The franchise must provide written notice to the state and district of any intent to move and of any negotiations involving this possible transfer. The agreement also stipulates that the district has the right to go to court to stop any such actions.

Where have we heard that before? Selig released this statement in connection with the sale:

> I am in full accord and pleased with the decision of the board of the Milwaukee Brewers to pursue the sale of the club. While it is personally difficult for me to bring to an end a 40-year association with Major League Baseball in Milwaukee and Wisconsin, this decision is one that I have seriously considered and strongly desired since I was elected commissioner six years ago. With the future of Brewer baseball solidified in Wisconsin, my overriding concern has been met. I have many wonderful and lasting memories of my time with the Brewers: from the 5 1/2-year struggle against seemingly insurmountable odds to return Major League Baseball to Milwaukee in the 1960s, which ultimately resulted in successfully acquiring the Seattle Pilots in 1970, to our great teams from the late 1970s through the early '90s, and our trip to the World Series in 1982, to the difficult process during the 1990s of seeking approval for the construction of a new ballpark and finally seeing Miller Park become a reality in 2001.

But above all, I will always remember with great fondness my relationship with the baseball fans of Milwaukee over two generations and with those players and employees who called Milwaukee home. . . . Now it is time for me to formally sever my ties to the Milwaukee Brewers Baseball Club. It is the correct decision for myself, my family and, while I have played no role in the administration of the Brewers since putting my ownership share in trust in 1998, I am convinced and have been for many years that it is in the best interests of the game. As commissioner, it is inappropriate for me to root for any one club, but I must admit, and I hope people will understand, that I will always have a soft spot in my heart for the Milwaukee Brewers.

Even his staunchest critics couldn't deny him that or fault him for it.

Columnists chimed in with their viewpoints as well, including Hofmann and Olson of the *Journal Sentinel.* Hofmann wrote: "The Seligs and their co-owners have made plenty of sacrifices for Milwaukee baseball, and this is the latest. Bad teams, bad crowds, bad economics, and bad public relations will form an avalanche eventually, and in the Brewers' case it took an incredibly long time. [Ulice] Payne wasn't the slide, but he was the gunshot that set it off. It's silly to say there's no connection."

And Olson's take included: "For all of their shortcomings, the Brewers' ownership group deserves credit for one major accomplishment that never can be overlooked or overstated. In the face of overwhelming odds, this group returned big-league baseball to Milwaukee and secured the future of the sport in this city for another generation."

So, while a myriad questions were created about an unknown future, general manager Doug Melvin knew what he needed to do with the product on the field, reacting to the news this way: "It really doesn't affect us right now," he said. "It usually takes a while to happen. I just hope the owners that come in have the same passion for the game as the Seligs have had. We still have to stick to our plans because the baseball side is going to sell the franchise. [The new owners] are going to want to see the baseball side is being run properly."

While Melvin tinkered with the roster, state politicians wanted to take a swing at how the team had managed its finances. In May, Assembly Speaker John Gard and Senate Majority Leader Mary Panzer pushed for a Legislative Audit Bureau review, and once the results of the number crunching started filtering out, Gard said his suspicions were confirmed that new ownership and investment were needed. "This audit shows that the problems facing the Brewers today are not the result of bad intentions or neglect, but rather the harsh by-products of a changed marketplace reality in Major League Baseball today," he said. "This review makes it clear that if the Brewers are going to be competitive and viable for the long term, new ownership with increased access to capital is essential."

Gard praised the Seligs for their efforts, but said it was time for change. "Unfortunately, the kind of ownership size, structure, and resources that worked for decades is a horse-and-buggy relic in today's turbocharged baseball marketplace. The audit makes it pretty clear the status quo is not an attractive option in Milwaukee and we need to do what we can to facilitate the sale of the team."

Panzer also voiced her opinion, saying that the sooner the team could be sold the better. "I believe what needs to happen is for the private sector to come forward and see what is out there for a potential owner or a consortium to bring new capital into the franchise. The public still wants a winning team in Milwaukee."

Wisconsin governor Jim Doyle, responding to reports that the Brewers had debt of more than $133 million in 2003 but had committed more cash to beef up their baseball operations, opposed any state effort to help the team. "We're not going to do anything to help them out," Doyle said from Madison. "I mean, this is a private business. The fact that they need to put more people in the stands and win more games, that's their responsibility, not the state's."

All of these financial woes occurred despite having Miller Park, which drew 2.8 million fans in its inaugural season. Hadrian Shaw of Shaw's Sports Business in California called the Brewers' situation a paradox: "Judging by the amount of debt that the club has incurred, it appears the Brewers couldn't afford Miller Park. On the flip side, given baseball's competitive balance issues, the Brewers couldn't afford not to build Miller Park."

In late June, Major League Baseball gave the green light to four national groups to pursue the sale, two of which featured prominent figures: Dan Gilbert, a Michigan-based multimillionaire who is chairman and founder of Quicken Loans, the nation's leading originator of mortgage loans via the Internet; and J. Christopher Reyes, a highly successful Chicago-area businessman who is cochairman of Reyes Holding LLC, a large food and beverage distribution company in Rosemont, Illinois. Later last summer, Los Angeles investor Mark Attanasio joined the equation, with he and Gilbert considered the front-runners.

The future appeared murky at best, according to many observers, including Tom Haudricourt of the *Journal Sentinel*. "The future of the franchise is definitely in question," Haudricourt said via phone interview. "The financial concerns outweigh the competitive concerns and the question is whether the market can sustain the team. With the sale, who knows what will happen? It doesn't look like there are any local buyers."

Haudricourt added that it's a matter of whether Melvin, Yost, and others can turn the team around quickly enough or if the franchise will continue to sink farther into its painful morass. "They had terrible drafts in the mid- to late 1990s and didn't have the money to bring in big-name players to pick up the slack," Haudricourt said. "They had injury problems with guys like Teddy Higuera and Juan Nieves, and they've been very poor at developing their own pitchers. But they've got the right baseball people in place who know what they're doing, and their drafts under Jack Zduriencik the last four years have been much better. Oakland and Minnesota are examples that their approach can be successful, and they've got a good farm system, although several prospects have suffered injuries this summer. This is a critical stage in franchise history. They're shooting for 2005 and 2006, but if they don't do it then . . ."

Fellow *Journal Sentinel* staff member Michael Hunt addressed the same issue late in 2003, writing: "Only two things matter. Can the kids play? If Rickie Weeks, Prince Fielder, Corey Hart, and the rest of the so-called super farm system develops, the latest five-year plan will have been vindicated. And can Melvin and Yost general manage and manage with limited resources until such maturation occurs? If not, there will be another valley purge. For if history has taught us anything, it is that the Brewers are defined by their spectacular pratfalls."

Meanwhile, the baseball owners extended Selig's contract as commissioner through 2009 after he had hinted that he would retire when his previous deal expired in 2006. Selig first took the job on an interim basis in 1992 after Fay Vincent's forced resignation and was elected in July 1998. In November 2001, his term was extended through December 31, 2006.

Now he can only watch as the organization that he built moves forward without him. "I've known him for 27 years, and I knew Wendy when she was a teenager," said Gregg Hoffmann. "Bud is like one of those Tommy Tippy dolls you can sock around and knock down, but it bounces back up. He is persistent and can take criticism without backing down. I think he and his fellow owners have made plenty of mistakes over the years, but I believe they are loyal to baseball and Milwaukee."

No one could argue with that about Selig, who remains steadfast in his belief that Wisconsin fans will again see a winner in Milwaukee. "After the Braves left, we worked hard for 5 1/2 years to get another team, and many times people said I was nuts, but we got the Brewers," Selig said via phone conversation. "And then most people said we wouldn't survive in a smaller market, but we did. We've had tough times, but we had very competitive teams here from 1978 to 1992, and those days will come back again for Milwaukee, as well as places like Pittsburgh, Cincinnati, and Detroit, and we're going to work hard to make it happen in this changing baseball landscape."

Attanasio, a 47-year-old investment banker, brought renewed hope for a brighter future in Milwaukee when his reported $220 million offer won the bidding war in late September. He assured the management team already in place and Brewers fans that payroll would increase. However, he also emphasized that the franchise would have to show vast improvement on the field for his additional cash commitment.

They can't expect miracles in an economic landscape in which the George Steinbrenners and the well-heeled owners of franchises in Atlanta, Boston, Los Angeles, and Chicago run the show, but all Brewers' fans have been asking for during the past 12 losing seasons is a competitive team in return for their investment.

The approval of Attanasio's ownership bid was a formality early in 2005, but he showed before the end of 2004 that he wasn't afraid to spend some cash when, with his input and approval, Melvin and his baseball folks pulled the trigger on several trades.

Those included shipping the immensely popular Scott Podsednik to the Chicago White Sox in a deal that gained them the right-handed, power-hitting bat of Carlos Lee, which the team needed so much after taking an offensive nosedive in 2004. The trade proved costly because the Brewers not only gave up their top base-stealing threat along with set-up reliever Luis Vizcaino. It also showed fans that the new regime wasn't afraid to spend money, with Lee's contract calling for an $8.6 million salary.

Melvin had earlier depleted his bullpen when he shipped Dan Kolb and his club record 39 saves to Atlanta for Jose Capellan, one of the top pitching prospects in the big leagues. Milwaukee then sent utility man Keith Ginter to Oakland for relief help in fellow righty Justin Lehr and minor league outfielder Nelson Cruz, a potential star for the near future.

The moves fit into Melvin and Attanasio's rebuilding plan, which features an infusion of younger guys with experience and a continual infusion of talent from its highly touted farm system, a combination they hope keeps the team competitive over the long haul.

Chapter Nine

Aaron and Yount and Many More

They were unselfish and team-oriented to the core. They were quiet but as competitive as anybody who played the game. They made mistakes, but seldom in the clutch. They had every reason to be boastful, yet humility was their middle name. Words can't describe the greatness of Henry Aaron and Robin Yount, except these three: Hall of Famers.

"Hammerin' Hank" and "Rockin' Robin." The former epitomized the Milwaukee Braves, while the latter did the same for the Milwaukee Brewers. They represented what was good about America's pastime, what was good about baseball in Milwaukee. They were separated by a generation, but not by the way they played.

Aaron was closing out his career with the Brewers in 1975–76, while Yount was barely beginning his. Aaron said he saw something special in the gangly kid even at that early stage. "You could see that there was greatness in him," Aaron said. "There was no question in my mind that he could be a Hall of Fame player."

Aaron's name has been tossed around with those of Ty Cobb, Babe Ruth, Joe DiMaggio, and a select few others as being the best player of all time. No one would suggest that Yount be included in that discussion because his career numbers didn't match up to Aaron's, but the way he approached life on and off the field were unmatched, leaving him in that next echelon of great players.

So it was only appropriate that on the eve of the first game at Miller Park, Commissioner Bud Selig unveiled monuments to Aaron and Yount, the greatest heroes in the city's baseball history. Aaron's bronze figure depicts the 23-year-old preparing to hit the 11th-inning homer in September 1957 that clinched the Braves' first National League pennant. Aaron also has statues in Eau Claire, Wisconsin, where he played his first season in the minors, and in Atlanta, where he broke Ruth's home run record. "I know one thing," Aaron said at the ceremony. "I played in Milwaukee and those people loved me, and I loved those people."

Meanwhile, Yount is displayed following through on his 3,000th hit in September 1992. "You've got statues all over the place," Yount joked to Aaron in his acceptance speech. "This is pretty intimidating for me. Having a statue out here at Miller Park next to probably the greatest player who ever played baseball. It just doesn't get any better than that."

HENRY AARON

"Hank Aaron could hit in a dark broom closet." Former Milwaukee Braves teammate Eddie Mathews said that in his 1994 book written with Bob Buege, and it was probably as good an illustration as any in describing the man who people called "the Hammer."

However, Mathews never had to face Aaron. In *The Braves Encyclopedia*, Saint Louis's Curt Simmons, who Aaron said gave him the most trouble of any pitcher, summed up the unenviable job of trying to get Aaron out when he said, "Throwing a fastball by Henry Aaron is like trying to sneak the sun past a rooster. He's the only ballplayer I've ever seen who goes to sleep at the plate and wakes up only to swing as the pitch comes in."

Aaron became much more of a pull hitter in his later years, but his success in the batter's box was attributed to his knowledge of his foes and arguably the quickest wrists ever to swing a bat, which enabled him to send rockets all over the diamond. The Mobile, Alabama, native became the game's all-time home run king, whacking his 715th in 1974 to surpass Babe Ruth's benchmark, despite receiving hate mail and death threats. He clubbed 18 more that season, his final one with the Braves, and combined for 22 in ending his career with two years with the Brewers to finish with 755. Aaron accumulated 6,856 total bases, 722 more than his nearest competitor, Stan Musial. He won home run titles in 1957, 1963, and 1966–67 and earned RBI crowns four times. Aaron averaged 33 HRs per year, hitting between 24 and 45 for 19 straight summers, including eight seasons of 40 or more.

Calling him a slugger or home run hitter paid him an injustice because, even though he was those things, Aaron was so much more. He turned in spectacular seasons and innumerable unbelievable performances, but the most remarkable aspect about Hank was his consistency. Aaron hit .300 or higher 14 times in finishing with a .305 lifetime average, including batting championships in '56 and '59. He surpassed 200 hits three times and reached double digits in triples three years and in stolen bases nine consecutive seasons. He also earned four Gold Gloves, including three in a row, and was an All-Star on 21 occasions.

Unfortunately, those talents were put on display in the postseason only three times. In 1957 he won the National League's most valuable player award and led the Braves to a World Series title with three homers, seven RBIs, and a .393 average against the Yankees. He finished with a .364 mark after Milwaukee dropped the Fall Classic to New York the next year. Then the Braves lost to the "Miracle Mets" in 1969 despite Aaron's hitting a homer in all three games and batting .357.

Aaron played semipro ball at age 15 and was the shortstop for two seasons with the Indianapolis Clowns in the Negro leagues. In May 1952, the Braves paid $7,500 for Aaron, who spent the next 18 months tearing up three leagues, including his first year with the Eau Claire Bears. He got his chance with the Braves in 1954 after Bobby Thomson broke his leg in spring training. He grabbed a spot in the lineup and never looked back.

While piling up numbers in the late 1960s and early '70s, the quiet star used his prowess on the field as a forum to become more outspoken about social issues and the lack of blacks in baseball management positions, saying in 1970, shortly after registering his 3,000th hit, "I have to tell the truth, and when people ask me what progress Negroes have made in baseball, I tell them the Negro hasn't made any progress on the field. We haven't made any progress in the commissioner's office. Even with Monte Irvin in there, I still think it's tokenism. I think we have a lot of Negroes capable of handling front-office jobs. We don't have Negro secretaries in some of the big league offices, and I think it's time that the major leagues and baseball in general just took hold of themselves and started hiring some of these capable people."

His pursuit of racial equality didn't deter his chase of Ruth's coveted standard. By 1971 and '72, talk of him possibly reaching the Babe's magical 714 heated up. Then he belted 40 round-trippers in 1973, the most ever for a 39-year-old, leaving him only one shy of tying Ruth. Atlanta opened the '74 campaign at Cincinnati, and Aaron reached the target when he lifted Jack Billingham's 3–1 pitch over the fence in his second at-bat, the first-ever homer hit at Riverfront Stadium. Controversy ensued when Mathews, the Braves' skipper, kept Aaron out of the lineup the next day, against the wishes of Commissioner Bowie Kuhn, in hopes that he would shatter the record at home. He did just that April 8 in a nationally televised contest against Al Downing and the Dodgers.

Aaron always credited Mathews for helping get him through those pressure-filled days during his race to number 715. "He got me through some tough moments as I approached the record," Aaron recalled in February 2001 upon hearing about Mathews's death at age 69. "He kept the writers and the wolves away and let me focus on what I had to do."

Aaron often returns to Milwaukee, as he did in August 2004 for a fundraising event to benefit his Chasing the Dream Foundation, which provides assistance to young people with limited opportunities so they may develop their talents, whether they are athletic, musical or something else. His visit included a stop at Miller Park, where he said Milwaukee always has held a special place in his heart.

"I'm always glad to come back to Milwaukee," Aaron said. "I've always considered this like home, and it was a great place for me. I enjoyed many triumphs here, including two [National League] championships. I can't say enough about the fans, who've welcomed me with open arms and treated me as well as anybody can."

ROBIN YOUNT

To fans in Beertown, "The Kid" always will be their MVP, a tag he earned during his incredible 1982 season. Yount won the first of his two American League MVP awards that year after leading the Brewers to their first and only World Series with a phenomenal season. He batted .331 with 210 hits, 46 doubles, 12 triples, 29 home runs, and 114 runs batted in. He scored 129 runs and stole 14 bases. He led loop shortstops with 489 assists and teamed with second baseman Jim Gantner to top the big leagues in double plays.

No game better typified the kind of summer he'd had than the regular-season finale. The Brewers had lost the first three games of the series at Baltimore, creating a tie with the Orioles in the Eastern Division. Yount smacked a home run against Baltimore ace and now fellow Cooperstown resident Jim Palmer in the first inning, added another HR and a triple, and scored four runs in the Brewers' 10–2 victory.

"He's the best ballplayer I ever saw," said Gorman Thomas, who Yount later replaced as the starting center fielder en route to winning his second MVP award in 1989. "Other people have their opinion and talk about different players. That's because they didn't see this guy."

Biased, of course, but his former teammates, many of them among the game's best during the team's six consecutive winning campaigns from 1978 to 1983, said Yount's value was measured never with statistics but rather by how he approached the game on a daily basis. He ran out every ground ball for 20 seasons, playing hurt and never complaining. And he never cared about personal accomplishments, because they didn't mean anything unless the team won.

That's how his fellow gladiators remembered Yount in several *Milwaukee Journal Sentinel* articles commemorating his joining baseball's hallowed hall in 1999, when he, George Brett and Nolan Ryan became first-ballot inductees. "As talented as he was, a lot of players, you may not want to be around them because they let it go to their head," said Larry Hisle, who played sparingly after a shoulder injury ruined the last several years of his career in Milwaukee (1978–82). "But Robin was as down-to-earth as anybody you ever met. If you didn't know who he was, you wouldn't even think he played in the major leagues. He had just the perfect attitude for an athlete."

Paul Molitor, who along with Gantner played with Yount for 15 seasons, related how Yount talked about how much fun it would be if they didn't keep track of batting averages and such things. "I probably learned more about the game from him than any other person—coach, manager, whatever," said Molitor, who was elected to the Hall of Fame in 2004. "It wasn't so much what he said to me. I just saw the way he was on a daily basis for 15 years."

A young Robin Yount avoids a sliding runner at second base in attempting to complete a double play during his rookie season, 1974.

Former Brewers pitcher Mike Caldwell said that Yount deserved every accolade bestowed upon him: "If you need a hero in baseball past, present or future, there's your man."

The only way that managers, medical staffers, and teammates could talk Yount out of playing, regardless of how bad he was ailing, involved going upstairs to the boss. And that didn't always work. Bud Selig said one incident described Yount's magnificent career. "Molitor and Gantner and [Cecil] Cooper were there, and as soon as Robin saw me he went, 'Awwwwww,' and he started moaning. 'You're not going to tell me what to do, I'm playing.' And I said: 'Robin, I just talked to Dr. [Paul] Jacobs, and they don't want you to play. Now this is for your own good.' And then he looked at me and said: 'Why shouldn't I play? I'm a ballplayer.' That said it all."

Indeed.

Yount finished his career after the 1993 season with 3,142 hits, the most ever by a right-handed batter in the American League at the time. He broke into the big leagues as an 18-year-old shortstop in 1974 after only 64 games in rookie league ball and became one of only three players to win MVP laurels at two positions; the others were Stan Musial and Hank Greenberg. A true testament is what others outside the Milwaukee organization said about Yount, including an article in the *Los Angeles Daily News* in April 2003: "Yount was the maestro of the intangible, that rare blend of leadership, on-field vision, and a ferocious desire to win."

"There was only one guy who went all out on every play, every day his entire career," Brett said during his acceptance speech at Cooperstown. "That was Robin Yount."

Yount never spent a day on the disabled list from 1978 to 1991. He holds team career records in runs (1,632), hits (3,142), doubles (583), homers (251), and RBIs (1,406). There was nothing more graceful than watching Yount go from first to third or leg out a triple, another category in which he tops the Brewers' charts (126). "Everybody's got something they can do in life, and it just happened that I could play some baseball," Yount said in 1988.

Tom Haudricourt, a Virginia native, has spent all but two of the last 20 years with the *Milwaukee Journal Sentinel* covering major league baseball in general and the Brewers in particular. He said nobody compared to Yount. "Robin was a franchise player, the epitome of what a ballplayer should be," Haudricourt said via phone. "He was the most selfless player I've ever seen. He was a throwback, and if you asked him if he'd trade being in the Hall of Fame for a couple of World Series rings, he'd do it without a doubt."

Hank Aaron paid Yount the ultimate compliment with these comments for a tribute publication upon the latter's reaching the 3,000-hit plateau: "I have often said, the greatest thing that ever happened to Milwaukee was that Robin Yount wanted to play his entire career with the Brewers. When I think of this franchise, I think of Robin Yount. That's the biggest tribute you can make to a player and to a club."

Twice the American League's MVP, always Milwaukee's MVP.

PAUL MOLITOR

It could have been a coincidence, but it's doubtful. Paul Molitor's last year in a Milwaukee uniform (1992) was the team's last winning season. It's no wonder he earned the nickname "the Ignitor," because the Brewers finished at .500 or better during 11 of his 15 summers in Beertown. He played in only 13 games in 1984 and missed significant time during two of the team's other three losing campaigns during his tenure.

The leadoff hitter for "Bambi's Bombers" and "Harvey's Wallbangers," Molitor ranked eighth on the career list with 3,319 hits. He batted .306 with 1,782 runs and 1,307 RBIs in 21 seasons for Milwaukee (1978–92), Toronto (1993–95), and Minnesota (1996–98). The seven-time American League All-Star was named the most valuable player in the 1993 World Series for the Blue Jays. He hit .418 in his two Fall Classic appearances.

With those kinds of credentials, it's easy to see why he was a first-ballot inductee into the Hall of Fame in 2004. He joined Robin Yount in Cooperstown, having announced in June 1999 at a ceremony at County Stadium in which his number four was retired, that he'd go in as a Brewer. Molitor was picked on 431 of 506 ballots (85.2 percent) cast by reporters who have been members of the Baseball

Paul Molitor was one of the best leadoff hitters in the American League; in 2004 he joined Robin Yount in the Hall of Fame.

Writers Association of America for 10 or more years. Dennis Eckersley was selected on 421 ballots (83.2 percent). A player must be chosen by at least 75 percent of the voters (380) for election.

Tom Haudricourt said that Molitor, a native of Saint Paul, Minnesota, was perhaps the franchise's greatest athlete: "He was a remarkable player. He was hurt so much early in his career that he didn't realize his full potential, but his career was odd in that he put up much bigger numbers in the second half of it."

Molitor received boos when he returned to Milwaukee in 1993 after signing as a free agent with Toronto, but fans can only cheer what he accomplished as a Brewer. He still ranks second all-time to Yount in games played (1,856), runs (1,275), hits (2,281), doubles (405), and triples (86). Molitor holds the top spot in club history in batting average (.303) and stolen bases (412) and is third in runs batted in (790). He led the AL with 136 runs scored in 1982. He became the third player after Ty Cobb and Honus Wagner to record 3,000 hits, 600 doubles, and 500 stolen bases.

It's little wonder that former teammates admired Molitor so much. After he moved on to Toronto, Brewers shortstop Pat Listach asked to wear number four in his honor. Center fielder Darryl Hamilton donned it when he played in Texas in 1996. "He's been a huge influence on my career," Hamilton said in '99. "I learned how to play from watching him and Robin. I know a lot of other guys who played with him would say the same thing. I'm glad they're finally [retiring his number]. I wish I could be there."

Hank Aaron (44), Rollie Fingers (34), and Yount (19) are the only other Brewers—all major league teams retired the Number 42 in honor of Jackie Robinson in 1997—to have their jersey numbers retired.

EDDIE MATHEWS

He had one of the sweetest swings in baseball, but this left-handed slugger became one of the game's most feared run producers because of his awesome power. Mathews burst onto the major league scene as a 20-year-old in 1952. He became the first rookie in big-league history to clout three homers in a game, accomplishing the feat at Ebbets Field in Brooklyn in the next-to-last outing of the season to finish tied for fourth in the National League with 25 round-trippers.

Born in Texarkana, Texas, but raised in California, Mathews threw aside any thoughts of a sophomore jinx with a vengeance, whacking a career-high 47 homers that led all of baseball in 1953, providing Braves' fans their first hero upon his arrival in Milwaukee. Mathews hit .302 and added a personal-best 31 doubles that season while driving in a club-record 135 runs. It proved to be the first of Mathews' nine consecutive seasons with at least 31 homers, a stretch that saw him surpass 100 RBIs five times. His best overall campaign came in 1959, when he set career highs in hits (182) and average (.306) while clobbering 46 HRs and finishing with 114 RBIs.

Not a great fielder when he started, Mathews worked on that aspect in becoming one of the game's best all-around third basemen. The only member to play in Boston, Milwaukee, and Atlanta, the hard-nosed and competitive Mathews also was the team's enforcer and took a leading role in several bench-clearing incidents in his day.

Johnny Logan, one of his roommates and his infield neighbor at shortstop, and several other teammates reminisced about Mathews and his all-out style after the latter passed away. "He'd knock them down with his chest and pick them up," Logan said of the 50 to 100 ground balls that Mathews took daily in spring training. "He broke his nose three times fielding balls. He'd work hard for a couple of hours, then we'd go to a bar and have a cold one. Actually, we'd have three or four or five."

Pitchers Warren Spahn and Lew Burdette knew they'd always have somebody in their corner if Mathews was anywhere in the vicinity. "Eddie was a tough competitor and a tough guy," Spahn said. "He didn't back down from anybody." "With Eddie, you never worried about anything," Burdette said. "If somebody charged the mound when you were pitching, you knew he was going to be there. Eddie used to tell me, 'Let the son of a gun charge you and get the hell out of the way.'"

Mathews finished with 512 homers, averaging just more than 30 per season during his 17-year career that ended with short stints in Houston and Detroit. He coached and managed in Atlanta before getting his call to Cooperstown in 1978.

"You can talk about those other towns, but there was nothing like Milwaukee when we played there," Mathews once said. "It wasn't just Milwaukee. It was the whole state of Wisconsin and surrounding states. It just went on and on. It was a joy to go to the ballpark in those days."

ROLLIE FINGERS

The game's first bona fide relief ace, Rollie Fingers was also famous for his handlebar mustache. But his right arm is what got him voted into the Hall of Fame in 1992, the same year the Brewers retired his number 34 despite his pitching less than four full seasons with the organization at the end of his 17-year career.

The lanky right-hander began his big-league career as a starter but helped make the Oakland A's back-to-back-to-back champions from 1972 to 1974 with his handiwork out of the bullpen. He retired after the 1985 season holding major league records for career saves (341) and World Series saves (seven). He registered 20 or more saves 10 times in posting a 114–118 record and 2.90 ERA. He reached double digits in wins on four occasions and posted a 1,299–492 strikeout-to-walk ratio.

After the 1980 season, San Diego believed that Fingers, 34, was past his prime and packaged him with former Oakland battery mate Gene Tenace to Saint Louis as part of an 11-player deal. Four days later, Fingers was on the move again, this time to Milwaukee in a huge seven-player swap.

Fingers proved to his previous employers and the rest of baseball that he still had plenty of arm left, leading the American League in saves with 28 while posting a magnificent 1.04 ERA. He was the major reason the Brewers of 1981 claimed their first postseason appearance. Fingers figured in 55 percent of the team's victories, earning the most valuable player and Cy Young awards. Despite pain, he registered 29 more saves in 1982 before being shelved early in September, thus missing the stretch run and Milwaukee's marvelous playoff journey that ended in its Game 7 loss to the Cardinals in the World Series, which many partisans believe wouldn't have been necessary had Fingers been available in the Brewers' bullpen.

He missed the 1983 season after elbow surgery. Fingers bounced back to post a 1.96 ERA while saving 23 games for a squad that won only 67 times in 1984. In 1985, age and injuries finally caught up to Fingers, who slumped to a 5.04 ERA, and he was released by the Brewers at the end of the year. However, with 97 saves, he still stands second to Dan Plesac (133) in team annals.

WARREN SPAHN

His numbers are mind-boggling. Warren Spahn, who played 20 of his 21 seasons with the Boston and Milwaukee Braves, won at least 20 games 13 times. The southpaw from Buffalo, New York, amassed 363 career wins, the fifth-highest total in major league history. He was inducted into baseball's Hall of Fame in 1973, the first year of his eligibility, garnering 83 percent of the vote.

Spahn signed with the Braves for $80 per month in 1940 but injured his arm twice during his first year of Class D competition. He won 19 games the next season and was invited to spring training. He started 1942 with the Braves, but manager Casey Stengel, who was angry because Spahn refused to brush back Pee Wee Reese in an exhibition game, sent him back to the minors, thinking he wasn't tough enough. Spahn finished 17–12 with a sparkling 1.96 ERA, while Boston captured seventh place. Stengel later said that shipping Spahn out was the worst mistake he ever made.

The ultimate competitor baffled hitters with his high-kicking delivery and array of pitches. He never wanted to leave a game, and he never wanted to leave the game of baseball. He won an incredible 177 games after his 35th birthday, including his 300th in 1961 at age 40.

Spahn's greatest season may have been 1953. He finished 23–7 with 24 complete games in 32 starts and led the National League with a 2.10 earned run average. He also went 23–7 in 1963, posting a 2.60 ERA. Not known as a strikeout pitcher, he still led the circuit in Ks from 1949 to 1952 and registered ERAs of less than 3.00 nine times and ended his career at 3.09. Spahn led the league in victories eight times, including five straight from 1957 to 1961. He tossed two no-hitters and completed an unbelievable 382 of his 665 career starts (57.4 percent), including at least 20 on 13 occasions. "He was so determined to complete nine innings," Logan said in 2003. "He never wanted to come out of a game. The way he looked at it was, 'If I start the game, I want to finish it.'"

Five days past his 40th birthday, the 14-time All-Star became the second-oldest pitcher, behind Cy Young, to throw a no-hitter when the Braves edged San Francisco, 1–0, on April 28, 1961. Two years later, at 42, he became the oldest 20-game winner in major league history.

His baseball accomplishments were remarkable enough, but the fact that he served a three-year tour of duty in World War II meant he didn't record his first big-league triumph until he was 25 in 1946. "You know he was in the army in his prime, and if you take those years back he probably wins another 30, 40, or 50 games, and that puts him above 400 [wins]," fellow Cooperstown enshrinee Phil Niekro said.

While in the service, Spahn did not sit on the sidelines. He served in Europe, where he was wounded, decorated for bravery with a Bronze Star and Purple Heart, and awarded a battlefield commission. He fought at the Battle of the Bulge and in the fight for the bridge at Remagen, where his company lost many men.

Many people have forgotten that Spahn was also a complete player. He established big-league records for pitchers by starting 82 double plays and hitting an NL-record 35 homers.

He once said, "When I'm pitching, I feel I'm down to the essentials—two men with one challenge between them." Spahn, who also saved 29 games, certainly won most of those challenges. He died at age 82 in November 2003.

CECIL COOPER

He was one of the quietest players to don a Brewers uniform, but his bat and glove made up for it with plenty of noise. "We had a lot of great ballplayers and he kind of got lost in the shuffle," former manager George Bamberger said. "If he had wanted to, there's no doubt in my mind he could've hit 35 to 40 homers a season. But he knew that wasn't his job. He was probably one of the best hitters I've ever seen."

"Coop" batted .300 eight times, including seven straight from 1977 to 1983, and was an annual Gold Glove candidate at first base. He contributed 20 or more homers five times and drove in 100 or more runs four times. He led the American League with 122 RBIs while hitting 25 homers and batting .352, second to Kansas City's George Brett (.390), in 1980. Cooper's brightest moment by far came when his two-run single won Game 5 of the 1982 American League Championship Series, lifting the Brewers into their only World Series appearance.

Cooper never sought the spotlight, preferring to let others in the clubhouse handle that part of being a pro player for one of the top teams in the game. "I would call myself a quiet assassin," Cooper said via telephone interview. "I was introverted, but I brought my game to the park every day and went about my job."

His Milwaukee career ended after the 1987 season. He sits in the top three in team history in average (.302), hits (1,815), runs (821), homers (201), RBIs (944), and doubles (345). "He was just a pure hitter," Robin Yount said. "He hit the ball to all fields, he hit for a high average, and had a lot of power to go with it. He was a great player."

JOE ADCOCK

He didn't hit for the highest average, and because of injuries, he usually didn't hit the most home runs. But Joe Adcock connected on some of the biggest and many of the longest round-trippers in Milwaukee Braves and National League history. Future Hall of Famers Hank Aaron and Eddie Mathews batted ahead of Adcock in the Braves' murderers' row offense in the 1950s and early 1960s, usually overshadowing the former farm boy who had attended Louisiana State University on a basketball scholarship before the Reds drafted him.

Adcock clubbed 239 of his 336 career long balls from 1953 to 1962, and he was involved in two of baseball's greatest feats while playing for Milwaukee. On July 31, 1954, against the Brooklyn Dodgers at Ebbets Field, Adcock tied the major league record of four homers in one game and also doubled to set a record of 18 total bases that stood until Los Angeles's Shawn Green lit up the Brewers for four HRs and 19 total bases August 23, 2002, at Miller Park. The four round-trippers made him one of only 10 big-leaguers to accomplish it in the twentieth century. And they were all off different pitchers: Don Newcombe, Erv Palica, Pete Wojey, and Johnny Podres. He would have been the only big leaguer to hit five if the double, which banged off the wall in left-center, had been a couple of feet higher.

Then, on May 26, 1959, at County Stadium, Adcock hit what he assumed was a winning homer against Harvey Haddix in the 13th after the Pittsburgh Pirates left-hander had pitched a perfect game through 12 innings. An error and an intentional walk had ruined the perfecto, and then Adcock ruined Haddix's no-hitter and handed him a defeat with one of his mighty swings. He was credited with a double because Aaron stopped running and Adcock passed him between second and third bases.

The six-foot-four-inch, 220-pound first baseman spent three nondescript seasons with Cincinnati, hitting a combined 31 homers, before joining the Braves just before their move to Milwaukee. He averaged 24 homers and 76 RBIs and sported a .285 average during his decade with the Braves, leading the team in long balls in 1956 (a career-high 38) and 1961 (35), the only two years he surpassed 100 RBIs.

Despite his clobbering 29 HRs and bringing home 78 runs, the Braves shipped him to Cleveland after he hit .248 in 1962. He spent one season with the Indians and ended his career with three years with the Los Angeles/California Angels. When he retired, Adcock was 20th on the all-time home run list, with many of his dingers having been mammoth shots. He was the first man to hit a ball into the bleachers in center field at the Polo Grounds in New York, a blast of more than 500 feet.

Regardless of how many accolades others received, his teammates knew how valuable Adcock was to the Braves' run of success. "I would classify Joe as an unsung hero," Johnny Logan said after Adcock died at age 71 in May 1999. "He not only hit home runs, but he hit the farthest home runs. This kid had baseball strength. He was one of the few real tall guys in our day. Joe was lanky, but when he put his 220 pounds into it, that was what you call a home run."

"I had the pleasure of knowing Joe as a teammate and a friend for many years," Aaron said. "As good a player as he was, he was an even better human being."

JIM GANTNER

Bob Uecker's assessment in *True Brew* was perfect when he described an intense infielder nicknamed Gumby. "Jimmy is a perfect example of how hard work pays off," Uecker said. "He may not have had the same tools as Paulie or Robin, but when it comes to heart and guts, no one is better."

"Jimmy was maybe everybody's favorite guy on the team," Paul Molitor said as he and members of the 1982 team gathered for a 20-year reunion. "He made you laugh, he made you appreciate work, he made you appreciate not taking things for granted."

Gantner never made the All-Star team, never batted .300, never scored or drove in 100 runs, never hit more than 11 home runs, and only twice had more than 150 hits in 17 seasons in the big leagues. But he was as valuable to the Brewers' winning teams in the late 1970s and early '80s as anybody because he did the dirty work without complaining. "I grew up in a big family, so nothing was given to you," Gantner said in *True Brew*. "You worked for what you got. That was my attitude. Take nothing for granted and keep going hard."

He did just that for 15 full seasons with the Brewers and parts of two others. The Eden, Wisconsin, native was drafted in the 12th round out of UW-Oshkosh in 1974. His first hit came September 3, 1976, against Detroit phenom Mark Fidrych. That year, the rookie got to pinch-run for Hank Aaron, one of his heroes as a youngster, after the latter reached base in his final at-bat with the Brewers.

Gantner made the team for good in 1978, which coincided with the team's rise from oblivion to division contender. He took over as the regular second baseman in 1981 and remained a fixture until retiring after the 1992 season. The Brewers have had eight different opening day starters since then.

"Jim Gantner was blue-collar, a perfect Brewer, which fit because he was from Wisconsin," Tom Haudricourt said. "I loved him because he was so gritty. He blew out his knee twice because he stood in there on double plays at second base. He, Robin, and Molitor were definitely the Three Amigos, the common threads for this organization."

Gantner hit a career-best .295 in 1982 and added a .333 average in the World Series. The next season was his best, when he batted .282, hit 11 homers, and drove in 74 runs. One might not know it, but Gumby is high on many team offensive charts: third in stolen bases (137); fourth in hits (1,696), runs (726), doubles (262), and triples (38); and sixth in RBIs (568). He was also one of the best defensive performers in either league and had arguably the best pivot turning double plays. His .992 fielding percentage was the all-time best for AL second sackers.

"I don't know if I was underrated or not," Gantner said in 2002. "That don't bother me if I was. I had fun. It was a great time. Nobody can take that away from me."

LEW BURDETTE

Gary Caruso, author of *The Braves Encyclopedia*, called Warren Spahn the most competitive player he'd ever seen. Most of it must have rubbed off on Spahn's good buddy, Lew Burdette.

Voted into the Braves Hall of Fame in 2001, Burdette won 179 games, which ranks fifth best in franchise history. And one of the reasons for his success was his friendly rivalry with Spahn, his roommate on road trips while playing in Milwaukee. "We used to see who could catch more fly balls in batting practice to determine who would buy dinner," Burdette said at the ceremony in Atlanta. "I really don't think anybody had more fun playing than we did. We really helped and prodded each other."

It definitely worked, as the two combined with Bob Buhl to average 50 wins per season from 1953 to 1961. Burdette, who played for the Braves from 1951 to 1963, led the National League in victories (21) in 1959 and in ERA (2.70) in 1956. He finished with 146 complete games and registered back-to-back 20-victory seasons in 1959–60 while recording at least 17 wins for six consecutive campaigns.

However, Burdette grabbed the spotlight during the 1957 World Series, throttling the high-powered Yankees three times in winning Games 2, 5, and 7, the latter two being shutouts. His Game 5 gem, a 1–0 decision, featured only 87 pitches and two fly balls to the outfield.

Too bad he couldn't have won Game 7 at County Stadium, where he said fans were number-one in his book. "Milwaukee truly was unequaled anywhere in the league at the time," he said. "The crowd would react to every pitch. You can talk about the Dodgers and their fans, or the Cardinals, but the Milwaukee crowds were the best in baseball."

AND MORE BRAVES
BOB BUHL

This right-hander from Saginaw, Michigan, was the third member of arguably baseball's best 1–3 punch during the 1950s and early '60s. From 1953 to 1960, Buhl had the highest winning percentage (.621) of anybody in baseball, including Warren Spahn and Lew Burdette.

If not for suffering arm problems several times, Buhl may have provided the difference in the Braves' winning two or three more pennants. He won 18 games in 1956 and '57. A line-drive hit off the index finger of his pitching hand in August meant he won only four times during the final eight weeks of the 1956 season, in which he finished 18–8 and the Braves ended up one game behind Brooklyn. He then missed a month of the 1957 campaign with shoulder trouble and wound up 18–7.

Then he made only 11 appearances and missed the 1958 World Series as the Braves failed to defend their title against the Yankees. Some say this power pitcher's herky-jerky motion contributed to his physical ailments, but his

Milwaukee career featured a 109–72 mark before he was traded to the Cubs in 1962. Buhl, who died in February 2001, was a Dodger killer, posting a 19–8 mark against them from 1953 to 1959, including eight wins in 1956 alone.

JOHNNY LOGAN

This shortstop was one of the feistiest players during an era of beanballs and fisticuffs, never backing down from anybody when the time came to partaking in extracurricular activities. Logan led the league in defense three times and made four All-Star teams. He reached double figures in homers six years, with his best season being 1955. He knocked in 83 runs and batted .297, both career highs. He also shared the top spot with 37 doubles and registered a 5-for-5 game in a 9–5 win over Cincinnati.

Traded to Pittsburgh for Gino Cimoli in 1961, he served as a backup infielder and pinch hitter through 1963 before playing in Japan for one season. Logan, who played with the minor league Brewers, has lived in Milwaukee since retiring.

DON McMAHON

This right-hander bounced around the minor leagues, mostly as a starter, and then served a two-year stint in the military before the Braves called him up in June 1957. He became the team's closer during a time before the term was used, notching nine saves with a 1.54 ERA during that short but wonderful first season in which he helped propel Milwaukee to a World Series title. McMahon worked five scoreless innings in three outings against the Yankees that October.

McMahon saved eight games the next season and then tied Lindy McDaniel of Saint Louis with 15 in 1959. His ERA ballooned to 5.94 despite 10 saves in 1960, but he bounced back for eight saves, six wins, and a 2.84 ERA in '61. After a slow start, Birdie Tebbetts shipped McMahon to lowly Houston early in 1962.

The fastball-curveball thrower bounced around the majors until 1974, when he was 44. In 1971, while with San Francisco, he topped the NL with nine relief wins and registered a career-high 19 saves.

DEL CRANDALL

This California native was known for his defensive play. He led the National League in fielding percentage four times and won four Gold Gloves. He caught three no-hitters while catching for the Braves: Jim Wilson, Warren Spahn and Lew Burdette.

Although he performed in the shadows of so many other stars in the explosive Milwaukee lineups, Crandall contributed three 21-plus-homer seasons, including 21 and 26 in 1954 and 1955, respectively. A backup with the team in Boston his first two years starting in '49, he rejoined the club after a two-year stint in the military. Crandall averaged 19 homers from 1953 to 1960 before suffering injury problems his final three years with the team.

Crandall appeared in eight All-Star games and smacked one homer in both of Milwaukee's trips to the World Series, although he hit only a combined .224. He became the Brewers' second manager, replacing Dave Bristol in late May of 1972.

BILLY BRUTON

This speedy center fielder was already a fan favorite when the Braves moved to town, having been a star with the American Association Brewers during the 1952 season in which he led the league with 130 runs and 211 hits while batting .325. He became an instant hero when he clubbed a solo homer in the 10th to win the Braves' first home opener. Bruton scored the second run of that 3–2 win and made the defensive play of the game in robbing Stan Musial of a hit with two men on in the eighth.

Bruton was the most serious base-stealing threat Milwaukee had; he led the NL in that category his first three years, even though the Braves weren't a running team. He missed the second half of the 1957 season, the World Series, and the beginning of '58 because of a knee injury. But he topped all players in the latter Fall Classic with a .412 average. His best season was 1960, his last with the team. Bruton led the NL with 112 runs and 13 triples and posted career highs in hits (180) and homers (12). Milwaukee then traded him to Detroit for second baseman Frank Bolling.

AND MORE BREWERS
GORMAN THOMAS

Robin Yount, Jim Gantner, and Paul Molitor were perfect for Milwaukee, but fans related to this slugging power hitter and outfielder, and still do when he shows up at Miller Park these days. Thomas floundered in the minor leagues, despite winning two home run titles, because he struck out a lot more often than not. He didn't get a full-time big-league job until George Bamberger handed him a starting assignment in 1978.

Thomas established a franchise record with 45 round-trippers in 1979. He also led the team with 21 in the strike-shortened 1981 season and with 39 the next year for the formidable Brewers' pennant-winning attack.

For his size, Thomas also was an above-average fielder and never met a wall he couldn't run into. His prowess diminished after he underwent rotator cuff surgery in 1984. In one of the team's most controversial trades, even though he was hitting only around .180, he was shipped to Cleveland in 1983 and then enjoyed a 33-homer season with Seattle in 1985.

JIM SLATON

This right-hander pitched for the Brewers from 1971 to 1977 and 1979 to 1983 and was a model of consistency whether in a starting or relieving role. Slaton won 117 games, toiling with the lowly Brewers during his first stint before recording a career-high 17 wins in '78 for the Tigers, who had obtained him for Ben Oglivie. Slaton came back to post his high-water mark for Milwaukee with 15 victories the next year against only nine defeats.

His career was curtailed in 1980 when he suffered a slight tear of his rotator cuff, but he bounced back to lead the crew with 14 wins in his final season in Milwaukee, all in relief. Slaton still holds down the number one or two positions in team record books in wins, appearances, games started, complete games, shutouts, innings pitched, and strikeouts. He finished with a 1.93 ERA in five innings of work in the American League championship series and was 1–0 and didn't allow an earned run in three innings of the World Series in 1982.

GEORGE SCOTT

"The Boomer," who had starred with the Red Sox in the mid- to late 1960s, gave the fledgling Brewers name recognition when he came to Milwaukee starting with the 1972 season. He also became the team's first big run producer and the first character in the clubhouse because of his colorful phrases and personality. He called his glove "Black Beauty," and it did the job, earning Scott several Gold Gloves.

Scott drove in 88 runs his first season and then batted .306 with 107 RBIs in 1973. He then tied Reggie Jackson for the AL homer lead with 36 long balls and topped the circuit with 109 RBIs in '75. Scott struggled to find his form the next summer and was sent back to Boston in the Cecil Cooper trade before the '77 campaign.

However, there's no denying he was the main man in the Brewers' lineup and in the dugout, and teammates and foes alike didn't want him mad at them. Despite his relatively short stay in town, Scott stood eighth in team annals in batting average (.283) and was 10th in hits (851) through the 2003 season.

First baseman George Scott wasn't only known for his bat; with the help of the the glove he called Black Beauty, he earned several Gold Gloves.

MIKE CALDWELL

In 1971, his first year of pro ball, Mike Caldwell made the jump from Class A ball to the San Diego Padres. He was subsequently traded to the Giants and finished 14–5 in '74. However, he underwent arm surgery and struggled, bouncing around to the Cardinals and Reds in 1977. He regained his form with Milwaukee in 1978, earning the American League's Comeback Player of the Year award with a 22–9 record, 2.36 ERA, and league-high 23 complete games. His .727 winning percentage (16–6) led the league in 1979, a season in which he won eight straight games. He won 17 games as Milwaukee clinched the East in 1982 and then won twice in the World Series against Saint Louis.

Caldwell is among the top 10 in most pitching categories for the club: 10th in appearances (239), third in starts (217), second in wins (102), first in complete games (85), second in shutouts (18), second in innings (1,603), and fourth in winning percentage (.560 at 102–80). His six shutouts in 1978, including three against the Yankees, is still a team standard.

139

TEDDY HIGUERA

Scout Roy Poitevint discovered this lefty sensation from Juarez of the Mexican League in 1983, and Higuera became arguably the best pitcher in Brewers history. He turned in the best rookie record in Milwaukee annals with a 15–8 mark, finishing second in rookie of the year balloting in 1985. The next year he became Milwaukee's third and last 20-game winner, going 20–11 with a 2.79 ERA. In '87, Higuera fashioned an 18–10 record, setting a franchise mark that still stands with 32 straight scoreless innings. His 240 strikeouts were also a team mark until Ben Sheets registered 264 in 2004.

The Brewers' ace went 16–9 with a nifty 2.45 ERA in 1988, but injury woes began in 1989 and haunted him and the team through his final season in '94. He bounced back with 11 victories in 1990, but a rotator cuff injury and surgery sidelined him most of 1991–92 and he never regained his stature. Higuera is fifth in career starts (205), third in victories (94), 10th in ERA (3.61), tied for fifth in complete games (50), third in shutouts (12), fifth in innings (1,380), first in strikeouts (1,081), and second in winning percentage at .595 (94–64).

NOT TO BE FORGOTTEN

Many other players deserve recognition for their roles with either organization, including Braves such as Wes Covington, Andy Pafko, Gene Conley, Bobby Thomson, Frank and Joe Torre, Ernie Johnson, Lee Maye, Frank Thomas, Tony Cloninger, Frank Bolling, Denny Lemaster, Rico Carty, and Denis Menke. And what about former Brewers such as Don Money, Ben Oglivie, Bill Travers, Jim Colborn, Lary Sorensen, Moose Haas, B. J. Surhoff, Dale Sveum, Greg Vaughn, Mark Loretta, Bob McClure, Johnny Briggs, Sixto Lezcano, Charlie Moore, Bill Wegman, Jeff Cirillo, John Jaha, Bill Castro, Dan Plesac, Jerry Augustine, Jeromy Burnitz, and Geoff Jenkins?

Chapter Ten

If You Build It. . .: County Stadium and Miller Park

People argued for years—politically, financially, and geograph-ically—about whether they should be built. Seven men died while working on the facilities. It took vision and courage by many, albeit a half-century apart, for them to become realities.

County Stadium and Miller Park were and are more than edifices of Milwaukee's skyline. Words such as community, history, and family come to mind. But these are only pieces of the fabric that is baseball.

For anybody who's ever attended a game in Milwaukee, it is more than that. It's dancing to your favorite polka music. It's a smoking tepee. It's watch-ing Bonnie Brewer whack an opposing manager's derriere with her broom. It's the Italian sausage winning by a nose. It's Gus the Wonder Dog. It's leder-hosen and good, old-fashioned gemutlichkeit.

And don't forget the beer and bratwurst.

COUNTY STADIUM

If people were sick of hearing or talking about funding for a new baseball park in the mid- to late 1990s, that was nothing compared to what hap-pened—and didn't happen—two and three generations earlier. Charles Whitnall talked about building a home for major league baseball back in 1909, but other city leaders didn't get serious about the idea until alderman Charles C. Schad introduced a resolution for a 50,000-seat stadium, at a cost of $300,000, on a 25-acre site at North 60th and West McKinley. That was in 1931. The Depression worsened and coffers emptied. Schad tried again four years later, but this time as a Public Works Administration project that would run around $700,000.

Henry Bendinger, owner of the American Association's Brewers, said he'd lease a new facility but favored a 40-acre parcel at North Hawley Road and West State Street. An application was received in 1938, but no more PWA projects were available. The county board authorized looking for a site and funding of up to $500,000. However, haggling over a site continued, and then discussions were tabled with World War II imminent.

Officials eventually settled on the Story Parkway land, and after bonding debates concerning street and transportation issues were ironed out, plans moved ahead in 1949.

Milwaukee newspaper columnist R. G. Lynch had this to say about these pioneers who depicted this as a historic juncture for the city: "Men of vision, the men who play important roles in the molding of Milwaukee for its future, stood in a row on a bluff overlooking the Menomonee River Valley Thursday afternoon . . . Men and trucks were working on the city dump, which has partly filled the old Story quarry, but the men on the bluff did not see the men and trucks. Their eyes were looking into the future—and they saw the steel and green grass of a stadium."

Milwaukee city officials look over the Story Parkway stone quarry in 1949, their top choice as a site for a new municipal stadium.

Ground was broken on October 19, 1950, and although steel shortages caused by the Korean War hampered construction, County Stadium was finally ready for the Brewers to move over from Borchert Field and begin play in 1953. Or so they thought. It turned out that Boston's Braves would become the new tenant for 13 seasons.

County Stadium was the first publicly financed ballpark in the country and ended up costing between $5 million and $6 million, the price of a decent starting pitcher in today's climate, a luxury that small-market teams such as the Brewers usually can't afford. The facility never won any beauty contests, but it assumed a prominent role during Milwaukee's post-World War II growth. "Here was a community, after the war, searching for an identity," Bud Selig said while reminiscing about his old home office while preparing to move into his new one at Miller Park. "The Arena was built and the library, the museum and the war memorial. And County Stadium became part of that growth. There were a lot of critics, not only of getting the stadium built but of where they were building it. That sounds familiar, doesn't it? Stadium controversies are a certainty of life, just like death and taxes."

Still, fans in Milwaukee and southern Wisconsin, many of whose allegiances favored the Cubs or the White Sox, got behind their new team as did few others in history, something that still amazed Tom Kaminski in the final days of the team's occupation in September 2000. "Everybody bent over backward for the team," said Kaminski, who was one of the batboys when the Braves arrived and later became an airline representative for the club. "County Stadium was nice and accessible, very convenient. People just wanted to be there." And people representing all walks of life, from the struggling blue-collar factory workers who formed the city's backbone to the well-to-do folks who traveled from their palatial digs along the lakeshore, people who were seldom seen together during the average day, came together for 9 or 10 or however many innings it took for

An aerial view shows County Stadium just about ready to welcome its first major league occupant, the Milwaukee Braves.

their Braves to win another one for "Bushville."

From 1953 until another expansion in '73, patients from the Veterans Administration Hospital could sit outside their rooms on Mockingbird Hill and view games for free from beyond the right-field corner. There was also Perini's Woods, a grove of spruce and fir trees behind the center-field fence that was planted in 1954 and replaced when bleachers were added seven years later. Also in 1961, a picnic area called Braves Reservation was added down the left-field line.

Frank Clines, a sports copy editor and occasional columnist for the *Milwaukee Journal Sentinel*, wrote these words in a September 2000 article: "The stadium itself was never much to look at. No ivy on the walls, no huge green wall in left field to gape at, no fancy facade on the upper deck, no towering office buildings or charming apartment houses just beyond the walls. Just a nice, useful place built by a town that wanted major-league baseball very, very much. County Stadium was, almost to the end, simply about the game—and about being with each other. And it was perfect for Milwaukee."

Those feelings and moments are etched in people's minds, especially somebody such as Selig, who was a fan long before he began fighting to keep the team from leaving. "When Billy Bruton hit the home run off Enos Slaughter's glove to win the game, it was just wild," Selig said of the Braves' first contest at County Stadium. "It became a love affair with the intensity that no one could have predicted."

Selig attended as many games as his studies allowed during the next several seasons, but his University of Wisconsin education took a distant second place on a chilly September evening in 1957 when Hank Aaron's dramatic home run gave Milwaukee its first pennant. Against his mother's wishes, even though she also was a baseball lover, Selig skipped an accounting class that evening and bought one of the few remaining tickets in the upper deck. "When Hank hit that home run, I remember sitting there and crying," Selig said. "I was so happy. It was really one of those great moments you never forget."

Which, to this day, makes the Braves' fall from their lofty pedestal so stunning and hard to understand. Despite repeating as National League titlists in 1958, the team failed to reach the two million mark in attendance for the first time in five years. A county board ruling in 1961 that prohibited carry-ins of beer only alienated more fans and widened the schism.

"There was a series of things that contributed to their demise in Milwaukee," Selig said. "It was like many things in life-all of the above. The Braves didn't promote very well. There was some shortsightedness in the public sector. It turned very negative. Then, they were gone."

And that was the beginning of a dreary, four-year hiatus in which religious gatherings, rock 'n' roll concerts, boxing matches, and anything else that would help pay the rent for an empty stadium tried to lure fans. The White Sox brought in almost 197,000 for 11 "home" games in Milwaukee while drawing only 393,000 the rest of the 1969 season in Chicago. Finally, the Pilots abandoned Seattle, changed their name, and called the place home for 31 years.

Their heroes didn't post a winning record until their ninth season, but when success-starved fans finally got a taste they reciprocated, making series against the Yankees and Red Sox in the late 1970s and early '80s into parties and opportunities to take their frustrations out on guys like Reggie Jackson. However, only one serious pennant chase (1992) and the loss of their most revered players—Robin Yount, Paul Molitor, and Jim Gantner—sapped much of the energy out of the franchise, the crowds, and, therefore, County Stadium. Opening day was always a big fiesta, but packed houses seldom gathered except for during the great home run chase between Chicago's Sammy Sosa and Saint Louis's Mark McGuire in 1998.

More than 73 million fans attended exhibition, regular-season, and postseason baseball and football tussles at County Stadium. And did they ever imbibe, to the tune of almost 36 million cups of what made Milwaukee famous, plus 10 million sodas. They couldn't drink and not eat, consuming 12.3 million hot dogs and 8.9 million bratwurst.

For those who played or worked at the stadium, it was tough to say goodbye. "It's like putting on an old pair of shoes," Gorman Thomas once said. "The new place looks fantastic, but this place is home."

It certainly was for Selig. "It may not have the history, tradition, and symbolism of Wrigley Field or Fenway Park, but in the end, it's where generations of people grew up," he said. "It's where we'll always have a lifetime of memories."

"It's time for it to go, but it's a place I'll always love," Selig noted on another occasion. "County Stadium produced, for two to three generations of people, great memories. It was a bond between fathers, mothers, and children. You can ask yourself, because of County Stadium, was Milwaukee and Wisconsin a better place to live? The answer is so clearly yes that it's not even worth debate."

A record crowd of 56,354 created another unforgettable memory, squeezing into the place for the Brewers' final game on September 28, 2000, most of them not caring that the team had fallen to Cincinnati (8–1) to culminate another losing season but waiting to pay tribute to the former stars as they assembled on the field one last time. The 100-minute farewell ceremony, a classic event for the ages, was emceed by Bob Uecker; former Braves play-by-play man Earl Gillespie; and Uecker's mentor, Merle Harmon and began with a 15-minute video presentation highlighting great moments in stadium history.

Then came the procession of luminaries, with Hank Aaron, Andy Pafko, Johnny Logan, Bob Buhl, Red Schoendienst, Lew Burdette, Del Crandall, Frank Torre, and Warren Spahn representing Milwaukee's first generation of ballplayers. Rollie Fingers, Darrell Porter, Jim Gantner, Danny Walton, Sixto Lezcano, Ken Sanders, Charlie Moore, Lew Krausse, Larry Hisle, Gorman Thomas, Jim Slaton, Don Money, Ben Oglivie, Jerry Augustine, Juan Nieves, Johnny Briggs, Cecil Cooper, Rob Deer, Ron Theobald, Harvey Kuenn's widow Audrey, Paul Molitor, Bill Castro, Moose Haas, Dale Sveum, Mike Caldwell, Tom Trebelhorn, and Robin Yount represented the second.

Yount brought the house down again with his second thrilling entrance aboard a motorcycle, causing the exact same goose bumps he did when he rode in from the bullpen during the post-World Series celebration in 1982.

Broadcaster Bob Uecker delivers a moving eulogy during closing ceremonies at County Stadium after the venerable park's final game, September 28, 2000.

So it was only appropriate that "the Kid" handed a flag, one that had passed through each of the former players' hands, to Mark Loretta for the current Brewers to take a short but sentimental journey.

"Fellas, twenty-five years ago I played my first big-league game here at County Stadium," Yount said. "It's a great honor to be selected to present this flag to you. Each of us has touched this flag today, symbolic of how County Stadium has touched us. Take this flag to Miller Park, your new home, with the same desire and dedication that has made us all proud to perform under it. And don't ever forget where it all started."

And the festivities concluded with Uecker's impassioned eulogy:

County Stadium, here you are in all your glory, silhouetted against the night. Forty-eight years have slipped away like a blink of an eye, yet the memories housed within your walls will live on forever. At first, you were called a jewel in the waiting, though soon a suitor would come forward. You promised to welcome all who visited, and they came—first, by the thousands, then by the millions.

A champion was born in your midst, and you stood proud, when the rest of the world wondered how. Yet those good times could not last. Brokenhearted, unwanted emptiness became sadness. Yet you never asked why. For perhaps, just perhaps, you alone knew that the spring would bloom again.

Oh, how you've changed, in so many ways, yet one thing remains: A bond between heroes and fans, and an ambition to succeed. It was here that boys became men, men became champions, and champions became legends.

It is a very sad time for me, for I have been here as a fan and as a player, and for the last 30 years as a broadcaster. But tonight is the final curtain. It's time to say good-bye. We will never forget you, for what was, will always be. So long, old friend, and good-night, everybody.

And with those touching last words, the final lights went out. The venerable stadium, which had twice welcomed major league baseball, had been laid to rest.

That evening and what it represented will remain in people's hearts. A few weeks later, in November 2000, hundreds of diehard fans attended an auction, making sure County Stadium would be stashed away in their basements and garages as they left the parking lot, cast in the shadows of Miller Park, with pieces of the stadium. Among the pricier items were Yount's locker ($3,150); a Harley-Davidson outfield wall pad ($1,000); a seat that Yount, Aaron, and Molitor had signed ($2,000); and the original Bernie Brewer chalet ($5,000). Bidding had begun on the Internet two months earlier and solicited more than 1,300 offers, mostly from Wisconsinites but also from folks as far away as California, Florida, and Australia. Bricks, urinals, coolers, a popcorn popper, the ticket printer, and even dirt were gobbled up, with proceeds helping to pay for the demolition of County Stadium and going to charitable causes.

"When they tear this old place down, they're going to take a piece of my heart with it," Aaron had said. On February 21, 2001, a crew from Midwest Rail and Dismantling pulled down the last remaining section of the stadium's upper deck.

"I drove out today on the freeway and I noticed there was no County Stadium, and it was one of the strangest feelings I've ever had," Selig said. "It's a little bit sad, to say the least, but happy in so many other ways looking at Miller Park. This is a very strange feeling. I have a lot of great memories. I know that Miller Park will serve the next two generations as proudly and as well as County Stadium served our generation. This wasn't unexpected, it's just eerie. But I'm so proud of Miller Park . . . people have a lot to look forward to."

At County Stadium, fans got to witness 211 of Eddie Mathews's home runs, 195 of Aaron's, and 124 of Yount's. They saw Cooper, Oglivie, and Sveum smack three round-trippers in a game. They watched as Jim Wilson, Burdette, and Spahn tossed a combined four no-hitters.

Cooper, like many of those players who performed across the parking lot from Miller Park, still has a soft spot for the old place. "Miller Park is a nice and beautiful new facility, but it's not County Stadium," he said. "That place had a different feeling. I got to know every nook and cranny."

Gregg Hoffmann did the same as a fan and as a journalist during his time living and working in Milwaukee, so he had plenty to reminisce about.

My favorite moment at County Stadium was my first game as a kid, with my dad. My hero, Eddie Mathews, hit a walk-off homer. I own the seats we sat in. Second would have to be the last out in the 1982 playoffs. I wanted to stand there and watch the spectacle but knew if I didn't hustle to the clubhouse I would never get in to do my interviews. That famous Easter Day game in 1987, when [Rob] Deer and [Dale] Sveum hit those homers, also was a thrill. Maybe my most consistent memory is getting to the ballpark early, often around 3 p.m. for a night game, and watching it come alive during the next few hours.

Hoffmann retired as a professor at UW-Milwaukee in 2004 and resides in Westby. He said any baseball park is one of the great places in the world, and you never know what you're going to see.

"I saw a lot of crazy things, but the weirdest were the time the skunk ran across the field and into the bullpen, when indeed the Brewers' pen did stink," Hoffmann said. "Then there was the dog they hired to chase away seagulls that were swarming in to catch some kind of insect that was hatching. The dog crapped in left field after running itself ragged between innings. Finally, I would pick Rick Manning being booed when he drove in the winning run with Paul Molitor on deck. The fans wanted to see Molly bat so he could extend his hitting streak to 40."

And as Frank Clines wrote, it was much more.

It was a place where, almost a half-century ago, love for a baseball team was so total, so innocent, that no way of showing it could be considered foolish. A place whose emptiness after just 13 seasons taught a painful lesson about that kind of trust. But ultimately, a place people returned to for another three decades, more skeptical but no less eager for fun. County Stadium was the old family home, creaky and dusty, renovations tacked on over the years, with an ancient black-and-white TV flickering away and a pair of worn-out shoes lying in the front hall. Drafty, cramped, even a little embarrassing after all these years. But ours.

But not anymore, as a new era began next door.

MILLER PARK

So many good things had happened there, but Bud Selig and his ownership group knew that County Stadium had outlived its usefulness, that baseball's big-dollar free agent system was already running amok and teams and cities such as Milwaukee were going to be trampled in the rubble if something didn't change. This was during the late 1980s, and Selig started sending out signals that his team couldn't survive much longer without a better revenue-producing facility.

In March 1987, the Greater Milwaukee Committee formed a task force to study the feasibility of building a new park versus renovating the rapidly deteriorating County Stadium. Partly because it estimated that renovations would cost $100 million and not fix all of the problems, the task force, in April 1988, recommended that a new stadium be built with the goal of having it ready for opening day 1992. Besides the existing site in the Menomonee Valley, members discussed three others: Oak Creek, downtown near the Summerfest grounds, and the County Grounds.

Arm wrestling and political maneuvering continued, with Selig strongly endorsing the current site in 1990 and shooting for opening day 1994. Private financing was still at the center of discussions, while talk of a roof entered the picture.

In 1991, Wisconsin governor Tommy Thompson unveiled a state development plan, and the assembly and senate approved financial assistance. However, obstacles emerged the next year, including environmental concerns over a rare rock formation and threatened wildflowers. The Brewers pushed back their calendar again, to 1996. Then politics got in the way as Milwaukee

Mayor John Norquist said other options should be explored, while state senator Gary George proposed a sports lottery to finance a downtown location. In 1994, the club called a press conference to announce that the facility should feature a convertible roof and that a combination of public and private funding would be needed. That fall the Green Bay Packers decided not to play any more home games at County Stadium, prompting those in the baseball community to act if they wanted to keep professional sports in the city.

In January 1995, the Brewers committed $60 million to $90 million for the cost of the stadium. Six financing ideas were introduced, including the state lottery, which was shot down in the April 1995 elections. In August, a memorandum of understanding stipulated a $90 million input from the Brewers and included a 30-year lease commitment. The package featured a one-tenth of 1 percent sales tax and hotel-motel room tax for Milwaukee and Waukesha counties to finance another $160 million. Washington, Ozaukee, and Racine counties were later added to the baseball district, while the hotel tax portion was eliminated.

Supporters received a boost from none other than one of Milwaukee's adversaries from the 1957–58 New York Yankees, Milwaukee native Tony Kubek, whose letter to the editor was published in the *Journal Sentinel* on September 18, 1995, and included these words:

Having spent 41 years observing the rapidly changing baseball landscape doesn't qualify one to be an expert on building a ballpark or, more to the point, making a definitive commentary regarding the socioeconomic impact on the area. However, as my former teammate and baseball scholar emeritus, Yogi Berra, once said, "You can see a lot by looking." I've done that on my walks and cab rides to and from ballparks in every city throughout the country, along with having conversations and interviews with baseball fans and non-fans alike.

Not so surprising to me, these people all manifested a deep feeling of pride in their community when talking about "their new ballpark."

Like Milwaukee, these cities have their share of warts. A new ballpark won't solve all of our ills but will certainly improve the quality of life for each of us. If we don't derive direct benefits from it, perhaps our grandchildren, a relative, friend, or neighbor a generation or two removed will.

What is happening in the cities mentioned above is a terrific testimony for why a new ballpark should be built and how it will be beneficial for all of us. Of equal importance, and perhaps paramount, is the question, for whom should the ballpark be built? Don't build it for the governor, the mayor, or the Brewers' ownership. Let's build it for ourselves. Let's maintain our reputation as one of the Midwest's finest places to be.

Regardless of who was on which side, the fate of the stadium—and of the team—wasn't decided until October 6 at the State Capitol. The assembly debated all day and voted 52–47 in favor of the financing plan. However, the senate chambers provided the real drama as members shot down the idea shortly after midnight before meeting in caucuses. The senate reconvened at 5 a.m., and Racine Republican George Petak changed his no vote to a yes, allowing the proposal to pass, 16–15. The brave reversal eventually cost Petak his seat in a recall election, but Thompson signed the legislation October 12. Then in March 1996, Miller Brewing Company announced a $41.2 million, 20-year naming rights deal. Miller Park was born.

Officials in Milwaukee continued to argue about financing alternatives and locations, prompting Selig and supporters to hold a press conference to plead their case. Chants of "Bud, Bud" were heard at the game that night, and eight days later 10,000 fans attended a rally that finally silenced the debate. Approximately 15,000 people showed up for the groundbreaking, which featured Robin Yount and Hank Aaron, on November 9, 1996.

Slowly fans and passersby could see something special going on as Miller Park began to take shape. For the umpteenth time a completion date was set: opening day 2000. But those dreams and the lives of three families were shattered July 14, 1999, when Big Blue, a 567-foot crane used to lift pieces of the roof, collapsed while installing a 400-ton structure. It hit a basket suspended from a crane inside the park, killing workers Jeffrey Wischer, William DeGrave, and Jerome Starr. Grieving started, as did the cleanup, a task that lasted six weeks, delaying construction and forcing the team to postpone its grand opening until 2001.

On July 30, 1999, all Miller Park workers received free admission to a game at County Stadium, at which a moment of silence was observed for their fallen comrades. Donations from ticket sales, fans, and employees raised $100,000 for the three families.

Meanwhile, the first roof lift since the accident took place in January 2000, and other tangible signs of progress sprouted up throughout the year, including Bernie Brewer's dugout and massive, high-tech scoreboard. Then came the emotional closing ceremony. As the last light standard at County Stadium went dark, fireworks exploded over Miller Park. As Gregg Hoffmann wrote in *The Making of Miller Park*, "It was a symbolic scene, of the old being replaced by the new, of an ending yet a beginning, of the transition in eras."

Baseball in Beertown

A sign announcing the Brewers inaugural game at Miller Park in 2001
provides a beacon of hope in the middle of a gray Wisconsin winter.

Hoffmann said the organization would have been forced to sell, relocate, or both had things not worked out the way they did. "I do believe the Seligs would have had to sell to somebody who would have moved the team if there was not a new stadium," he said in 2004. "I loved County Stadium, but if people saw it in its bowels, like we did every night, they would have known it was a dump. It was a year or two away from dropping concrete like Wrigley is now."

The 43,000-seat park is definitely a state-of-the-art facility. It features 550 TV monitors and 2,000 stereo speakers, 10 escalators, 30 permanent concession stands, 66 restrooms, kids' interactive areas and a fan zone, restaurants, a retail outlet, and many more amenities. And don't forget the problematic roof, which covers about 10 acres and weighs 12,000 tons. And which, despite a few leaks, has prevented any games from getting rained out and has made it much more comfortable for fans early and late in the season.

Opening day finally arrived on April 6, 2001. A crowd of 42,024 watched the Brewers get revenge against Cincinnati for the setback in the County Stadium finale, posting a 5–4 victory over the Reds. While most fans loved the new digs, the team and its fancy playground had its share of detractors, as these letters to the editor of the *Milwaukee Journal Sentinel* proved.

Such Extravagance Not Necessary

I attended the first exhibition game at Miller Park, and it was obvious that this stadium is quite an engineering feat. From another perspective, this multimillion-dollar structure appears to be an example of grotesque overkill for providing 18 men a place with which to play a game as well as a blatant example of abusing the political process. The considerations such as computerized vendors, waiters delivering food and beverages right to one's club seat, or the limited access to the luxurious .300 Club are either unavailable or unaffordable to the average fans, taxpayers, and ticket holders who had stadium financing crammed down their already overtaxed throats. This speaks to the elitist nature of professional baseball, not to mention the overt hijacking of the political process by special interests. Clearly, the interests being served here are those of Major League Baseball, corporations, politicians, and other privileged types.

—*John T. Sau, Milwaukee*

It's Wonderful but Something's Missing

The new stadium is certainly a work of art and unbelievable engineering. Something is missing, though. St. Paul, Minn., where I grew up, had a stadium with a board fence. Kids could look through the knotholes and get a glimpse of Babe Ruth, Dizzy Dean, and his brother, to name a few. That is what is missing in the new stadium: knotholes.

—*Don J. Eggum, Waukesha*

Baseball Out of Reach for Some Families

Once again, Milwaukee has built something that may be out of reach for the poor—Miller Park. Let's do the arithmetic. Let's say a family of five wants to sit in the terrace outfield box area at $14 per ticket. That's $70. Add to that the cost of overpriced refreshments, and you're well over $100. Because of league expansion, we have a lot of good amateurs with very few greats like those of yesteryear. My sense is that the prices to watch these amateurs are inflated to the point where the poor may be left out. Perhaps the league could provide discounted tickets for those on disability incomes or for those who are unemployed yet want to be a part of a wholesome activity—American baseball.

—*David M. Molling, Milwaukee*

No Surprise that Brewers Can't Compete

Those of us who opposed the building of Miller Park would hardly call the Journal Sentinel's *April 5 front-page article "Baseball Isn't Safe at*

Home" news. The fact that the Brewers can't compete in the major leagues has been known for years and is exactly why Miller Park is a fool's panacea and a waste of taxpayers' money. If by some fluke the Brewers have a good year, any player with big numbers will play for the Yankees or the Braves the following year. Bud Selig was able to fool taxpayers into giving their money away, but he won't have as gullible an audience when he asks George Steinbrenner to give up his.

—Mark Altendorf, Eagle

Obviously the cost of attending a game is a major factor, especially for the thousands of fans who have to pay for gas and drive hundreds of miles from the hinterlands of the Badger State. And sure, every park has its quirks and nobody's going to like everything. Change is inevitable. For example, Bernie Brewer's family sent him away for the weekend so the TLC crew of "While You Were Out" could modernize his schmaltzy chalet and giant beer mug into an upscale joint with a slide, balloons, and light show. So what? It's a good thing because it means the good guys have just hit a homer or won the game.

The replay board's high-definition clarity is much better than the black-and-white version at County Stadium. Every seat in the place points toward second base, and the front row is 60 feet from home plate, which is six inches closer than the pitcher's rubber. The homier, old-time feel and look of the stadium is worth the price of admission.

Fans found more good than bad, as more than 2.8 million flocked in to see Miller Park during the team's first season there. That's almost 500,000 more than the 1983 high-water mark at County Stadium. Certainly the novelty has worn off during the past three seasons, but methinks that's due more to bad baseball than anything else.

Dale Hofmann said fans will grow to appreciate Miller Park in time, but winning sure wouldn't hurt.

Miller Park has seemed jinxed at times, with the accident, roof problems, controversies over finances, etc., but overall I think it is a great place that someday will be appreciated more than it is today. The ballpark was built for the community, not the Seligs or millionaire players. The 1/10th of a cent [sales tax] never broke my bank when I lived in Milwaukee County.

The bitterness over Miller Park did sour me a little on Milwaukee as a baseball town. The Braves are one of the great stories in the history of baseball, but Milwaukee is a bit of a front-runner town now. Nevertheless, there are a lot of people who would like to be good baseball fans if the

Brewers ever give them something to get excited about for a full season. Maybe if the team is sold, and the new owners have deeper pockets, that might happen.

Regardless, Bud Selig said that both ballparks have stood and will stand the test of time and remind people how important baseball has been and what it's meant to the city and state.

"There have been so many wonderful players and so many great moments here," Selig said via phone. "People with vision and courage built County Stadium not even knowing they'd get a team, and then the Braves came along. And then we got the Brewers. And despite everything we went through to get Miller Park. The important question is whether having a major league team made Milwaukee a better place, socially, economically, or whatever, and the answer is an unequivocal yes."

Bud Selig gets a standing ovation before
Milwaukee's first game at Miller Park in 2001.

On This Date

August 21, 1866. The Forest City Club of Rockford, Illinois, visited Milwaukee and defeated the local Cream Citys, 24–10. Future Hall of Famer Albert Spalding pitched for Forest City.

July 30, 1869. The Cincinnati Red Stockings, the first team made up of all professional ball players, stopped in Milwaukee as part of its yearlong nationwide tour. The Red Stockings whipped the Cream Citys, 85–7, and went undefeated on their 65–game tour.

1904–1916 and 1922–25. Harry "Pep" Clark played in more games (1,834) than anybody in American Association history, all for the Milwaukee Brewers.

April 15, 1921. The Brewers claimed a 7–4 victory in nine innings against Saint Paul in a game played in the snow and 30-degree temperatures. A crowd of 176 showed up. Umpires asked Milwaukee owner Otto Borchert and he said, "Play ball." Snow piled up to the top of the fences overnight, so Borchert had trucks haul it away. Games were postponed for five days.

1926. The Milwaukee Brewers established an American Association record with a 21-game winning streak.

1927. Harry Riconda finished 255-for-722 for a .353 average, topping the Brewers with 18 triples and a franchise-record 57 doubles, which led the league.

1928. Bevo LeBourveau, who compiled a .358 career average in AA play from 1924 to 1933, hit .399 in 266 at-bats for Milwaukee in 1928, his first of two years with the club. It was the highest Brewers mark since George Stone's .405 in 1904.

1931. Anton "Tony" Kubek batted .357 in 280 at-bats in his first full season with the Brewers. He finished above .300 the next two seasons, spending six years (1930–35) with the club. He was the father of former New York Yankees star turned broadcaster Tony Kubek.

1936. Forest "Tot" Pressnell, Joe Heving, and Luke "Hot Potato" Hamlin each won 19 games (against a combined 35 losses) in helping the Brewers to a 90–64 finish under Al Sothoron. Milwaukee native Chet Laabs, who later played for Detroit and Saint Louis in the majors, swatted a league-leading 42 homers while driving in a team-topping 151 runs and batted .324.

1937. Milwaukee native Ken Keltner, who later played 12 of his 13 big-league seasons with Cleveland, led the Brewers with 27 homers and 120 runs while batting .310. He also topped the AA with 92 strikeouts.

1938. Brewers' pitcher Whitlow Wyatt dominated AA batters, leading the league with 23 victories, a .767 winning percentage (only seven losses), 32 starts, nine shutouts, 208 strikeouts, and a 2.37 ERA. Wyatt compiled a 106–95 mark in the majors from 1929 to 1945 in a career that included stops in Detroit, Chicago (AL), and Brooklyn.

1945. Brewers outfielder Lew "Noisy" Flick cranked a league-high 215 hits and topped the AA with a .374 average in 575 at-bats. He led the team with 32 doubles and 10 triples and was second with 90 RBIs.

1950. Len Pearson, the Brewers' first black player, was a first baseman who hit .305 in 223 at-bats.

April 23, 1954. Henry Aaron clubbed the first of his 755 major league home runs, a solo smash against Vic Raschi, as the Braves defeated the Cardinals, 7–5, at Sportsman's Park in Saint Louis.

September 6, 1954. Eddie Mathews powered Milwaukee to a doubleheader sweep of the Cubs, 13–2 and 6–1, at County Stadium. Mathews finished with eight consecutive base hits before lining out in his final trip to the plate. The attendance of 43,207 pushed the Braves over the two million mark for the first time. The triumphs also stretched the hosts' winning streak to nine games.

September 22, 1954. What a wacky finish—almost. Cincinnati and Milwaukee battled until the ninth inning at County Stadium. In the top half, the Redlegs put runners on first and second and Bob Borkowski struck out on a wild pitch. Braves' catcher Del Crandall retrieved the ball and fired to third to nail the lead runner. Meanwhile, Borkowski took off for first—illegally, because that base was already occupied with less than two outs. He drew a throw, which hit him in the back and rolled into right field, so he and the man on second scored. The umpires ruled both runners out, thus giving Milwaukee a 3–1 victory. However, Cincinnati protested and because five teams were affected, NL president Warren Giles upheld the protest, even though he believed the correct call was made. The game was played two days later, with the Braves hanging on for a 4–3 win.

May 26, 1956. Cincinnati pitchers Johnny Klippstein, Hersh Freeman, and Joe Black combined to no-hit the Braves for 9 2/3 innings. Klippstein walked eight in seven hitless innings before he gave way to Freeman for one. Black then walked two during his stint and finally gave up a two-out double to Jack Dittmer in the 10th and two more hits in the 11th to lose, 2–1. Hank Aaron's triple and two intentional walks set up Frank Torre's game-winning single. This was the eighth no-hitter lost in extra innings and the only combined-effort one. Milwaukee starter Ray Crone didn't allow a run until Wally Post's RBI double with two outs in the ninth. Torre knocked in both of Milwaukee's runs.

May 30–31, 1956. Neither team brought much pitching to this doubleheader slugfest at Wrigley Field. Chicago's Russ Meyer dished up consecutive homers to Eddie Mathews, Hank Aaron, and Bobby Thomson in the first inning. Meyer hit the next batter, Billy Bruton, with a pitch. Bruton charged the mound, and both players were ejected after the ensuing fight. The Cubs pushed across three runs in their half of the first against Bob Buhl, and reliever Turk Lown homered in the second for his first big-league round-tripper. Thomson added another home run, but the Braves lost the opener, 10–9. However, Milwaukee hung on to win the second contest, 11–9. Fifteen home runs in the two games, including Thomson's four, established a major league record for a twin bill. All but three of them were solo shots. The rivals continued pounding away the next day as the Braves claimed a 15–8 victory that went to Lew Burdette. Chicago's Paul Minner absorbed his 12th straight setback to the Braves, a streak that started August 29, 1951.

June 17, 1956. First baseman Joe Adcock and the Braves handed new manager Fred Haney two victories on his first full day in the dugout, posting 5–4 and 3–1 victories at Brooklyn's Ebbets Field. Adcock smacked 3 of his record 13 homers in the historic park before 34,394 fans. In the first game, his game-winning ninth-inning homer off Ed Roebuck landed on the roof, making him the only slugger to accomplish the feat. The ball left the field at the 350-foot mark in left field, clearing the 83-foot wall.

April 21, 1957. Warren Spahn got the victory as Milwaukee stayed unbeaten at 4–0 with a 3–1 triumph over Cincinnati at County Stadium. Base-running gaffes helped do the Reds in. Reds' base runner Don Hoak broke up a double play by fielding Wally Post's grounder and flipping it to Braves shortstop Johnny Logan. Hoak was called out for interference, but Post was given a single. During Milwaukee's 5–4 decision the day before, Cincinnati runner Johnny Temple let Gus Bell's ground ball hit him, with the same result: Temple was called out for interfering and Bell was awarded a single. Four days after the second incident, Major League Baseball adopted a rule that prohibited runners from interfering with a batted ball in any way.

May 24, 1957. Cubs rookie Frank Ernaga belted a solo homer in the second inning and followed with an RBI triple in the fourth, both against Warren Spahn, as Chicago prevailed, 5–1, at Wrigley Field. Ernaga hit only one more HR in his career.

May 26, 1957. At Wrigley Field, 20-year-old rookie Dick Drott struck out 15 Braves, including Hank Aaron and Billy Bruton three times apiece, en route to Chicago's 7–5 victory in game one of a doubleheader that the Cubs would sweep with a 5–4 verdict. Drott's 15 Ks set a Cubs twentieth-century mark for nine innings (since broken by Kerry Wood) and was one shy of John Clarkson's 1886 club mark. He went on to win 15 times, the most for a Cubs rookie since Pat Malone earned 18 victories in 1928.

July 31, 1957. The Braves and pitcher Bob Buhl stopped Pittsburgh, 4–2. Bucs manager—and future Milwaukee skipper—Bobby Bragan was ejected in the bottom of the fifth for making obscene gestures. Before departing, he strolled onto the field while sipping an orange drink through a straw and offering the umpires a taste. Two days later, Bragan was fired.

June 23, 1958. Carlton Willey of the Braves pitched a 7–0 shutout against the Giants in his first major league start. The 27-year-old right-hander allowed six hits, including Willie Mays's 1,000th career hit. Willey received help from Joe Adcock, playing left field for the first time since 1952, who climbed the fence to snag a ball. Don McMahon relieved Willey, becoming the first pitcher to be driven to the mound—a motor scooter with sidecar delivered him from the bullpen.

May 26, 1959. Harvey Haddix of the Pirates pitched a perfect game for 12 innings at County Stadium, only to lose in the 13th. Felix Mantilla reached on an error to open the last inning. A sacrifice and an intentional walk to Hank Aaron brought up Joe Adcock, who drilled one out of the park in right-center for what everybody thought was a 3–0 victory. However, Aaron started to leave the field, and Adcock passed him on the base path. Both were called out as Mantilla scored, officially making it 1–0. Lew Burdette went all 13 innings for his eighth win, scattering 12 hits. As a consequence of the base-running blunder, the Braves stranded a National League record-low one runner. Haddix's gem made him the ninth pitcher to lose a no-hitter in extra innings. Making his effort even more remarkable was the fact that the Braves' hitters apparently knew what was coming: In 1993, Bob Buhl said that Milwaukee's pitchers stole signs from Smoky Burgess, who could not crouch down all the way. They placed a towel on the bullpen fence in certain ways to signal fastball or breaking ball.

August 2, 1959. Lew Burdette was the beneficiary of Billy Bruton's offensive explosion as Milwaukee gained a split of a twin bill against Saint Louis at County Stadium. The speedy Bruton laced three triples, two of them with the bases loaded, to help the Braves spank Cardinals' starter Vinegar Bend Mizell during an 11–5 victory. Saint Louis had won the opener, 4–3.

August 15, 1960. Eddie Mathews, always ready to protect his teammates in a scuffle, got into one of his own in the first game of a doubleheader at Cincinnati's Crosley Field. Reds' star Frank Robinson slid hard into third base in the seventh inning of the hosts' 5–3 win, prompting an exchange of punches. Robinson came out on the short end of things, sustaining a swollen eye, bloody nose, and jammed thumb. However, Robinson came back to smack a home run and double in the nightcap, a 4–0 decision in which Cincy hurler Bob Purkey got the shutout despite giving up 11 hits.

May 3, 1961. Mel Roach's misplay in left field ended Warren Spahn's bid for a second straight no-hitter, but it didn't cost the Braves a 4–1 victory over the Dodgers. Spahn settled for a two-hitter in his showdown against Stan Williams.

August 17–20, 1961. Offense reigned despite a pitching matchup of Milwaukee's Bob Buhl and Braves' nemesis Robin Roberts of Philadelphia. In the first contest of a five-game series at County Stadium, the Braves pulled out a 7–6 victory in 11 innings. Al Spangler singled home the winning run after the hosts overcame a 6–4 deficit in the eighth inning when Joe Adcock slammed a two-run homer against Art Mahaffey. Milwaukee won the second game, 4–1, behind Lew Burdette. Tony Cloninger allowed 13 hits, but the Braves hung on for a 4–3 decision in game three. The Phils rallied in the ninth but stranded 11 runners. Hard-luck loser Frank Sullivan allowed only seven hits as the Braves scored all of their runs in the third inning, the big blow being Frank Thomas's two-run homer. Milwaukee extended the Phils' losing streak to 23 games, a modern big-league record, while extending its winning string to 10 games with Warren Spahn's 5–2 triumph in the first of two Sunday encounters. Philadelphia stopped the bleeding with a 7–4 win in the finale.

September 19, 1961. The Giants clobbered Warren Spahn for four homers, including Willie Mays's grand slam, and rallied in the last two innings for an 11–10 win at Candlestick Park. The foes combined for eight HRs and 57 total bases, but the short ball pulled it out for San Francisco as future Brewers' skipper Harvey Kuenn delivered a tie-breaking single in the eighth and Ed Bailey smacked a bases-loaded single in the ninth.

April 30, 1962. Philadelphia finally figured out a way to defeat Warren Spahn, posting a 6–4 triumph at Shibe Park after dropping 11 games in a row to the Braves' ace lefty. Milwaukee also shipped Bob Buhl to the Cubs for pitcher Jack Curtis. Buhl was coming off his first losing record since 1954 but would be a solid starter for Chicago with 51 victories during the next four seasons. Buhl also set a major league mark of futility as a batter, going 0-for-70 during the year.

May 29, 1962. Chicago's Ernie Banks made a spectacular return after being beaned May 25, clubbing three homers and a double against the Braves at Wrigley Field. Three other Cubs hit long balls, but Milwaukee received homers from Amado Samuel, his first in the big leagues; Joe Torre; and Joe Adcock in the visitors' 11–9 win. Chicago outhit the Braves, 15–8, but Andre Rodgers's error opened the gates for six unearned runs in the third.

June 12, 1962. Lew Burdette silenced the powerful Dodgers' bats while his teammates pounded Johnny Podres at County Stadium, 15–2. Milwaukee's Aaron brothers, Hank and Tommie, belted homers in the same game for the first time. They did it two more times that year. Hank registered three hits and drove in three before retiring in the seventh for pinch hitter Lee Maye, the first of six batters who ended up pinch-hitting for Aaron in his career.

July 11, 1962. Tommie and Hank Aaron formed a winning combination again for the Braves when they became the first brothers since Paul and Lloyd Waner in 1938 to hit round-trippers in the same inning, teeing off in the bottom of the ninth. Hank's grand slam provided the difference as Milwaukee rallied past the Cardinals, 8–6.

July 26, 1962. Warren Spahn not only did his part on the mound for Milwaukee, but he crunched his 31st career homer off Craig Anderson during a 6–1 home victory against the Mets. Spahn's HR set a National League standard for pitchers. It was also New York's 11th straight loss.

May 4, 1963. Milwaukee starter Bob Shaw placed his name in the record books for something he would have liked to have forgotten. Shaw shattered the existing mark for balks in a game when he was called for five during a 7–5 setback to the Cubs at County Stadium. He committed three in the third inning alone, tying the big-league standard that had been established the previous week.

May 21, 1963. Jim Maloney of the Reds outdueled Bob Hendley at County Stadium in a 2–0 Cincinnati victory. In the process, Maloney tied the modern major league record with eight consecutive strikeouts, sending Braves hitters down from the first to the fourth innings. Maloney finished with 16 Ks but needed relief help from Bill Henry, who retired the last two Milwaukee batters.

June 28, 1963. Warren Spahn won more games than any left-handed pitcher in history (363), but he always had trouble against the Dodgers, especially on the road. However, he didn't on this day at Dodger Stadium. He and the Braves, kicking off a six-city, 21-day road trip, earned a 1–0 decision against Don Drysdale, tossing a three-hitter. It was the first time Spahn, who entered with a 19–34 mark overall against L.A., had beaten the Dodgers on their home grounds since August 21, 1948. He had lost 14 consecutive times, nine at Ebbets Field in Brooklyn and four at Memorial Coliseum and one at Chavez Ravine in Los Angeles. Milwaukee scored the game's only run on Joe Torre's sacrifice fly after loading the bases in the first inning. It was Spahn's 58th career shutout and the Braves' third in their last four outings.

August 23, 1963. Warren Spahn registered his 601st career start, a modern National League record, passing Grover Alexander's previous mark. The Braves downed the Dodgers, 6–1, in Los Angeles.

September 8, 1963. Milwaukee downed the Phillies, 3–2, at Shibe Park to give Warren Spahn, who improved to 20–5, his 13th consecutive campaign of at least 20 wins, which tied Christy Mathewson's NL standard. Gene Oliver smacked a two-run homer in the eighth inning against Dallas Green. At 42, Spahn became the oldest 20-game winner in major league history.

September 1, 1964. Former Braves backup catcher and current Brewers broadcaster Bob Uecker clubbed his first homer of the season and then singled in the winning run in the ninth to give Saint Louis a 5–4 victory over Milwaukee at Sportsman's Park as the Cards moved past San Francisco and into second place behind Philadelphia.

September 26, 1964. At Shibe Park, the Braves and Phillies set a major league record by using 43 players in a nine-inning contest. Milwaukee's total of 25 and eight pitchers matched NL marks. Rico Carty's three-run triple in the ninth against Bobby Shantz, in for starter Art Mahaffey, lifted Milwaukee to a 6–4 win. It also was Philadelphia's sixth straight setback during a 10-game losing skid that would see the Phils lose the pennant to the Cardinals despite holding a 6 ½-game lead with two weeks remaining in the season. Joe Torre contributed three hits for the Braves.

June 8, 1965. The Braves unleashed their awesome power as Joe Torre, Eddie Mathews, Hank Aaron, and Gene Oliver crunched homers in the 10th inning of an 8–2 victory over the Cubs at Wrigley Field. The feat established a big-league mark for the most home runs in an extra inning.

July 8, 1965. Mike De La Hoz's heroics carried the Braves to a 9–8 triumph over the Astros at County Stadium despite Joe Morgan becoming the first Houston player to register six hits in a game. De La Hoz smacked a pinch-hit homer in the eighth inning, tied the game with a single as the Braves tallied three times in the ninth, and then scored the winning run after singling in the 12th.

August 18, 1965. Milwaukee moved into first place with a 69–49 record as Tony Cloninger won his duel against Curt Simmons, 5–3, at Sportsman's Park. Hank Aaron hit what he thought was a home run, but umpire Chris Pelekoudas nullified it, saying that Aaron had stepped out of the batter's box when he made contact.

September 11, 1965. Tony Cloninger's masterpiece gave the Braves their second consecutive one-hitter against the Mets, which tied a major league standard from 48 years earlier. Hank Aaron contributed two hits, a stolen base, an RBI, and a run scored before leaving the 9–0 victory for pinch-hitter John Blanchard. The day before, Wade Blasingame, Billy O'Dell, and Phil Niekro combined for a 3–1 win over New York.

May 30, 1970. A wonderful moment occurred for the Brewers' franchise, but it was a scary one for the Tigers. Detroit starter Les Cain loaded the bases before fanning Danny Walton and Jerry McNertney, but Roberto "Baby" Pena lined the ball 382 feet to right-center. Al Kaline and Jim Northrup collided while attempting to make the catch as the ball tipped off Northrup's glove and rolled to the wall. Pena circled the bases to give Milwaukee a 5–2 lead on the franchise's only inside-the-park grand slam at County Stadium. Meanwhile, Kaline was supine on the grass, gasping for air and turning blue from swallowing his tongue. Detroit left fielder Willie Horton arrived and forced open Kaline's mouth, and Brewers' trainer Curt Rayer did the rest. Kaline remained conscious and was taken to Lutheran Hospital; he was released the next day. The Brewers fell behind twice after that but rallied again for a 9–7 win.

September 3, 1970. Minnesota's Leo Cardenas knocked a pitch off the foul pole in the eighth inning, but the umpires ruled it a foul ball. Twins' manager Bill Rigney and Bob Allison argued that it should have been a homer and were tossed for their efforts. Cardenas ended up striking out. Phil Roof and Roberto Pena homered to lead the Brewers to an 8–3 victory.

March 6, 1971. In an exhibition game in Mesa, Arizona, the A's and Brewers tested Oakland owner Charlie Finley's idea of using three-ball walks. The A's won 13–9 in a game that featured 19 free passes, essentially ending the experiment.

May 12–13, 1972. The Brewers and Twins battled for 21 innings before the 1:00 a.m. curfew halted play with the score knotted at 3-all. The rivals picked action up the next day, tying a major league record of combining for seven intentional walks in an extra-inning game. Minnesota tied its club mark of 23 stranded runners. Milwaukee scored in the 22nd inning to post a 4–3 victory at Metropolitan Stadium. The Twins won the regularly scheduled contest, 5–4, in another 15-inning marathon. The two games lasted nine hours, 23 minutes to set an American League record for innings played in two days.

August 1, 1972. Manager Billy Martin had his Detroit Tigers employ stalling tactics while trailing by several runs in a game threatened by rain. Meanwhile, Del Crandall and his Brewers tried to speed the game up. The contest at Tiger Stadium lasted six innings, with Milwaukee claiming a 9–0 victory. Umpire Frank Umont recommended a fine of $1,000 for both managers.

April 15, 1973. Seldom-used Milwaukee rookie Gorman Thomas belted his first big-league homer off Baltimore ace Jim Palmer to tie the Orioles in the ninth inning. Pedro Garcia delivered the game winner in the 11th, 4–3. Thomas finished the season with two homers and 11 RBIs. Baltimore gained a split of the twin bill with a 5–4 win.

July 7, 1973. Eddie Rodriguez notched his first major league win as the Brewers unloaded on 18-year-old rookie David Clyde during a 19–5 triumph over Texas at County Stadium. Rodriguez registered a complete game, while Milwaukee whipped the Rangers behind a five-run sixth and seven-run seventh. Bobby Coluccio whacked a grand slam, and Don Money smacked a three-run shot.

August 6, 1973. In Milwaukee, 33,337 showed up for an exhibition game between the Brewers and the Atlanta Braves. The Brewers claimed a 7–5 victory despite a homer from then-Atlanta slugger Hank Aaron in the fourth and final such contest between the teams.

June 19, 1974. Kansas City's Steve Busby allowed only a second-inning walk to George Scott in dominating the Brewers during a 2–0 no-hitter at County Stadium. Busby became the first major league pitcher to toss no-hitters in his first two years.

July 7, 1974. Don Money established a major-league record for consecutive errorless games (78) by a third baseman as Milwaukee claimed an 8–5 win in a doubleheader split against the Twins at County Stadium. Money ended the campaign with just five errors, which broke George Kell's standard from 1950. Money set the National League mark with 10 errors with the Phillies in 1972.

May 31, 1975. Kansas City defeated the Brewers, 7–5, in a game that bridged the generation gap. Home run leaders Hank Aaron and the Royals' Harmon Killebrew were in their 22nd big-league seasons while winning pitcher Lindy McDaniel was playing in his 21st. All three were in the majors before Brewers' shortstop Robin Yount was born.

June 6, 1975. Hank Aaron spoiled Nolan Ryan's bid for his second no-hitter in a row with a single in the sixth inning at Anaheim Stadium. Ryan allowed one other hit in California's 6–0 victory.

September 28, 1975. Milwaukee fired manager Del Crandall two hours before game time, with Harvey Kuenn filling in as the Brewers won their season finale, 7–0, against Detroit. Larry Anderson made news when he became the third pitcher in the twentieth century to throw a shutout in his only major league starting assignment. George Scott drove in two runs to give him the league's RBI crown with 109.

April 10, 1976. The Brewers suffered a controversial 9–7 setback to the Yankees at County Stadium. New York was ahead by a 9–6 score, but the Brewers had the bases loaded in the bottom of the ninth. Because of the crowd noise, Yankees relief pitcher Dave Pagan didn't hear first baseman Chris Chambliss call for a timeout. Pagan delivered a pitch to Don Money, who promptly deposited the offering into the seats for a grand slam. However, umpires nullified the clout and sent Money back to the batter's box, where he hit a sacrifice fly. The Brewers unsuccessfully protested the outcome.

September 3, 1976. Mike Hegan hit for the cycle and brought home six runs as the Brewers whipped Mark Fidrych and Detroit, 11–2, at Tiger Stadium. Jerry Augustine got the win for Milwaukee to improve to 8–9, while Fidrych slipped to 15–7.

May 22, 1977. Boston had claimed a 10–9 verdict the day before a Sunday doubleheader at Fenway Park. In the twin-bill opener, the Red Sox outlasted Milwaukee, 14–10, as the teams tied a major league record with 11 home runs, six from Boston. Dwight Evans crushed one of them over the new upper section of the center-field wall, about 20 feet to the right of the flagpole. The foes combined for 23 homers during the last three contests of the four-game series. Milwaukee gained a split as Eddie Rodriguez stopped the slugging barrage with a 6–0 win in the second game, beating Fergie Jenkins.

August 14, 1977. The Indians teed off on Milwaukee pitching during a doubleheader sweep at Cleveland Stadium, posting 12–4 and 14–5 victories. In the nightcap, Cleveland pounded Brewers' lefty Bill Travers for 18 hits and 14 runs.

July 27, 1979. A back-and-forth game ended with 47,928 people yelling "Coo-oo-oop!" after Cecil Cooper hit a ninth-inning homer off New York reliever Goose Gossage, his third blast of the night, for a 6–5 Milwaukee victory. What happened to the Yankees' Reggie Jackson made everything sweeter. Mike Caldwell's pitch in the fourth inning sent Jackson sprawling. Jackson popped up on the next pitch and flipped his bat toward Caldwell, who promptly smashed it to the ground and broke it. Jackson charged the mound and was ejected when the brawl was over.

May 31, 1980. Milwaukee pounded the Red Sox, 19–8, at Fenway Park despite the fact that its pitching staff allowed six homers. Boston clubbed four in the fourth inning, including consecutive blasts from Tony Perez, Carlton Fisk, and Butch Hobson, and still lost big.

June 5, 1982. Robin Yount, Cecil Cooper, and Ben Oglivie cracked consecutive homers in the seventh inning as Milwaukee whipped the A's at Oakland-Alameda County Stadium, 11–3. Ted Simmons and Gorman Thomas also smacked long balls to back Bob McClure's third win of the season. It was the second time in a week that the Brewers' sluggers belted three homers in succession.

July 3, 1982. Pete Vuckovich improved to 10–3 after shutting down Boston, 7–0, in front of a record County Stadium crowd of 55,716. The victory allowed Milwaukee to move into a tie for first place with the Red Sox.

July 18, 1982. The Brewers completed a rare five-game series sweep of the Chicago White Sox and moved into sole possession of first place in the American League East with a 9–3 win before 46,455 fans. It was the Brewers' eighth straight win.

May 9, 1984. The longest—and slowest—game in American League history ended in the 25th inning when Chicago's Harold Baines homered off Chuck Porter to give the White Sox a 7–6 victory over the Brewers. It was the latest homer as far as innings in history.

Bernie Brewer was a fixture at County Stadium and carries on that tradition at Miller Park, celebrating Brewer home runs and victories with a trip down his slide.

169

The game fell one inning shy of the major league mark but was the longest by far in time: eight hours and six minutes. The contest was suspended a day earlier after 17 innings with the score tied at 3. Both teams scored three runs in the 21st inning. The Sox lost a chance to win in that inning when runner Dave Stegman was ruled to have touched third-base coach Jim Leyland, which led to a Sox protest. Tom Seaver pitched the final inning to earn the victory and then won the regularly scheduled game, 5–4. Chicago's Tom Paciorek set a major league record as he entered in the fourth inning and registered nine at-bats.

May 20, 1985. The Indians-Brewers contest at Cleveland Stadium became the first one rained out during the season, ending a record string of 458 big-league games played since opening day without a washout. Since 1900, no season had survived without at least one April shower.

May 13, 1986. Seattle downed Milwaukee, 8–5, in the Kingdome with the help of an unusual 3–6–1–2–4 triple play in the first inning. After Randy Ready and Ernest Riles walked to open the game, Cecil Cooper bounced a grounder to first baseman Alvin Davis, who threw to second to force Riles. Cooper beat the return throw to first, but Ready was thrown out trying to score and Cooper was gunned down going to second.

August 17, 1986. Steve Carlton, only 5–12 entering the contest, picked up his first American League victory in Chicago's 7–4 decision over the Brewers at Comiskey Park. It was Carlton's 320th win of his Hall of Fame career.

July 26, 1987. Paul Molitor, hitting .348, tied a major league record by stealing second, third, and home in the first inning of Milwaukee's 7–4 triumph against Oakland as Teddy Higuera improved to 10–7 in this contest at County Stadium.

August 19–20, 1987. Paul Molitor collected four base hits to extend his hitting streak to 34 games, tying Dom DiMaggio for the 11th spot on the all-time list. The Brewers defeated Cleveland, 13–2, on the road as Rob Deer cranked a grand slam. Deer duplicated the feat the next day as Milwaukee cruised again, 13–2. Deer became the 11th player in history to hit grand slams in consecutive games.

April 20–21, 1988. Baltimore established a major league record for futility, losing its 14th consecutive decision to open a season, dropping an 8–6 contest at County Stadium. The 1904 Washington Senators and 1920 Detroit Tigers each lost their first 13 games of those seasons. Bill Wegman improved to 1–2 for Milwaukee, which handed Mike Boddicker his fourth straight setback to start the year. Milwaukee's Chris Bosio improved to 3–1 the next night as the Brewers won 7–1 to extend Baltimore's misery, which reached a big-league-record 21 games before it ended.

May 28, 1988. Milwaukee's Odell Jones made his first start since 1981 a game to remember, improving to 3–0 after no-hitting the Indians at Cleveland Stadium for 8 1/2 innings. Ron Washington broke up Jones's bid with a pinch-hit single. Dan Plesac recorded the save in the 2–0 victory.

June 5, 1989. Milwaukee slapped the Blue Jays with a 5–3 loss to open the Toronto SkyDome. Baseball's newest and most modern stadium at the time featured a $100 million, fully retractable roof; a hotel; the world's largest video display board; and a Hard Rock Cafe. Construction crews worked around the clock to get the park ready. Both teams skipped batting practice because the fences were being painted. Don August got the win, while Jimmy Key suffered the loss.

June 7, 1989. When it rains it pours, at least for a while. Toronto catcher Ernie Whitt contributed three hits and drove in three runs as the Blue Jays defeated the Brewers, 4–2, in the first game ever played indoors and outdoors in the same day. With dark clouds threatening, workers began closing the roof in the fifth inning. The operation began at 8:48 p.m. and ended at 9:22, which proved to be too late to prevent a brief stoppage of play because of the rain.

April 16, 1990. The Brewers accumulated 20 hits, but no home runs, in blasting Boston, 18–0, at Fenway Park. Dave Parker notched four hits, highlighted by three doubles, in Milwaukee's largest shutout margin ever. Teddy Higuera was the easy winner over Mike Boddicker. Milwaukee scored against all five Red Sox hurlers.

July 8, 1990. The Brewers, trailing 7–0 in the third inning, scored 20 unanswered runs, including 13 in the fifth inning, to win 20–7 over California at County Stadium. This was the largest swing of runs since 1980 and wasn't topped in the '90s. The Angels' Bert Blyleven was seeking his 279th career win but didn't get out of the fourth. He won only once the remainder of the season.

May 1, 1991. Milwaukee outlasted the White Sox, 10–9, in a six-hour, five-minute contest that lasted 19 innings, the longest in the American League since the two clubs played 25 innings May 8, 1984. Willie Randolph drove home the deciding run at County Stadium.

September 3, 1991. Milwaukee's Jim Gantner doubled and smacked his first homer since 1987, a span that had stretched to 1,762 at-bats without a dinger, in a 5-3 victory over Oakland at County Stadium. Two days later, Gantner hit another HR. Robin Yount drilled a three-run homer against A's relief ace Dennis Eckersley with two outs in the ninth inning. Eckersley joined Yount in the Hall of Fame in 2004.

April 9, 1993. Brewers' outfielder Darryl Hamilton placed his name in the American League record book by handling his 541st consecutive chance without an error. Milwaukee defeated the Athletics, 6–5, in Oakland.

April 14, 1993. Pitcher Graeme Lloyd and catcher Dave Nilsson formed the first all-Australian battery in major league history during the Brewers' 12–2 loss to California at County Stadium. Both of them pitched in the ninth inning after the Angels scored five runs in the eighth and six more in the ninth. On April 30, Lloyd became the initial Aussie to win a big-league game during Milwaukee's 5–4 triumph over Texas.

May 28, 1993. Robin Yount and the Brewers downed George Brett and Kansas City, 5–1, at County Stadium in the first meeting of two 3,000-hit players since 1925. Cal Eldred got the victory, while Kevin Appier suffered the loss.

June 7, 1993. Cal Eldred defeated Seattle, 5–3, for his seventh triumph of the season. Not important, you say? Well, it gave Eldred 20 victories in his first 30 career big-league appearances, tying him with Boo Ferriss (1945), Russ Ford (1910), and Nick Maddox (1908) as the quickest hurlers to reach that plateau. Doug Henry notched his 10th save in this game at County Stadium.

April 11, 1994. Milwaukee upended the Rangers, 4–3, in the opener at the Ballpark in Arlington, Texas, as Jaime Navarro outpitched Kenny Rogers. A fan named Hollye Minter, posing for pictures, fell some 35 feet from the railing of the right-field home run porch. She broke her right arm, her ribs, and several bones in her neck.

April 27, 1994. Minnesota's Scott Erickson made history, hurling a 6–0 no-hitter against Milwaukee, the first time a no-hitter was accomplished in the Metrodome. Erickson struck out five and walked four in the Twins' first no-no in 27 years.

July 14, 1994. Another oddity found only in a domed stadium occurred twice during the course of Milwaukee's 6–4 victory over the Twins. Two batted balls hit off the Metrodome's ceiling: Kent Hrbek's fly ball bounced off for a double, while Brewers' first baseman Kevin Seitzer managed to catch Pedro Munoz's popup.

June 22, 1995. Milwaukee just couldn't avoid being around for stadium mishaps. Two acoustic panels fell from the roof of the Toronto SkyDome, injuring seven fans during the seventh inning of the Brewers 9–0 victory that completed a three-game sweep of the Blue Jays.

July 22, 1995. Chicago shortstop and current White Sox manager Ozzie Guillen shoved Brewers third baseman Jeff Cirillo to touch off a bench-clearing brawl that featured both skippers, Milwaukee's Phil Garner and Chicago's Terry Bevington, swinging at each other. Wilson Alvarez and Chicago notched a 4–2 win over Steve Sparks.

July 30, 1995. Chili Davis of the Angels was charged with disorderly conduct after California's 8–3 triumph at County Stadium. Davis allegedly slapped a fan who was taunting him. Davis also registered a hit at the plate.

October 1, 1995. Boston's Chris Donnels drilled a homer in the ninth inning for Boston's only run during an 8–1 loss to the Brewers and Scott Karl. It was Donnels's last big-league at-bat. Pitcher Bill Wegman, inserted into right field, watched the ball sail over the wall. Wegman, who had played in the Milwaukee organization since 1981, was making his last major league appearance.

May 15, 1996. Milwaukee waited out a two-hour delay because of fog at County Stadium. Then the Brewers played like they were still in one as the White Sox clobbered them 20–8, scoring six times in the second inning and six more in the sixth. Frank Thomas led Chicago's charge with six RBIs. The visitors' outburst tied a 1975 mark for most runs scored against Milwaukee.

July 16, 1996. Jeff D'Amico benefited from the Brewers' offensive fireworks at County Stadium. Milwaukee didn't score in the first two innings but dented the scoreboard every at-bat after that in nailing down a 20–7 victory over Detroit. Greg Vaughn knocked in five runs to push his league-leading total to 88, while Jose Valentin registered four hits.

April 25, 1997. The Indians ripped Scott Karl and the Brewers, 11–4, clouting a club-record eight homers. Third baseman Matt Williams smoked three HRs to lead Cleveland's barrage, while David Justice added two round-trippers. Milwaukee went deep three times, giving the Central Division foes a major league record-tying 11 for the game. Orel Hershiser improved to 2–0, while Karl dropped to 0–4.

June 13-15, 1997. Jeff D'Amico and Milwaukee downed Terry Mulholland and the Cubs, 4–2, in the opener of a series at Wrigley Field. Chicago then won the final two games 9–5 and 4–3, respectively. The teams drew 112,690, only 7,638 shy of the Wrigley record of 120,328 for a three-game series, which was set in 1994 against Cincinnati.

July 28, 1997. Milwaukee defeated Toronto, 9–3, to cap a doubleheader sweep at County Stadium. However, the talk of the day was game one, a 1–0 Brewers triumph that saw rookie hurler Steve Woodard, recalled from the minors that morning, outduel Roger Clemens. Woodard allowed only one hit, a double to Otis Nixon, in eight innings. Mike Fetters got the save with a hitless ninth. Clemens dropped to 16–4.

April 23, 1998. Brewers outfielder Marquis Grissom cranked his 103rd career homer during Milwaukee's 2–1 win over the Dodgers. He surpassed Lou Piniella's record for most dingers without a multiple-HR game. Grissom eventually reached 109 career home runs before hitting two in a game September 26 of that year. Jose Mercedes got the victory, while Hideo Nomo was slapped with the loss at County Stadium.

August 1, 1998. Although Milwaukee suffered a 5–4 setback at home to Arizona, Brewers right-handed pitcher Bronswell Patrick delivered a home run against Felix Rodriguez in the fifth inning. It was the first round-tripper for a Milwaukee pitcher since Skip Lockwood connected off Detroit's Joe Niekro on August 11, 1971.

April 23, 1999. Steve Woodard hurled a 9–1 victory at Pittsburgh's Three Rivers Stadium, snapping Milwaukee's National League record streak of 113 games without a complete game. Third baseman Jeff Cirillo powered the visitors' attack with three hits and four RBIs, including a double and a home run.

May 20, 1999. New York Mets third baseman Robin Ventura slugged a grand slam in both ends of a doubleheader sweep of Milwaukee, 11–10 and 10–1, becoming the first player in history to do so.

June 15, 1999. Pitcher Jim Abbott, born without a right hand, registered his first major league hit. Unfortunately, he fell to 1–6 as Milwaukee dropped a 7–4 decision to the Cubs at County Stadium.

July 1, 1999. The Brewers trounced the Cubs, 19–12, as shortstop Jose Valentin smacked a pair of two-run homers, one from each side of the plate. Second baseman Ron Belliard and catcher Dave Nilsson finished with four hits apiece as Belliard brought home five runs. The Brewers knocked around Steve Trachsel for 10 runs in 3 2/3 innings, saddling him with his National League-high 11th loss. The Brewers collected 21 hits for the second time in three nights at Wrigley Field. Chicago's Mickey Morandini sent two into the seats in a contest that featured eight homers. Sammy Sosa, who singled twice, had his streak of four straight games with a homer stopped. Milwaukee had won the series opener, 17–6, two nights earlier.

July 10, 1999. Detroit whipped the Brewers, 9–3, drawing 25,374 fans at Tiger Stadium. That enabled the club to top the one million mark in attendance for the 35th consecutive season, the longest such run in American League history.

September 18, 1999. Chicago's Sammy Sosa belted his 60th homer of the season to become the first big-leaguer to reach that milestone twice.

However, Milwaukee, behind Kyle Peterson, claimed a 7–4 triumph at Wrigley Field.

September 24, 1999. Houston outfielder Bill Spiers, who played for Milwaukee from 1989 to 1994, was attacked by a fan in the sixth inning of the Astros' 9–4 victory at County Stadium. His teammates left the bench and bullpen to aid Spiers, who suffered a welt under his left eye and a bloody nose but stayed in the game. His assailant was charged with two counts of assault after being taken into custody.

April 3, 2000. The Reds and Brewers played to a 3–3 tie in a contest that was called in the sixth inning because of rain. It was Ken Griffey Jr.'s debut in Cincinnati and the first tie game on opening day in 35 years.

May 11, 2000. Another game between the Brewers and Cubs, and another slugfest at Wrigley Field. Milwaukee drubbed Chicago, 14–8, in what became the longest nine-inning matchup in National League history. The four-hour, 22-minute contest included 35 hits and 19 walks. Milwaukee's Mark Loretta finished 5-for-5, while Glenallen Hill of the Cubs crushed a 490-foot homer that landed on the roof of a three-story building across Waveland Avenue.

May 22, 2000. Milwaukee claimed a doubleheader sweep over Houston at County Stadium with a 6–1 victory in the nightcap. The Brewers got all of their momentum in the opener, rallying for seven runs in the ninth to deadlock the game at 9. Jose Hernandez won it with a solo homer in the 10th. It was a club-record rally for the ninth inning.

June 27, 2000. The Atlanta Braves backed off from their decision to bar four team announcers from their chartered flights after the broadcasters had raised questions about the catcher's box at Turner Field. After station WTBS discussed the width of the box in a game against the Brewers three days earlier, Skip Caray, Pete Van Wieren, Joe Simpson, and Don Sutton were booted off a flight to Montreal and were forced to grab a commercial flight. The station had aired a video showing that the box was four to five inches smaller than it was the previous night, which is when Milwaukee had griped about where Atlanta catcher Javy Lopez had been setting up. Opposing teams had long said that Braves pitchers had received an extra-wide strike zone. The video was shown after a rare balk call against Fernando Lunar, the Braves catcher. Home-plate umpire John Shulock ruled that Lunar set up with his right foot outside the 43-inch-wide box. The balk led to Milwaukee's first run in a 2-1 Brewers victory. Shulock ejected Braves manager Bobby Cox during the ensuing argument.

May 15, 2001. The Brewers accumulated 22 hits during a 14–10 triumph at Veterans Stadium in Philadelphia. Milwaukee blew an eight-run lead before going ahead in the 10th inning on Richie Sexson's double. Tyler Houston collected five hits, while Devon White clubbed a grand slam for the visitors.

July 31, 2001. Not only did Milwaukee lose a 5–1 decision to Florida, but also Brewers manager Davey Lopes was suspended for two games and fined by the commissioner's office for threatening to have his pitchers hit Rickey Henderson of San Diego two days earlier. Lopes became upset when the all-time base-stealing champion took off for second during the seventh inning of the Padres' 12–5 win.

August 22, 2001. Cubs right fielder Sammy Sosa ripped three homers for the second time in two weeks as he carried Chicago to an easy 16–3 victory over Milwaukee at Wrigley Field. Sosa missed out on an opportunity to tie the big-league mark of four round-trippers in a game because he was removed in the sixth inning.

September 10, 2001. The Cardinals shut out the Brewers, 8–0, as Darryl Kile pitched six innings for the win at County Stadium with the help of Mark McGwire's 24th homer. Jamey Wright lost the game, failing to plunk any batters and ending his possible major league record of hitting a batter in 10 straight games.

May 23, 2002. Shawn Green of Los Angeles finished 6-for-6, including four homers, and knocked in seven runs while setting a major league record of 19 total bases. Green ended up 9-for-14 with six round-trippers in the three-game series at Miller Park.

September 17-18, 2002. Ben Sheets became the first Milwaukee pitcher since 1997 to reach 200 innings pitched during a game against Houston. Lefty Glendon Rusch joined Sheets the next night, marking the first time that two Brewers hurlers reached that milestone in the same season since Ben McDonald and Scott Karl achieved it in 1996.

September 13, 2003. Richie Sexson became the first Brewers player to register two 40-homer campaigns when he blasted one at San Francisco. About two weeks later he reached the record of 45 for a season that he hit in 2001 and shares with Gorman Thomas (1979).

Bibliography

BOOKS

Aaron, Hank, with Lonnie Wheeler. *I Had a Hammer: The Hank Aaron Story.* New York: HarperCollins, 1991.

The Baseball Encyclopedia. 10th ed. New York: Macmillan, 1996.

Buege, Bob. *The Milwaukee Braves: A Baseball Eulogy.* Milwaukee: Douglas American Sports Publications, 1988.

Carlson, Chuck. *True Brew: A Quarter Century with the Milwaukee Brewers.* Dallas: Taylor Publishing Company and the Milwaukee Brewers Baseball Club, 1993.

Caruso, Gary. *The Braves Encyclopedia.* Philadelphia: Temple University Press, 1995.

Chadwick, Bruce. *Baseball's Hometown Teams: The Story of the Minor Leagues.* New York: Abbeville Press, 1994.

Everson, Jeff. *This Date in Milwaukee Brewers History: A Box Seat for 18 Seasons of Brewers Baseball 1970–87.* Appleton, WI: Everson House-Graphic Communications, 1987.

Gurda, John. *The Making of Milwaukee.* Milwaukee: Milwaukee Historical Society, 1999.

Hamann, Rex, and Bob Koehler. *The American Association Milwaukee Brewers: Images of Baseball.* Charleston, SC: Arcadia Publishing, 2004.

Hoffmann, Gregg. *Down in the Valley. The History of Milwaukee County Stadium: The People, the Promise, the Passion.* Milwaukee: Milwaukee Brewers Baseball Club and *Milwaukee Journal Sentinel,* 2000.

Hoffmann, Gregg. *The Making of Miller Park.* Milwaukee: Milwaukee Brewers Baseball Club, 2001.

Mathews, Eddie, and Bob Buege. *Eddie Mathews and the National Pastime.* Milwaukee: Douglas American Sports Publications, 1994.

McCann, Dennis. *The Wisconsin Story: 150 Stories/150 Years.* Milwaukee: *Milwaukee Journal Sentinel,* 2001.

Obojski, Robert. *Bush League: A Colorful, Factual Account of Minor League Baseball from 1877 to the Present.* New York: Macmillan, 1975.

Robin Yount: The Legend Lives On. Milwaukee: Milwaukee Brewers Baseball Club, 1992.

Schoor, Gene. *The History of the World Series: The Complete Chronology of America's Greatest Sports Tradition.* New York: William Morrow, 1990.

Stout, Glenn, and Richard A. Johnson. *Red Sox Century.* Boston: Houghton Mifflin, 2000.

20th Century Baseball Chronicle: A Year-by-Year History of Major League Baseball. Montreal: Tormont Publications, 1992.

Wells, Robert W. *This Is Milwaukee: A Colorful Portrait of the City That Made Beer Famous.* Garden City, NY: Doubleday, 1970.

NEWSPAPERS

Capital Times (Madison)
Janesville Gazette
La Crosse Tribune
Manitowoc Herald-Times
Milwaukee Journal
Milwaukee Journal Sentinel
Milwaukee Sentinel
San Francisco Examiner

Washington Post
Wisconsin State Journal

WEB SITES AND OTHER SOURCES

Atlanta Braves
BaseballLibrary.com
Milwaukee Brewers
Major League Baseball
OnMilwaukee.com
Milwaukee Brewers media guides

Index

Covington, Wes, 19, 21-23, 25, 33, 35-38, 43-46, 140
Cox, Bobby, 177
Crandall, Del, 13, 15-17, 21-23, 25, 29, 40, 43-46, 52, 56, 136-137, 146, 159, 166-167
Crim, Chuck, 72, 74-75, 92-93
Crone, Ray, 16-17, 19, 159
Crowe, George, 16
Cruz, Enrique, 110
Cruz, Nelson, 119
Curtis, Jack, 162

D

Dalton, Harry, 57-59, 63, 65-66, 68, 71, 77, 80
D'Amico, Jeff, 98-99, 104, 106, 174
Darwin, Danny, 71
Davis, Alvin, 170
Davis, Chilli, 173
Davis, Dick, 62
Davis, Doug, 108, 110-111
Davis, Joel, 73
Davis, Ron, 79
Dean, Dizzy, 153
Deer, Rob, 71-75, 92, 146, 148, 170
DeGrave, William, 151
DeJean, Mike, 106-108
De La Hoz, Mike, 165
De La Rosa, Jorge, 109-110
De Los Santos, Valerio, 100
Dent, Bucky, 60
DiMaggio, Dom, 170
DiMaggio, Joe, 121
Ditmar, Art, 45
Dittmer, Jack, x, 10, 13, 159
Donatelli, Augie, 37, 39
Donnels, Chris, 173
Downing, Al, 51-52, 123
Doyle, Gov. Jim, 117
Drago, Dick, 57
Dressen, Charlie, 23-25,
Drott, Dick, 160
Drysdale, Don, 22, 164
Duren, Ryne, 43-45

E

Easterly, Jamie, 65
Eckersley, Dennis, 128, 172
Edwards, Marshall, 66, 83-84,
Eggum, Don J., 153

Eisen, Thelma "Tiby," 7
Eisenhower, Dwight, 86
Eldred, Cal, 95-96, 98-101, 103, 172
Ellis, Michael, xi
Erickson, Scott, 173
Ernaga, Frank, 160
Evans, Dwight, 168
Eveland, Dana, 112
Evers, Johnny, 6

F

Farrell, John, 73
Favre, Brett, 104
Felder, Ken, 114
Felder, Mike, 70, 92
Ferriss, Boo, 172
Fetters, Mike, 95-99, 174
Fidrych, Mark, 134, 168
Fielder, Prince, 112, 118
Fingers, Rollie, xiii, 58, 63-64, 66, 68-71, 77-80, 86, 88-89, 128-130, 146
Finley, Charlie, 166
Fischer, Hank, 30
Fisk, Carlton, 169
Fitzgerald, Ed, 48
Flanagan, Mike, 66
Fletcher, Scott, 94-95
Flick, Lewis "Noisy," 3, 158
Florie, Bryce, 98
Ford, Russ, 172
Ford, Whitey, 37, 39, 42-45
Forsch, Bob, 85
Fossas, Tony, 75
Fox, Chad, 99-100, 106
Foxx, Jimmie, 24
Franklin, Wayne, 109
Freeman, Hersh, 159
Frisella, Danny, 56
Fuss, Mike, ix-xi

G

Gallardo, Yovani, 112
Gamble, Oscar, 78-80
Gantner, Jim, 59, 64-66, 69-71, 73-75, 83-84, 86, 88, 92-95, 124-126, 133-134, 137, 145-146, 172
Garcia, Pedro, 53-54, 56, 166
Garcia, Ramon, 98
Gard, John, 116-117
Garner, Phil, 91, 93, 101, 173
Gehrig, Lou, 31

185